Pam Buttre

Pam Buttrey, who grew up in F
was a head occupational ther;
in adult mental health in South London, and a member of the *Positive Futures* team from 1989 to 1992 during Cane Hill Hospital's closure programme. With an MA in English Local History from the University of Leicester, she now researches local history as well as house histories and genealogy.

More details about Pam Buttrey, can be found at www.mcfadden-buttrey.com

Titles

Lyss Place: Peace and Turmoil
among the Gentry in Liss from 900 AD

With Sue Hutt

I've Got a Job to Do!
A Study of the Clubhouse Model

With D. Meredith McFadden

Salt & Silk
Silk & Sons

Cane Hill Hospital:

The Tower on the Hill

by

Pam Buttrey

© Pam Buttrey 2010
Cane Hill Hospital: The Tower on the Hill

ISBN 978-0-9549582-3-7

Published by Aubrey Warsash Publishing
PO Box 3186
South Croydon
Surrey CR2 6UW
United Kingdom

The right of Pam Buttrey to be identified as the author of this work has been asserted by her in accordance with the Copyright, Designs and Patents Act 1988.

All rights reserved. No part of this publication may be produced in any form or by any means – graphic, electronic or mechanical including photocopying, recording, taping or information storage and retrieval systems – without the prior permission, in writing, of the publisher.

A CIP catalogue record of this book
can be obtained from the British Library.

Book designed by Michael Walsh at
THE BETTER BOOK COMPANY
5 Lime Close, Chichester PO19 6SW

and printed by
IMPRINTDIGITAL.NET

Seychelles Farm, Upton Pyne, Exeter, Devon EX5 5HY

Contents

Introduction ii

Chapters
1   The Background 1
2   Planning the Asylum.. 6
3   Opening Cane Hill 16
4   Staff and patients 1888-1889 25
5   Overcrowding 36
6   A time of change 1889-1899 43
7   Staff and patients 1890-1900 50
8   The daily routine 60
9   The new century 1900-1914...................................67
10 Law and disorder 76
11 Progress and development 85
12 The patients' lot 94
13 World War One and its consequences...................107
14 War and asylum..118
15 Portnalls 129
16 Attitudes in the 1920s 134
17 From asylum to hospital 143
18 The Board of Control 153
19 The Estate 162
20 From gas to electric 168
21 Freedom for some...174
22 Occupational therapy 184
23 World War Two and its aftermath 188
24 The National Health Service 1948-1960...............200
25 Activity and rehabilitation...................................212
26 Planned reduction...220
27 The Hospital Management Team..........................227
28 The nurses' view – how did we do it? 233
29 Planned closure 236

Appendix: Description of Cane Hill in 1887
by A. Henry Frend..240
Bibliography...246
Notes..249
Index..262

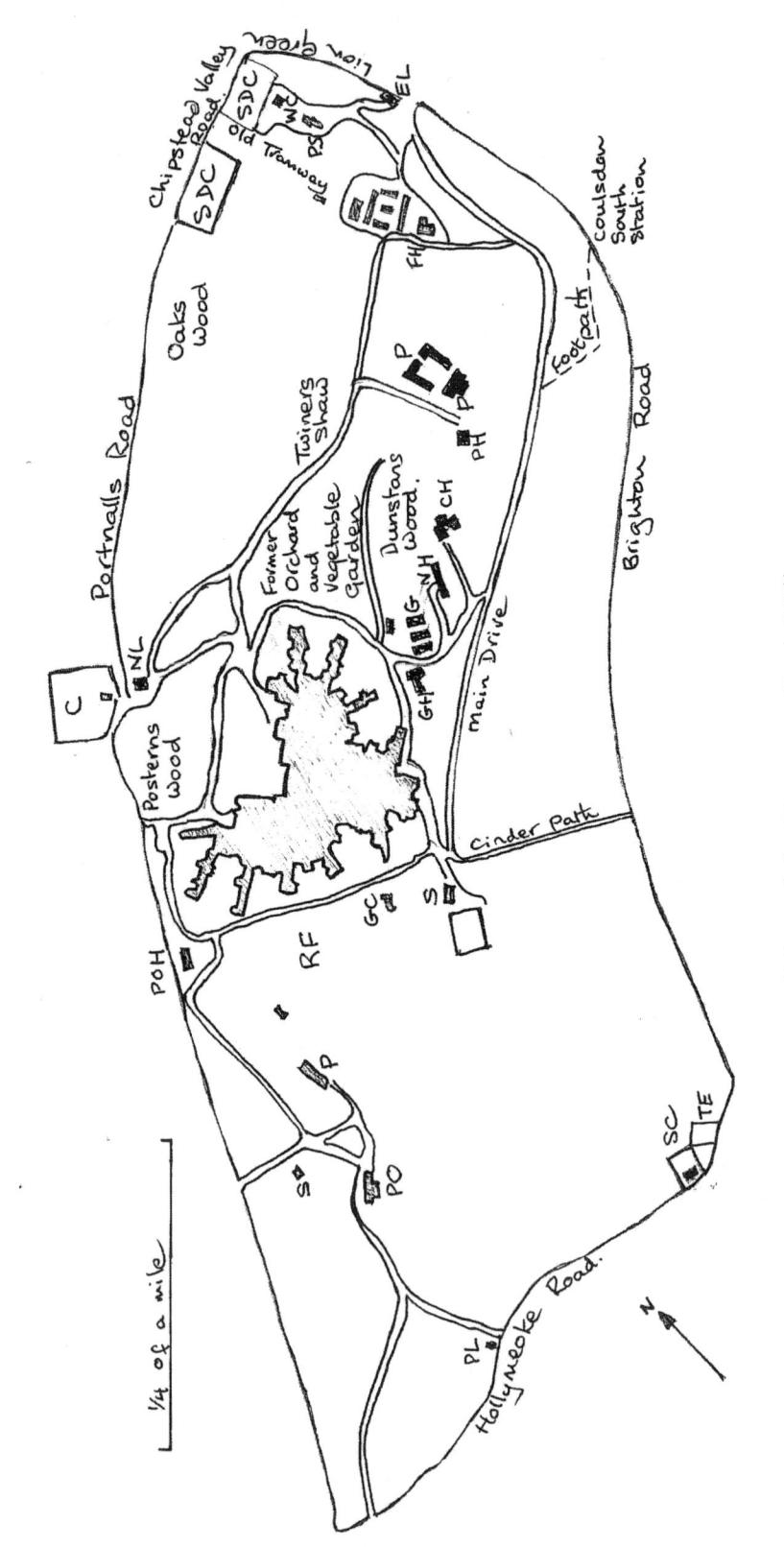

Map of the Estate at Cane Hill

Map of the estate at Cane Hill

Key:

C	Cemetery
CH	Cottage Hospital
EL	East Lodge
FH	Farm House
G	Greenhouses
GC	Glencairn
GH	Garden House
NH	Nurses Home
NL	North Lodge
P	Piggeries
PH	Pigman's House
PL	Portnalls Lodge
PO	Portnalls
POH	Postern House
PS	Pumping Station
RF	Recreation Field
S	Stables
SC	Stoney Cottages
SDC	St. Dunstans Cottages
TE	PO Telephone Exchange
WC	Well Cottages

Introduction

In April 1989, I went to work with what became known as the *Positive Futures* team, administrators and clinicians working to plan and set up services for long term patients living in Cane Hill Hospital who would move to Bromley, and to help these people to readjust to living in the London Borough of Bromley.

Some fifteen years later, finding that Cane Hill was one of the few mental hospitals not to have had its story published, I began to research its history, initially as part of an MA dissertation about pauper lunatics in Croydon. As so often happens, one thing has led to another! Now, most of the hospital buildings have recently been demolished and the site faces a new future.

With growing interest in family history, many have found an ancestor who spent time in Cane Hill, either as a member of staff or as a patient. Patients' case records were destroyed, but patients and staff registers survive for much of the period up to 1948. Some limited details for early admissions to Warlingham Park Hospital, then known as Croydon Mental Hospital, who were formerly at Cane Hill Hospital, can be found in Bethlem Royal's Archives, and in the minutes of Croydon's Board of Guardians. Despite the valiant efforts of Julian Pooley at Surrey History Centre, many other records appear to have destroyed in Cane Hill's last days.

Most of the hospital's surviving records are deposited in Croydon Local Studies and Archives, while the hospital's committee meetings up to 1948 are in the London Metropolitan Archives. Because of overcrowding, some of those admitted to Cane Hill were moved to other asylums, especially to Fisherton House in Salisbury, but also to asylums in Gloucester, Lancaster, Worcester, Birmingham, Leicester, West Yorkshire and elsewhere. Probably, references to patients can be found in their records. In the World Wars, patients came to Cane Hill from other London asylums, and some from Gibraltar.

Throughout its existence, its medical superintendents and their successors, its senior staff and management committees endeavoured to provide a high standard of treatment, although nowadays, we might not always approve of their methods.

As I read the records, I realised that I had been taught about the development of diagnoses, labels and treatments, but knew little of earlier life in mental hospitals, apart from what staff and patients told me. My aim has been to find out as much as possible about the day to day life of its patients and staff, and the hospital's relationship with its neighbours in Coulsdon. I discovered that, although for many years the main building was locked to stop patients getting out, the boundaries of the estate had to be fenced to stop local people getting in, because of repeated thefts and vandalism. There are a vast number of stories, and it has only been possible to include some as examples.

I am indebted to Chris Bennett and his staff at the London Borough of Croydon Local Studies and Archives Service for their help, interest and encouragement, to the staff of the The National Archives and the London Metropolitan Archives and to Colin Gale at Bethlem Royal Archives. When I questioned whether there were Commonwealth War Grave's headstones in its cemetery, as some service men admitted to Cane Hill in the two world wars died there soon after, I found Adrian Falks has campaigned for recognition of such men, and I am grateful for the information he has given me, including stories from relatives of these men.

Thanks are due to former staff and patients of Cane Hill who told me about life there – they will know who they are – and to Barry Vines who told me about the patients' social activities. I greatly appreciate the encouragement and interest of Chris Mansi, Tracy Simpson, Nathan Pathananthan and John Wates at Community Options, soon to celebrate its twentieth anniversary in November 2010.

Pam Buttrey
Croydon
September 2010

Chapter 1: The background

'. . . a lunatic asylum is intended to be not merely a place of security but a place of cure . . . The recovery of the curable, the improvement of the incurable, the comfort of all the patients, should . . . be steadily kept in view'. John Conolly, 1847.[1]

William Tuke (1732-1822) founded the York Retreat in 1792 where mentally ill patients were 'treated with all the kindness which their condition allows'. His approach, known as 'moral treatment', used gentle persuasion to instil 'self-restraint', with rewards for acceptable behaviour, in conditions as close as possible to ordinary life.

The asylum, with light, homely well-ventilated buildings, was seen as the most therapeutic setting for the insane. Mechanical restraints, including straitjackets and locked gloves, were discontinued, work and leisure being seen as therapeutic. Patients' previous occupations provided trades necessary to run an asylum, such as painting and decorating, tailoring, baking, brewing, farming, gardening, cleaning and shoemaking, maintaining skills while acknowledging that it reduced running costs. Books, games and amusements were equally important. The Commissioners in Lunacy commented, in 1844, on the consequences of lack of employment:

The lunatic is left to pass his time listless and unoccupied only with the delusions that disturb him, and which thus, being diverted by no amusement or employment in the course of time become strengthened, and not to be removed.[2]

Moral treatment was introduced into other asylums, including Hanwell in Middlesex where John Conolly (1794-1866) was medical superintendent. It led to the 1845 Lunacy Act which defined three groups of insane people who could be confined in an asylum: 'lunatics, idiots, or persons of unsound mind'. A lunatic 'sometimes is of good and sound memory, and sometimes non compos mentis'. An idiot's mind was from birth 'so deficient as to be incapable of directing him in any matter which requires thought or judgement', being less able to reason than an imbecile. A 'person of unsound mind' had a permanent intellectual deficit caused by an event after infancy.[3]

A pauper lunatic was a person certified as insane, whose care and maintenance was paid for wholly or partly from public funds through the Union. Many pauper lunatics, or their immediate family, had incomes. In 1855, the Commissioners reported that relatives of 'tradesmen, or thriving artisans' were admitted to asylums as pauper lunatics, being unable to afford the charges in private licensed houses. In 1875, the Crown's judiciary stated that people were 'chargeable' to the parish or Union if they, or their close relatives, could not afford the cost of care as a private patient.[4]

Magistrates, responsible for county asylums, were authorised to admit pauper lunatics for care and treatment. Poor Law guardians, aware of disgruntled ratepayers, generally saw the 'dangerous insane' as a priority, while medical superintendents wanted to treat 'curable' cases.

The 1845 Lunacy Act authorised Commissioners in Lunacy, hereafter known as Commissioners, to inspect county asylums and private licensed houses in England and Wales. They could remove lunatics from the latter, but rarely did so, and transfer lunatics from workhouses to asylums, subject to an appeal by Guardians to the Home Secretary. Asylums and workhouses could disregard their recommendations and, with only six Commissioners, rural Unions were only visited every few years. The Local Government Board had the most influence as it could insist on the Commissioners' recommendations being acted on, using the authority of the Home Secretary. It authorised new building, expenditure, and staff appointments.

From the 1860s, with overcrowding and insufficient staffing, mechanical restraints and seclusion were reintroduced in asylums and workhouses. In 1870, Andrew Wynter wrote that more than a third of chronic 'harmless and quiet' patients in asylums, could live safely in ordinary homes. Plans were made for interim placements between asylum and home, and the Mental Aftercare Association (MACA) was formed, but those running asylums were usually reluctant to discharge patients.

Large sums of money had been expended in building in asylums, and senior staff had a vested interest in keeping them open, having built careers there. Most medical superintendents preferred to create domestic settings within the asylum, with increased employment opportunities and less use of restraint, which became 'custodial warehouses'.[5] However, at Cane Hill, the sub-committee appeared willing to discharge provided they had suitable accommodation, and sent people to MACA's hostels from an early date, while Dr Moody helped people to resettle in the community. Parole and trial leave, as preparation for discharge, were used with some patients. From 1874 onwards, Guardians received 4s a week from central government for each pauper lunatic in an asylum, which became an incentive to admit and keep them there.

Many pauper lunatics, experiencing poverty, bad housing and working conditions and malnutrition, were thin and weak on admission, and a period of good food, fresh air and exercise was seen as essential to recovery. In 1887, Dr Cassidy of Lancaster extolled the 'embarrassment of riches' of improved methods including massage, shower baths, experiments with electricity and drugs.[6] Others used drugs, such as chloral hydrate, to quieten and sedate violent patients, an alternative to mechanical restraint.

People were more accepting of admitting the insane to asylums. The General Inspector of the Local Government Board reported in 1877: 'I . . . think there is a disposition among all classes now not to bear with the troubles that may arise in their own houses'. Male wage earners tended to be admitted more rapidly than women, to be 'cured' in order to earn a wage, although there were more female admissions.[7] Mentally ill people often displayed physical violence towards their families, which could not be easily managed in small houses, particularly if there was heightened emotional expression within the household.

Psychiatry became increasingly interested in eugenics. Henry Maudsley (1835-1918), previously a medical superintendent, became a widely read author on lunacy. Expressing contrasting views to moral treatment, and the ability of a person to improve himself, in 1873, he wrote that

> . . . I believe it to be not less true, that in consequence of evil ancestral influences, individuals are born with such a flaw or warp of nature that all care in the world will not prevent them

from being vicious or criminal, or becoming insane . . .

And, a year later

. . . we would not willingly select for breeding purposes a hound that was deficient in scent, or a greyhound that was deficient in speed, or a racehorse that could neither stay nor gallop fast. Is it right then to sanction propagation of his kind by an individual who is wanting in that which is the highest attribute of man – a sound and stable mental constitution?[8]

A growing belief that insane people threatened society, and should be discouraged from producing children, led to increased hospitalisation. As the numbers of pauper lunatics in asylums and workhouses rose, so did costs. The authorities economised, using long term patients as unpaid workers and reducing the quantity and quality of food.

There is a general consensus, amongst those writing about workhouses in the nineteenth century, that Guardians preferred to keep pauper lunatics in workhouses, often in poor conditions, as it cost less, while those with learning difficulties could do jobs in the workhouse instead of paid staff. Norman Longmate quoted the chairman of Braintree's Board who, in 1895, refused to agree to an imbecile going to an asylum for he 'could be kept at the union house for less than half the cost at the asylum'.[9] However, using information to a select committee in 1877, Andrew Scull wrote that

there is considerable evidence that workhouse authorities, too, sought to use asylums to 'relieve their wards of many old people who are suffering from nothing else than the natural failing of old age'. . .[10]

Peter Bartlett suggested the process of becoming a pauper lunatic generally began when family, or occasionally neighbours, approached the Poor Law relieving officer who arranged for two medical certificates to be signed, usually one by the Poor Law medical officer and another by an independent doctor.[11] Following the 1890 Lunacy Act, a certificate from a physician was sufficient. The relieving officer took the lunatic, with the certificates, to the local magistrate who signed an admission order to the asylum but, sometimes, refused. The asylum's visiting committee decided discharges from the asylum, following the medical superintendent's report.

A complex administrative process was set up by central government in which no one person, or group of people, was responsible for the admission, care, treatment and discharge of pauper lunatics. All were regularly encouraged by the Commissioners to provide high standards, based on 'moral treatment', the medical superintendent being autonomous in deciding the type of treatment. As for the initial decision to admit, Adair, Melling and Forsythe suggest that

> The journey to the asylum was directed not merely by the broad market, class and ideological dynamics that have been traced in some accounts, but also by a complex interplay between local kinship or community ties and the evolving institutions of the Poor Law which demarcated the boundaries of social regulation in people's lives.[12]

Chapter 2: Planning the Asylum

Surrey's first county asylum opened in Wandsworth, in 1841, for 350 patients. Known as Wandsworth Asylum, it was enlarged several times to meet a steadily increasingly demand for beds.[1] Brookwood Asylum, near Woking, opened in 1867 as the second asylum for Surrey, taking pauper lunatics from West Surrey.

Soon, Wandsworth's accommodation was again insufficient and patients were sent to other county asylums, and to private licensed houses. In 1874 that, with nearly 1,000 patients, it was filled with long-term patients 'in a state of confirmed sanity' whereas beds should be for acute cases sent long distances to licensed houses. Its committee requested the county's magistrates to build a third asylum 'on the grounds of humanity' to provide 'better care and more frequent cures'.[2]

In early 1875, the Guardians of St. Saviour's Union wrote to the other Unions in Surrey about the recent increase in charges by proprietors of licensed houses to 19s 3d a week for care and maintenance, compared with 10s 6d in the county's asylums.[3] St. Saviour's Union wanted support in persuading the magistrates to increase accommodation in the county's two asylums.

The Croydon Advertiser reflected current opinion in deploring the increase in lunacy, which

> Physiologists ascribe to the great mental excitement which men now undergo in the endeavour to regulate their actions to the pace of steam machinery, to severe and protracted brain work, and to intemperate habits of many who are engaged in sedentary occupations.

It saw intemperance as the main cause, hoping 'the steady, persistent operation of moral influence and the spread of education' would make the next generation 'soberer and wiser' and that 'many sad aspects of insanity ... will disappear'.[4]

From 1875 to 1883, the Commissioners in Lunacy consistently

reported favourably on Wandsworth Asylum, its interiors being 'cheerful and comfortable', and 'the demeanour of the patients . . . has been very satisfactory' although, in 1880, corridors in the basement were overcrowded with beds.[5]

In late May, the magistrates' 'Committee appointed to consider the question of providing further accommodation' reported that it had considered accommodating large numbers of pauper lunatics in workhouses, but Guardians repeatedly refused to build 'lunatic wards', while the medical superintendents of Wandsworth and Brookwood believed only 10 patients were suitable for lunatic wards in workhouses. Several large Unions urged the immediate building of a new asylum.

The Committee decided against enlarging the existing two asylums, each already containing over 1,000 patients, because 'such economy would be dearly purchased at the cost of efficiency and of that personal supervision by the Medical Superintendent, the importance of which it is difficult to exaggerate'.[6] They recommended building a third asylum, of a similar size with about the same number of patients. The committee would select and purchase a site, at a cost not exceeding £12,000.

Their recommendations were accepted at the midsummer quarter sessions. Dr Alfred Carpenter (1825-92), a committee member and one of Wandsworth Asylum's visiting committee, expressed his support. A medical practitioner in Croydon, he was a Liberal, a local magistrate and an ex-officio member of the Croydon Union's Board of Guardians. He had previously objected to a new asylum as

> A certain class of people, not paupers, were striving to get their relatives confined in lunatic asylums, because they were eccentric and troublesome. Magistrates should not sign orders simply for those reasons, and unless the person brought before them was homicidal, suicidal, or destructive, they ought not to be kept in lunatic asylums at the expense of the ratepayers.

He believed the increase in the number of lunatics in Surrey, from 1,202 in 1854 to the present 3,200, was largely due to living longer and to more humane treatment than some had at home. The increase could be greatly reduced if magistrates took more care when signing certificates for admission, but evidence showed him that a new asylum was necessary. 'Curable cases' should go to asylums at the earliest possible moment, but it was impossible to admit them 'until they had become almost incurable', which greatly contributed to the present 'block'.[7]

In July, Croydon's Guardians, now able to admit to Brookwood and Wandsworth, looked forward to a new asylum. Despite an increase in rates, they saw savings as they would not need to use licensed houses. *The Croydon Advertiser* extolled nearby Caterham Asylum, built by the Metropolitan Asylums Board for 2,000 patients, 1,900 being imbeciles and the remainder 'chronic' lunatics. Most of its food was raised on its estate, reducing costs to a minimum, 'the fact of cures being frequent among the class of people who are classed in the workhouses as 'chronic' proves the beneficial result of country treatment combined with labour where practicable'.[8] A delegation from the Guardians of the Croydon Union to Caterham Asylum believed its methods could be imitated 'as a proof of the humanity of the present age', and cost only 9s per head per week, resulting in outstanding cabbages and savoys: two cabbages together weighed 46½lbs.[9]

Many of Surrey's Unions objected to a new asylum, suggesting more pauper lunatics could be cared for in workhouses, at home by relatives or boarded out in cottages and, in September 1875, held a conference at Wandsworth Board of Works, attended by Guardians from Godstone, Guildford, Richmond, Chertsey, Dorking, Wandsworth, Clapham, Farnham and Camberwell Unions.[10] The conference asserted that it cost 11s 3d a week to keep a lunatic in an asylum, but only 6s 3d in a workhouse. Croydon's Guardians, who did not attend, doubted that staffing costs were included, which would almost double the cost, while 'lunatics were people who required a great amount of supervision, and an extra amount of nourishment in order to facilitate the chances of recovery', and bedridden patients 'could not be so well treated anywhere as in a proper asylum'.

St. Saviour's and Reigate Unions expressed their confidence in the magistrates and the chairman of Croydon Union's board called the conference 'a sort of underhand meeting', its Guardians re-affirming that a third county asylum was 'absolutely necessary'.[11] The magistrates, ignoring the views expressed at the conference, went ahead to look for suitable land. They tendered in local newspapers for 100 to 150 acres suitable for building and agriculture, with good access and no public footpaths.

When extensions opened at Wandsworth and Brookwood in December 1875, the medical superintendent at Wandsworth reported that, of 133 of Surrey's pauper lunatics transferred from licensed houses to Wandsworth, 27 were infested with vermin and, in nine cases, he saw no symptoms of insanity.[12] Five women, belonging to Croydon Union, came from Fisherton House, a private licensed house in Salisbury, with nits in their hair, including Elizabeth Barden, 66, a plasterer's wife, certified in 1869 on grounds of 'domestic trouble' who now showed 'no signs of insanity', and was discharged in February 1876 as 'recovered'.[13]

Acquiring the land

The Commissioners wrote to the magistrates in November expressing their wish to 'eliminate' from asylums 'large proportions of harmless imbeciles, idiots and epileptics, demented persons and those labouring under chronic insanity' in order to stop the extension of costly asylums. Patients 'in a fit state for home' ought to be discharged, with a liberal weekly allowance, to their families while relieving officers should ensure that single pauper patients had adequate relief and not be placed with strangers.

The Commissioners considered that, unless intermediate asylums such as Caterham Asylum were provided, large wards in workhouses should be set aside for harmless and incurable patients 'conducted with liberality' for

> one who, under the influence of a full and varied diet, of ample air and exercise, with suitable employment and supervision, and with cheerful surroundings, may be classed as 'quiet and harmless', is very liable, on the removal or serious modification of these conditions, to become morose, dirty, and destructive, or even violent and dangerous, and in fact unfit for anything but a return to the Asylums.

When the Commissioners recommended an 'inexpensive and homely' asylum, the chief requirement being dormitories and day rooms, the magistrates replied that they were 'more interested than anyone else in making the buildings as inexpensive as possible', and that the reasons which prevented chronic cases being discharged equally demanded the provision 'of single rooms and all other appliances for excitable, violent and troublesome patients'.

The magistrates' committee looked at many estates but, in early 1876, with ten less pauper lunatics in the county than a year earlier, they decided not to purchase land until numbers increased again. On 1st January 1876, there were 3244 pauper lunatics but, a year later, with 3346, the magistrates took immediate steps to find a site. They were advised by Mr Charles Henry Howell (1824-1905), the surveyor of public buildings for Surrey and consulting architect to the Commissioners in Lunacy who had already designed asylums at Brookwood, Moulsford in Berkshire and Beverley in the East Riding of Yorkshire.

Mr Edmund Byron, of Coulsdon Court, was lord of the manor of Coulsdon. In April, his agent offered to sell 131 acres, 2 rods and 7 poles of land in Coulsdon, including timber and farm buildings, for £70,700, and was willing to sell more for another £1,000 as a footpath ran through the part where the asylum would probably be built, which would need to be closed or diverted. It was probably part of the Portnalls estate which, in the tithe map of 1870, consisted of 356 acres. It included 'Cane Hill and rough', the nearest field to today's Coulsdon, then known as Smitham Bottom. It was decided to withhold the offer unless Mr. Byron would include more land for that amount. The committee knew him well, for he was a fellow magistrate.

Next, Mr Byron suggested selling more land than the magistrates wanted, the offer only being open for a short time as he would otherwise want a new tenant for the farm, the price being 'very low considering the locality and beautiful site and the prices which have and are being obtained within a very short distance of it'.

The magistrates responded by considering enlarging Wandsworth and Brookwood Asylums: each would have an additional 500 beds. However, Mr Howell recommended that it would cost more than building a new asylum and that, whatever Mr Byron claimed, farming in Surrey might not be profitable 'entirely with hired labourers, but with a large amount of labour at your disposal [in the form of patients], some advantage ought to be derived from the production of milk, butter, pork and vegetables'. Taking his advice, they looked at other properties, but eventually decided on part of the Portnalls estate.[14]

In the meantime Byron had sold Portnalls, including its farm, to Joseph Tucker, a member of the Stock Exchange, who sold the land in 1878. In the 1881 census, Joseph Tucker, aged 49 and born in Stoke Newington, lived at Portnalls with his wife, four daughters and his heir Horace aged 8, his sister and four female servants. David Lingen, his tenant, was at Portnalls Farm, now 165 acres, with his family. He employed four men and two boys: one farm labourer was at Portnalls Cottage, and a cowman lived on the estate, as did Tucker's gardener, all with families.[15]

With Mr Howell as architect, building eventually began. In June 1880, the magistrates wrote to the Chief Commissioner of the Metropolitan Police requesting a strengthening of the police force in Coulsdon 'for the protection of the inhabitants', namely the labourers, in the temporary shanty erected for their use. In October, there were nearly 300 men on site, many with their families, including Frederick W. Holmes, the architect's clerk of works and George Harvey, foreman of the excavators.

Howell planned the building as a 'radiating pavilion asylum' with blocks of wards, of different sizes and designs, coming off a D-shaped internal corridor. Each ward had access to an airing court where patients could walk and sit, supervised by attendants. The female wards, on the south side, were separated from the male wards by a series of buildings running down the centre with the administrative block at the front and, behind it, the chapel, the dining hall, kitchens, bake house, butchers, stores, engineer's department and laundry. The asylum was built on two arable fields: Snagging Grove, bordering Portnall Road, and Doctors Commons running down to the present Brighton Road, and on Dunstans Wood. A well close to Lion Green would provide sufficient water, the water tower providing the necessary pressure.

In October 1882, Dr James Matthew Moody was appointed, from 44 applicants, as medical superintendent. Aged thirty and single, he had been a junior and was currently a senior assistant medical officer at Brookwood Asylum, having worked there since 1876. It was noted that he had experienced being there during the building of its extension. Born in Ireland, as were his parents, he was brought up in Essex, the younger son of a Royal Navy Fleet Surgeon. In 1885, he married Alice Harriett Frend, of Worplesdon in Surrey, a daughter of an architect and surveyor. He began at Cane Hill in February 1883.

The Clerk of the asylum, Mr Ralph also came from Brookwood.

The Railway

Lord Monson, chairman of the committee, met with Sir Edward Watkin, chairman of the South Eastern Railway Company in June 1880, to discuss the name and site of a railway station to be built near to the asylum, Sir Edward promising to see Mr Laing, chairman of the London, Brighton and South Coast Railway.

Both could see the potential: With a small goods yard, it could help in recruitment as potential staff would not feel isolated while the railway company would not only look forward to business from the asylum, but knew that usage would grow as people wanted to live near to stations.

There was discussion of a branch line to the hospital. In April 1882, Mr Howell enquired into constructing a railway from the London and Brighton line to the main buildings. In July, he reported that the suggested route would entail the considerable cost of building a viaduct or high embankment which would be 'a disturbance and danger to patients' and seriously reduce the amount of land intended for cultivation. Although a gas works was being built at the asylum, it was decided not to construct a railway, it being cheaper to cart coal and other goods a mile from Stoats Nest Station. With a goods entrance made on Chipstead Road, about 200 yards south-east of North Lodge, Croydon Highways Board were asked to construct a granite tramway on the steepest part of the road. There would be a tramway in the yard leading to the stores. Nothing came of the tramway, and it would be a few years before a railway station opened.

Negotiations took place with Mr Tucker to buy more of Portnalls Farm, adjoining the asylum's estate. He was anxious to sell but, in October 1882, was unable to give the magistrates possession of land in the conveyance lying within 40 rods of the farm house as his tenant, Mr Lingen, would not surrender his holding. Mr Tucker was instructing his solicitors to take proceedings against Mr Lingen, but the committee needed immediate possession of the land. Shortly after, Mr Tucker was able to move the temporary fence so that all the purchased land could be enclosed and, in February 1883, it was decided to purchase from Mr Tucker for £12,250. Comprising about

35 acres, it included five cottages, pasture, woodland, meadow, stables and a lodge.[16] Mr Tucker proceeded to rebuild Portnalls House in the 1880s.[17]

Problems continued in October, regarding a small piece of land, known as the Old Tram Road, there being no proof that its owners ever purchased it, although the tenant was prepared to make a statutory declaration that he had rented it for many years. It was a small part of a large field which might have been subject to a payment of £25 a year to a parish on Sussex, but the vendor offered indemnity.[18]

In 1883, the contractor auctioned his buildings: brick and tile erections comprising the general office, canteen, stables, clerk of works office, and weather board and felt roof constructions consisting of the engine shed with brick pit, mill and carpenter's shop, lime shed, mortar shed, three smiths' shops, portable office. He also sold two useful horses, iron cisterns, trollies, sleepers, new and old doors and sashes, 55 scaffold poles, 300 scaffold boards, 5 dobbins, barrows, putlogs, trestles, a large quantity of centres, 20 stacks of good firewood and various miscellaneous effects.[19]

At the Midsummer Session in 1883, the magistrates decided that Cane Hill Asylum would admit all the pauper lunatics from Dorking, Epsom, Godstone, Reigate and Croydon Unions, the last being the largest Union. A maximum of 110 from St. Olave's Union and 220 from St. Saviour's Union would go to Wandsworth, with the remainder from those two Unions going to Cane Hill.

The Local Community

In October 1882 Mr Stewart, the rector of Coulsdon, wrote to Lord Monson of 'the hardship it would be to the parishioners if the parish church yard was used as a place of interment for the patients', especially as the church was two miles away 'by a narrow and hilly lane': parishioners strongly objected to the annoyance to which they would be subjected if the churchyard was used by the asylum. The Commissioners in Lunacy regretted the parishioners' views, but would not oppose a burial ground at the asylum.

The first patients arrived in December 1883. By the end of January 1884, four patients having died, the rector wrote to ask that the asylum's cemetery be opened as soon as possible so that it would be unnecessary for patients to be buried in the parish church yard.

The committee decided on a cemetery 'laid out to produce rather a soothing than depressing effect' and planted so as not to be seen from the wards. They asked Mr Tucker, the neighbouring landowner, for about two acres. He offered 1½ acres for £75 but, in April 1884, agreed to two acres for the same price. In October, it was decided that unclaimed bodies of people dying in the asylum be handed over for 'the purposes of anatomical examination', which continued into the twentieth century, and, a month later, that the cemetery should have its own mortuary and chapel.[20]

The asylum committee did not yet feel a need for a boundary wall. Replanting hedges and erecting fencing would be 'sufficient to keep out an intruding public', although a wall could be considered in the future if the local population increased.[21] They wanted to reduce the sense of restriction for the patients: the airing courts had 'sunk walls in order not to obstruct the view or give an air of confinement. Where the level of the ground requires it, they have cuttings on both sides' (see Appendix 1).

In January 1884, the medical superintendent reported mischief caused by gypsies camped near Farthing Down. A month later, Dr Moody reported that he would prepare, for the next meeting, a letter to the Master of the Hounds to stop them entering the asylum's estate while hunting.[22] A year later, two men were employed to repair boundary fences. There were two lodges and, by 1887 East Lodge at the main Brighton road entrance was occupied by the clerk of the works and North Lodge, at the goods entrance, by the engineer.[23]

Mr Stewart wrote to the committee in December 1888, about the very large percentage of children in the school at Smitham Bottom whose parents worked at the asylum. Opened in November 1886 in a corrugated iron mission hall in Brighton Road, it was known as the Cane Hill Church of England Mission School. He asked 'that the Committee may be pleased to make a Subscription to the Friends of the School'. The committee replied that they regretted they could not legally make a grant but that 'if they had the power they would have had great pleasure in making a contribution'.[24]

Final preparations

In October 1883, an order was made for clothing, and for material to make clothes at the asylum, for patients and staff. For the men, it would be corduroy, blue cloth (indigo), blue striped shirting, Welsh flannel, Turkey twill, handkerchiefs, Drab Jean, blue serge lining, braces and grey knit stockings. The women would have twill cotton print, Winseys, brown cloth (to make strong dresses), blue serge, brown twill, chemising, striped cotton for night gowns, cap muslin & gathering, apron check, gingham for sun bonnets, stays, handkerchiefs, neck shawls, large shawls, grey calico and brown hosiery. Headwear consisted of felt hats, straw hats and straw bonnets.[25] Footwear was purchased from prisons, presumably made by prisoners: boots and shoes from Pentonville and slippers from Wakefield.[26] In January 1884, it was decided that the male attendants' uniforms would closely resemble those of the Army Hospital Corps. A bow would be removed from the female attendants' morning dress, and the apron bib enlarged.

Sets of games and amusements were purchased for the wards: 50 draughts, 24 dominoes, 10 chess men, 50 besique, 50 draughtboards, 24 happy families, 24 cribbage boards, 25 dice in boxes and 2 footballs. There would be billiard tables and daily newspapers. Weekly magazines included *Punch*, *Fun*, *Judy*, *Funny Folks*, *Pall Mall Gazette* and *Field* while monthly periodicals included *Cornhill Magazine*, *Harper's*, *Leisure Hour* and *Band of Hope*.

An organ, built twenty-five years earlier for St. John's Church in Hampstead, was purchased for the church. Seed was bought for planting to provide vegetables for six months: onions, turnips, carrots and three types of potatoes.

The first patients arrived on 20 December 1883; twenty pauper lunatics transferred from Brookwood Asylum. Local Unions would be charged 11s 8d a week for each pauper lunatic, but received 4s for each one from central government, while those from Unions in other counties would be charged 14s. Patients were transferred in groups from other asylums and private licensed houses. Croydon Union, in late 1883, had pauper lunatics in county asylums in Northamptonshire, Norfolk, Warwickshire and Essex, the borough asylum in Portsmouth, five licensed houses, including Fisherton House in Salisbury, and the Western Counties Idiot Asylum near Exeter, as well as in Wandsworth and Brookwood Asylums. In January 1884, there were '64 attendants, nurses, artisans and servants ... and a number of patients are daily employed in the laundry and domestic offices'.[27]

Chapter 3 Opening Cane Hill

Journalists from the *The Croydon Advertiser*, who visited Cane Hill Asylum in January 1884, wrote that Mr Howell, the architect, had 'achieved an undoubted triumph, having arranged a model institution as near to perfection as human ingenuity can get' in a place where 'the air is purity itself', while Dr Moody was 'a treasure of no small worth' having the entire confidence of the visiting justices. It would hold about 1,150 patients, but could be enlarged to take 2,000. The newspaper believed that the magistrates 'have been economical and expeditious to a most creditable extent. Seldom has a county got better value for its money, and never, we believe, has money been more judiciously expended' providing it could be done for the inmates without extravagance. Built by Mr. J.T. Chappell for £198,640, it was claimed to have some of the finest brickwork in the South of England.

The buildings covered about twelve acres, with over three miles of corridors. With a large number of small court yards, it was designed so that as much light as possible could enter the building. The chapel, designed in the early English style, could hold about 800 people while the recreation hall, which could seat 500, had a stage and proscenium, orchestra pit, dressing rooms and a balcony for visitors. Larger than most London theatres, staff and their friends could perform. The first concert would be held that evening.

The kitchen, built beside the dining-room, was 90 foot long and 80 foot wide, and designed to feed 2,000 patients and about 250 attendants. Roasting spits were turned by a miniature steam engine which powered a coffee mill and a mincing machine. Two gas ovens, used to cook meat for the senior staff, could turn out about 100 joints at the same time. A row of six coppers would be used to make tea, coffee and cocoa and to boiling soap, meat and other foods.

The store yard lay alongside, surrounded by storerooms. The general store-room, 'over which Mr Thompson, the genial steward, presides', was filled with 'heavily stacked shelves and cupboards' and 'clothing of every description'. There were three large larders, and the butcher's shop

> in which it is proposed to kill beasts, when the asylum is a little more fully occupied, is so designed as to keep the sun out, and make the visits of blow flies impossible, although the draft of cold air is continuous. At Cane Hill, the air is purity itself, and we should imagine the building will be almost as valuable as a refrigerator.

They were equally enthusiastic about the 'machinery department' which was 'perfect', where a small donkey-engine pumped water into four enormous boilers supplying steam to heat the whole building, as well as 'for many other useful purposes'. Nearby, a twelve-horse power engine operated the machines in the laundries, necessary 'in an institution of great magnitude, in which cleanliness is regarded as second only to order and discipline':

> The washing machines are of enormous capacity, and the power is turned on and off with the greatest ease. The clothes pass through a rubber wringing machine, and fall into the rinsing troughs below, whence they are subsequently transferred to centrifugal wringers, in which the surplus water is cast away by the force of motion only, and without any kind of pressure. The drying-room is fitted up with 'horses' on trollies. When filled with clothes, these are pushed over hot air gratings, and no matter what the weather may be outside, rapid drying is assured.

There was a drying ground outside, and ironing and sorting rooms

> 'fitted up with the greatest possible regard for economy, time and labour. A number of patients were busy ironing as we passed through, and seemed perfectly contented and happy. Some of them conversed rationally on general subjects, and it was really difficult to believe that they were really insane at all'.

The journalists continued their tour and visited the wards, where the day rooms were

> large airy compartments, admirably fitted up with everything that could be reasonably thought of for the comfort of the inmates.

There is a bagatelle table provided, while in the matter of tables and seats great good taste has been displayed; we noticed with pleasure that Carter's invalid chairs are provided for some of those most afflicted. The wards are all that can be desired, and the dormitories most comfortable. The arrangements for suicidal patients are at once complete and effective. Each patient has a separate apartment with a door, from which the panels have been removed, so as to at once make inspection easy and sure . . . a lamp is so fixed over the door that the light falls on the bed. This is placed on the floor, and there is thus no bedstead to be broken up and made use of as a weapon of self-destruction. Padded rooms are provided, the side and floors being covered with thick india rubber, against which a violent patient might knock himself a dozen times without sustaining the least injury.

Every towel rail was fitted with a key, 'so that the inmates cannot get it out to make an improper use of'. 'Grandmaster' keys, issued only to doctors, opened every door, but keys supplied to heads of departments fitted their own locks only. Letters sent to patients were not checked, 'but it is necessary that all epistles from inmates to their friends should be read through, or serious trouble might be caused, while threatening letters would be common'.

The journalists saw the attendants' recreation rooms, the housekeeper's 'very snug' quarters, and the servants' bedrooms, those staff responsible for maintaining the building and services, rather than working with the patients. Each contained two beds with

> very comfortable sprung mattresses with every possible convenience, though nothing can be said to be of an extravagant or luxurious character. Dr, Moody himself superintended the furnishing of every room in the building, and common sense, and good taste, to say nothing of marked ingenuity everywhere prevails.[1]

A deputation of Croydon Union's Guardians visited, declaring themselves 'highly pleased with the arrangements made for the comfort and welfare of the patients'.[2] They would visit twice a year, always praising the condition of the buildings and patients, not enquiring into their treatment.

Building and equipping continued, such as a shower bath, a form of treatment, window blinds and sewing machines.[3] They acquired cricket equipment, seating for the airing courts and a greenhouse in early 1884 and, the next year, a shelter and sunshade for Male Airing Court No. 1. In 1886, gravel was bought to complete airing courts G & H on the female side and H on the male side.[4]

The farm and gardens provided work for patients and supplemented the diet, but it was necessary to obtain food locally such as in 1884 when Mr Thomas Brooke of the Red Lion in Coulsdon offered to sell 40 or 50 tons of potatoes at 87s 6d a ton. It would be accepted provided he delivered about a ton a week for the next year. Mr Brook of Tanfield Dairy in South Croydon would supply milk at 1s 1d a gallon for 9 months, while Mr Tucker offered to sell about 70 acres of grass.[5]

The General Post Office (GPO) agreed to provide a private telephone line between the asylum and Stoats Nest Station.[6] In 1885, the house committee bought a mare to draw light goods from the station. Every day, it would take swill from the asylum to the farm, and the steward and bailiff could use it to go to Croydon and elsewhere on business. It would also be used for light work' and assist the other horses. The asylum's carriage would meet committee members at Caterham Junction, now called Purley Station, on meeting days, leaving the station at 10.10 a.m. and 11.20 a.m. It could not be used by staff without permission in writing from Dr. Moody. The stableman's duties included driving the carriage and attending to Dr. Moody's horse and dog cart, assisted by a patient, and working in the medical superintendent's house, cleaning knives and boots. Dr. Moody had a messenger who also worked in the garden.[7]

Already in February 1884, male staff members had formed a band, a bandsman receiving 6d for each practice and the bandmaster 1s. The first fete was probably held in 1884 for, the following year, Dr Moody was authorised to hold 'the customary fete' for the patients, to hire swings and to provide prizes to a value not exceeding £3.[8] The next year, he was allowed to arrange the church choir's annual excursion.[9] In 1886, he could provide a plain luncheon and a pint of stout to each person playing cricket at the asylum.[10] Staff competed with local teams and those from other asylums. To celebrate the Queen's Jubilee in the summer of 1887, there was 'Christmas fare', afternoon sports and evening entertainments for the patients. All staff, attendants and their families would have a 'ball and tupper'.[11]

In 1885, it was decided to erect a building for photography, as a photograph was taken of each patient and kept with the case notes.[12] The same year, plans commenced to build cottages for 20 married attendants, to cost £3,750, but at least one would continue to sleep on each male ward.[13] While twelve cottages would have a living room, kitchen scullery and two bedrooms, capable of being divided into three bedrooms, four cottages would be 'half houses' for attendants without children.[14] All gardens were to be kept neat and tidy. The rent would be 4s a week for cottages and 3s for the 'half houses'. Attendants living there could come and go by the main roads in the grounds, but no children or family members were to trespass on the estate.[15]

The State Legislature in Pennsylvania, looking to build an asylum, wrote to Dr. Tuke of Lyndon Lodge, Hanwell, West London for advice. In his reply in 1887, Dr. Tuke wrote that he considered the best asylum in England, with regard to the architecture, was Cane Hill: '. . . it has borne the test of experience in all its main features and that in some points of detail in which the original design admits of improvement, the necessary alterations are made in the plans which I have prepared'.[16] He included comments from Dr Moody: "My experience of Cane Hill is all in its favor. I find a very workable asylum". A description of Cane Hill by an architect, a relative of Mrs Moody, which accompanied Dr. Tuke's letter, is in Appendix 1. It had already been decided to enlarge the asylum to take an additional nine hundred patients.

The Commissioners in Lunacy

Two Commissioners in Lunacy, (hereafter referred to as Commissioners), visited annually and made a report which could include criticism and recommendations. They could not enforce them, but the Local Government Board could take note and do so.

On their first visit, in July 1884, they observed that 'The high and airy position of the Asylum and the dryness of the soil should, with the good sanitary conditions, render it a very healthy abode'. Mr. Green and Miss Woodward, the head attendants seemed 'zealous and intelligent'

The Commissioners were satisfied with the patients' dress and their care, their demeanour being 'very good and quiet', with 71 per cent of males and 57 per cent of females employed: 'We cannot urge too strongly the importance of useful employment in the treatment of the insane'. No patients complained of ill-usage or want of care. Dinners were good and sufficient, workers having extra, and were served on the wards, but the Commissioners hoped that the large recreation hall would be used for associated dinners, meals where both sexes could meet.[17]

Although this suggestion was repeated the following year, the committee did 'not see their way at present to adopt the recommendation' but agreed to screens between the baths on the female side, patients having complained on both visits, and to an airing court for the male infirmary, which would be made as soon as possible.[18] There was a need to make walkways in the woods and along the boundary of the estate, to provide 'extended exercise' for the patients. They noted good furniture on the wards, although there was too much on the male epileptic wards, newspaper desks and chairs for the sick. Picture frames were being made. This time, nearly ¾ of patients complained of tainted meat while the Commissioners noted that their clothing, while fairly good, could be improved, particularly for the females, with more varied fabrics. Despite these comments, progress was 'highly creditable' to the committee and medical superintendent.

There were 429 male and 563 female patients, a total of 992, of which 128 were epileptic while 10 males and 14 females were actively suicidal. 60 per cent of the females and 80 per cent of the men were employed. Of 347 women, 166 did needlework, probably sewing, 105 were ward cleaners, 44 were in the laundry and 32 in the kitchens and offices. As for the men, 34 were ward cleaners while 232 worked on the land and at the farm, a few being lodged in the bailiff's and gardener's cottages. Three greenhouses produced plants and flowers for the wards. In the summer, men working on the land had a drink of oatmeal or lime juice sent to them in the morning and afternoon.[19]

For the rest of the 1880s, the Commissioners praised what they saw at Cane Hill, with little criticism. In 1886, the patients' conduct was very good, largely due to the staffs' tact. There were few complaints by patients, although one old man reported an attendant. It 'raised the suspicion of unnecessary violence and the attendant was warned'. Several patients had black eyes, attributed to fellow patients; the Commissioners believe that having more staff would reduce such incidents - there were 44 male and 53 female attendants. Each year, it was reported that no seclusion or mechanical restraints were used. In 1885, three men and fifteen women died of exhaustion following an episode of mania of depression, perhaps an indication that medication was not used routinely to sedate patients (see Figure 2). In the early years of Cane Hill, they were not admitting large numbers of people with senile dementia; only 9 died from senile decay. As no case notes have survived, diagnoses are not known but, each year, the Commissioners listed causes of death. In 1885, with a high than usual number of deaths, the causes were as follows:

Figure 1. Causes of deaths of patients in 1885 [20]

Cause	Males	Females	Total
General Paralysis	27	6	33
Epilepsy	1	6	7
Other forms of brain disease	7	9	16
Exhaustion after mania and melancholia	3	15	18
Pulmonary consumption	8	11	19
Other forms of lung disease	2	5	7
Disease of heart	1	4	5
Disease of abdominal organs	1	6	7
Senile decay	5	4	9
A fatal casualty (patient jumped through a window)	1		1
Suicide by hanging	1		1
Totals	57	66	123

There were fewer male patients and more females in 1886, namely 442 men and 601 women, a ratio which would continue. 380 men, being most of the male patients, but only 394 females were employed. It was important that men should retain their work skills in order to obtain employment after discharge.

Figure 2 Employment of Patients on 10 June 1886 [21]

Men
340 – on the land
55 – workshops
37 – offices
16 – coal carriers and wood choppers
32 – wards (12 – hard workers, 20 light workers)

Women
88 – sewing in wards
65 – sewing in workroom – hoped to increase the numbers by providing another workroom
53 – laundry
27 – kitchen
27 – knitting, mending and quilting
34 – assisting in offices
85 – ward workers (70 hard workers, the remaining contributing little assistance)

Female patients now had more varied dresses, and there were pianos in two female wards. There was a library with 'well chosen books'. Dayrooms were 'decorated economically and in good taste' while a door from the female airing courts to the recreation field enabled even the most 'refractory' women to have 'proper out-door exercise'. There were to be more airing courts 'with extensive views, swats and sunshades'. Two female airing courts were 'well-timbered', which would 'yield an agreeable shelter on sunny days'.152 men and 291 women were allowed to walk beyond the estate.[22]

In 1887, 601 patients walked twice a week beyond the airing courts while 236 men and 185 females walked weekly beyond the estate, although it is not known why there were fewer women at a time when their numbers were increasing. Similarly, 29 men had parole within the grounds and 23 beyond.[23] The following year, the committee were 'contemplating a good walk around the boundary' which, in the view of the Commissioners, 'greatly facilitates a system of extended daily exercise for the patients, to which we attach much importance in the treatment of the insane and the making of the walk affords occupation for the men'. The gardens and grounds had been abundantly planted. About 600 patients walked out weekly beyond the asylum and airing courts, but the Commissioners' recommendation for daily walks beyond the airing courts had not been taken up. Now, 73 per cent of males and 70 per cent of females were employed, and they reported that patients were well supplied with amusements in the wards, the recreation hall and out of doors.

Chapter 4: Staff and patients 1883-1889

The Staff

Dr. Moody was initially appointed with a salary of £700 a year, a large detached house and garden, just south of the main building, lighting, fuel, and laundry as well as farm and garden produce from the estate. In 1887, his annual salary increased to £900. All staff received annual increments up to a maximum salary.

There was one other doctor, a senior assistant medical officer, employed at £150 a year, increasing to £200 plus his board, food, laundry etc. Dr David George Thomson, and most of his successors, stayed for a few years before becoming medical superintendents elsewhere.

The chaplain, John Charles Crawford, received £250 a year, an unfurnished house and garden and lighting. From 1888, he was given fuel and milk and, from 1889, vegetables. James Lake Ralph, the Clerk, commenced at £150 and George Gilbert Thomson, the steward and storekeeper at £100, increased in 1885 to £150, with a furnished house, light, fuel, laundry, and farm and garden produce 'at market prices'. The housekeeper, Eliza Powell, began at £60 a year, and the dispenser at £65, both with 'all found'. A laundress was paid £30 a year including beer money. The male and female head attendants commenced at £65 a year, and assistant matrons at £60.[1] The salary of junior attendants is not known but, a decade on, male second class day attendants started at £29 a year and females at £18, while male first class day attendants began at £36 a year and females at £25.[2]

A wide range of workers were necessary, including an estate manager, a lodge keeper, a back door keeper, hall porters, a boy messenger, house boys, an engineer, stokers, fitters, a tin man, cooks, bakers, scullery men and maids, a laundry superintendent, a laundry mistress, laundry men and laundresses, sewing room staff, work room assistants, laundry maids, kitchen maids, hall maids, mess room maids, house maids, firemen, bricklayers, painters, carpenters, a shoemaker, a tailor, an upholster, gardeners, stablemen and stockmen.

Many, mostly men, were dismissed for a variety of misdemeanors: a large number, all second class attendants, were found 'intoxicated' and some showed 'roughness to patients'. William Davies 'boxed a patient's ears' and Joseph Herbert Tuohey ill treated a patient. Frederick Edward Chapman climbed out of the window in his room and left the asylum without permission, taking the mess boy with him and using bad language in a local public house, while John Mackie 'objected to going to work'.[3] A messenger boy was prosecuted in 1887 for opening letters to patients and one to a nurse, and for stealing a packet of cigars belonging to a male attendant.[4]

In May 1886, Frederick Paine, a joiner, taken on in the winter because he was unemployed, on Mr. Edridge's recommendation, was considered to be the ringleader 'in creating and fostering the present discontent among the men'. He was 'discharged' a month later.[5] As for the female staff, Emma Bearman, Kate Hill and Emily Sargeant 'conspired to prevent the work of the ward being carried out', while Mary Harman showed 'incompetency and carelessness in her work'. Mary Warne was dismissed for 'dishonest conduct towards the workman with whom she usually dwelt' while Emily Clara Tupper lent keys to a patient enabling her to escape, and was fined the cost of the patient's recapture. All were second class attendants, but it was Charge Nurse Esther Ann Woodhall who was 'intoxicated when at Gloucester on duty'.[6] The number of staff dismissed, mainly second class attendants, steadily increased, reaching a peak in 1888, intoxication being the most common cause. Anne Stanley, 'under the influence of drink', gave drink to a female patient while James Carson left the asylum without permission, and was intoxicated on duty.

That same year, the wife of Thomas Reynolds, an attendant, informed Dr Hill, the deputy medical superintendent, that her husband took a tablecloth and comb from the asylum. Dr Hill reported to the committee that Reynolds had an exemplary character, while his wife appeared to be a jealous and hysterical woman. Reynolds appeared before the committee, saying he did not know how the property came into his house, and could only suggest that his wife took them 'to trump up this present charge'. The committee decided the evidence was insufficient in view of his 'high character' both in the army and at Cane Hill. Eventually, he was apprehended by the police and convicted.[7]

All such incidents were reported by the medical superintendent to the county's magistrates who were responsible for running the asylum, and ready to dismiss staff discovered to have flouted the regulations. When the Commissioners visited in 1887, there were 457 male and 618 female patients, looked after by 40 male and 50 female day attendants and, at night, 6 male and 7 female attendants, half of the male attendants and over half of the female attendants having been there less than a year.[8] The following year, there were sufficient attendants who 'appear to be composed of a respectable class of persons'.[9]

The Committees

There were three committees, made up of the same magistrates, all male: the visiting committee, the house committee and the general committee. The functions of each seem to overlap but the former was mainly responsible for major policy and planning decisions while the house committee visited selected parts of the asylum each month. Matters of discipline and issues concerning individual staff and patients were mainly discussed by the house committee. Lord Monson was chairman when the asylum opened, Lieutenant Colonel Leopold Richard Seymour taking the chair in his absence. Major General Thomas Harmer Sibley became chairman in May 1884. They resolved to have at least two local magistrates who included Mr Jabez Spencer Balfour, Mayor of Croydon in 1883-4, Dr Carpenter, a medical practitioner, and Mr Thomas Edridge, a ship owner, all living in Croydon.

Almost without exception, the house committee considered all was satisfactory. In 1884, they commented that ornaments and pictures made a great improvement. They talked with patients who, invariably, were observed as quiet and orderly. In 1886 all the wards were clean and orderly and the patients 'contented and well cared for'. The asylum's discipline was well maintained and the general management reflected well on the medical superintendent and his staff.

There were occasional criticisms, which initially concerned food. In 1884, it was of good quality but they suggested how it could be delivered to wards and served up. Shortly after, serving up still needed to improve: 'the meat was said to be hot, but nearly, if not, cold', but it appeared to have been resolved as there was no further mention.

They recommended changes, often following escapes and suicides. In 1885, they instructed that the engineer should check locks as some were defective and, in 1888, greenhouses were neglected with broken pipes and unpainted shelves while plants in the middle green house were 'in a very bad state and in no way to be accounted for by their having been in the wards'.

The Patients

Case notes for patients at Cane Hill having been destroyed, any information about a person's illness can only come from information kept by other institutions which may have survived. Cane Hill's admission books have limited information, only recording the patient's name, dates of admission, discharge or death, and the responsible Union. Those transferred to other asylums were described as 'not improved'. Similar books maintained by Wandsworth Asylum are more detailed and earlier information about patients transferred to Cane Hill in 1883-4 is found in them.[10]

There may be mention in Union records, such as those kept by Croydon's Board of Guardians which included admissions and discharges to asylums. Patients, or their immediate relatives, were expected to pay towards maintenance and care in the asylum, if there was any available money, savings, investments or property, and the Guardian's committee minutes may have detailed information.

In July 1887, Mary Ann Perry of 55 Upland Road, Croydon was admitted to Cane Hill. Her husband Henry John Perry, a labourer with the London, Brighton and South Coast Railway Company, earned £1 2s 0d a week and offered to pay 4s a week towards her maintenance, probably with 'persuasion' from the Relieving Officer. He would have been made aware that a refusal might lead to an appearance before the magistrates and perhaps imprisonment, the fate of several men who refused to pay.[11] In June 1886, proceedings began against four men who refused to contribute, including John Ball of Bridge Terrace Cross Roads, Croydon, whose wife was in Cane Hill. He would end up in prison.[12] James Best of Brigstock Road, Croydon, also with a wife in Cane Hill, asked the Guardians for permission to emigrate with their two sons. They would not impede his request, but trusted he would send payments once he was in a position to do so.[13] Sometimes, a working man, his wife in Cane Hill with no one to look after his family, had to admit his young children to the workhouse.

The Guardians accepted that not all relatives could pay. Henry and Richard Thomas were ordered to pay 5s a week until the arrears for their father's maintenance was paid, or they would be summoned before the magistrates, but Richard was excused payment for the time being. Some applications for a reduction or removal of payments were accepted: Edward Sewell, approached to contribute towards the maintenance of his thirty year old daughter Jessie Sewell, was later considered unable to pay.[14]

When Alwyn Baker of 1 Padua Road, Penge was admitted in 1886, his wife offered to contribute 5s a week from his weekly pension of 19s 2d, as did Henry R. Taylor' wife, who offered 4s a week from her allowance from the Foresters Society. Both offers were accepted.[15] Some patients had their own income: Sarah Wilson was entitled to money from 'cottage property in Wales and other sources'.[16] In 1888, an application was made to the magistrates to obtain the interest on her investments.[17]

Occasionally, minutes from the Guardians' meetings described patients. Matilda Goddard was admitted from Croydon in September 1884 'with very bad varicose veins and in feeble health suffering from delusional mania'.[18] When Ellen Todd wrote to the Guardians in Croydon in 1885, asking to be allowed to enter the Workhouse instead of being detained in Cane Hill, the Guardians' Clerk sent a copy of the letter to the Asylum's Clerk. Dr. Moody replied that 'She has Chronic Delusions and is not a fit case for discharge from an Asylum'.[19]

The Unions expected asylums to admit children, often only five years old, and young people with learning difficulties, described as idiots or imbeciles, who could not be looked after at home, although the visiting committee at Cane Hill became increasingly unwilling to accept them. There were two wards for those with severe epilepsy which contained, in 1885, 67 males and 61 females.[20]

Ann Kilminster, admitted to an asylum in 1877, was transferred from Peckham House in March 1884, a private licensed house, to Cane Hill. Aged about 27, she was 'epileptic, and of weak and undeveloped mind although capable of assisting to some extent in the domestic work of the house'. In May, she was found to be pregnant and, according to her own account, the father was an outdoor servant at Peckham House whose work brought him 'to the neighbourhood of the kitchen where the patient occasionally was. He thus found the opportunity of intercourse with her'. Ann's statements varied and it was not clear if it had happened more than once.

He was dismissed immediately. The visiting committee and Croydon Union's Guardians sought the advice of the Commissioners, the Crown's law officers and an eminent criminal lawyer as to whether he could be prosecuted, but were advised that he could not be charged under the Act concerning the abuse and ill treatment of insane patients in licensed house and hospitals. The Commissioners wondered if Ann's mental state would allow her to appear in Court, and if there was any corroborative evidence.[21] In their annual report, they repeated an earlier recommendation that the law be amended.[22] Ann's daughter, Maud, was born on 4 September at Cane Hill, but Ann died on 13 September 'from puerperal peritonitis of five days duration'.[23] Maud died soon after.

'Recovered'

Between 1883 and 1892, an average of 39.73 per cent of those admitted to county and borough asylums in England and Wales as pauper lunatics were discharged as 'recovered', most having spent between a few months and up to eighteen months in an asylum.[24] Similar results were achieved at Cane Hill, 38 per cent of those admitted from the Croydon Union being discharged as 'recovered'.[25]

Alfred Ferrier, aged 27, a pauper lunatic belonging to the Croydon Union, was admitted to Wandsworth Asylum in June 1871. In the 1871 census, taken in April, he was a labourer living in Love Lane, Mitcham with his wife Ellen and three young children, the youngest being Alfred aged 8 months. He was discharged as recovered but readmitted in January 1875 as a gas stoker with 'mania – hereditary', having been ill for six weeks. Discharged six weeks later, he returned to Wandsworth Asylum in February 1877, having had mania for 28 days, and spent 5 weeks in the asylum. He was readmitted in September, being weak and having 'dementia', probably a psychotic illness, for 5 days. Five weeks later, he was discharged and in May 1881 readmitted, being well nourished with a three day history of mania. In early April, the 1881 census showed him as a bricklayer's labourer, of 14 Smiths Buildings in Mitcham with Ellen and five children aged from 15 to 1 year old. Again, he spent about five weeks in Wandsworth Asylum with mania.[26]

In October 1887 he was readmitted to Cane Hill, and discharged in March after 5½ months. Two months later, he was readmitted and remained until March 1889. The reorganisation of local government and asylums, in 1889, meant that pauper lunatics belonging to the Croydon Union who did not live in the parish of Croydon, were transferred to other asylums.[27] For Alfred, it was Brookwood Asylum where he died in 1895. However, prior to his admission in May 1888, his six earlier admissions were relatively short and he returned to his family and employment. The visiting and house committees were keen to discharge whenever possible, but carefully ensured a patient was well enough, and could live somewhere suitable with enough care, generally with their family.

Trial Leave

Patients were sent on trial leave, usually for a month at a time, after which they sent a certificate from a medical practitioner or personally returned to the asylum. If the patient's mental state was satisfactory, an order of discharge was signed. In October 1885, nine patients discharged after a trial, all 'voluntarily express their thankfulness', as did 3 women in 1888, who 'expressed their gratitude for the kindness and attention shown to them' whilst in the asylum.[28, 29] Patients received an allowance while on trial which, until 1888, depended on money collected by Dr Moody.[30] In 1884, Charles Morris was discharged with 10s, part of the money being used to redeem tools left with the stableman at the Greyhound Tap in Croydon.[31]

In December 1884, the visiting committee invited Joseph Berry's wife and mother-in-law to their meeting, to obtain their opinion about his condition and whether anybody would take responsibility if he was sent out on leave. Dr Moody, present at the meeting, saw Berry on 29 January 1885 and recommended that he remain at Cane Hill as he still had delusions, and no relative had offered to look after him.[32] In August, he was on leave in Colchester, in the care of his cousin, Mr Slaughter, who reported that he was doing very well.

In September 1885, the Commissioners in Lunacy wrote to Dr Moody, Mrs Berry having called at their office 'in a state of great alarm': 'she went in fear of her life' because of her husband's violence. He had been sent out on leave, without her knowledge. Mrs Slaughter wrote to Dr Moody that Berry wanted to go to London to get work, and that his old delusions about trade unions and his wife had reappeared.

Joseph Berry was returned to Cane Hill, and a letter sent to the Commissioners to explain the care with which the committee twice considered his case, the reasons why they sent him out on trial, and the conditions of the trial. A letter sent to Mrs Berry, in February 1886 informed her that he was out on trial for a month, with the intention of extending the period of leave in the future, and an undertaking that he would not approach his wife and children. Mr Slaughter would care for him and find employment.

On 11 March, Berry wrote that his leave expired that day. He was well, employed by his cousin, and enclosed a signed certificate from a surgeon in Colchester that his mental state was satisfactory, which they would check to ensure it was genuine. Mrs Berry appeared before the committee, expressing fears about her safety, but was reminded that her husband agreed to stay away, and would be returned to the asylum if he did so while on leave. They assured her there was no reason to fear him. Berry's trial was extended until 15 April, when he appeared before the house committee and was discharged.[33]

A few patients escaped, most being 'recaptured', and responsible, or irresponsible, attendants were disciplined. Amelia Brindley escaped in October 1885, and Daniel Styles, admitted in December 1883, escaped in August 1887. Neither were found or readmitted.[34]

Suicides

Patients thought to be actively suicidal were supervised day and night. Seven men and one woman committed suicide, which were fully investigated, and reported to the Commissioners. Two were in 1884: in April, Edwin Toovey Ashfield threw himself from a window, after which all first and second floor windows were blocked so that they could not be opened more than four inches. In 1885, all first and second floor windows were to be blocked immediately.

However, in 1886, when a man died apparently attempting to escape, he fell from a first floor window in the day-room of a ward, the lower sash being unlocked.[35] Two men hung themselves in 'slop closets': in the first incident, the inquest jury requested the attendants be exonerated while, the second time, the attendant was severely reprimanded.[36, 37]

Emma Saunders aged thirty, admitted in 1887 with melancholia, was on an observation ward in 1889 as she was recognised to be actively suicidal. Asking to help the dormitory nurse, after making a few beds, she slipped into a store cupboard where she hung herself using binding tape which she had secreted. Two nurses were dismissed, and the nurse in charge was severely reprimanded.[38]

W.B, aged forty-seven, was admitted in June 1888, with his first 'attack of melancholic mania'. Considered suicidal, he was initially kept under continual supervision but, after three weeks, allowed to work outside supervised by a male attendant. With eight other patients, he was 'stone picking and wheeling' a few yards from the railway line when he escaped through a hedge while the attendant's back was turned, and 'placed or threw himself deliberately in front of a train and was killed'. A fence was erected along the boundary with the railway, Dr Moody ordering that 'similar gangs of working patients should be guarded by two attendants'.[39] As employment was seen as an important part of treatment, efforts were made to reduce risk rather than further restrict a patient's routine.

Little is known of other forms of treatment. The Commissioners consistently reported no use of seclusion, namely the use of solitary confinement during the day, or mechanical restriction, but there were padded rooms on wards and strong dresses were ordered. In 1885, the house committee instructed that all cases of blistering and the use of shower baths be recorded.[40]

While about a third of admissions were discharged as 'recovered', most patients became long-term. Andrew Wynter had observed, in 1870: 'This is the class of people that form at least 90 per cent of the inhabitants of our asylums, chronic and incurable cases that no treatment will ever improve . . .'.[41] In 1889, the asylum contained 'many aged and broken down cases'.[42]

Most deaths in asylums were of those with general paralysis of the insane, which emerges in the last stages of syphilis. Such people required constant nursing care and supervision and were mainly men but, in 1889, a woman M.M., aged 42, had been in Cane Hill for sixteen months. On her ward, a bath in the bathroom adjoining the ward lavatory was two-thirds full of boiling water, there being no water supply in the scullery for a few hours. She was taken to the lavatory, 'having been dirty and requiring washing and changing'. The nurse partly undressed her, leaving her briefly in the charge of a patient who was assisting in washing her, while she went to fetch clean clothing: 'the poor woman having sight of the bath in the adjoining room through the open door walked up to it, stepped into the water and was seen by another patient to slip down into it'. Nine hours later, she died of severe scalding. The charge nurse was censured and the nurse dismissed for leaving the bathroom door unlocked.[43]

Visitors

Family members visited, a few complaining after listening to their relative. In 1886, Mrs Eliza Hall complained of the ill treatment of her niece Bessie Matilda Wood. They appeared together before the house committee, where it was reported that Bessie had a delusion that people constantly threw dust at her, and was struck on two occasions by female patients, when she wrongly accused them of throwing dust at her. The first time, her nose was bruised and, the second time, her skin: 'Injuries were of a very trivial nature and the patient now seems quite free from any side effects'. The interview resulted in an order being signed for her discharge into her aunt's care.[44]

In July 1888, Martha Bravery told her husband, in the Clerk's presence, that 'she came to the Asylum a prudent and honest woman to her husband . . . but she had been dishonoured by some of the Attendants with the knowledge of the Medical Officers'. She appeared before the committee, still alleging it, but 'upon asked to name the Attendants, she states that she would not have known that she had been dishonoured had not the Lord revealed the fact to her'. The committee were convinced 'by the Patient's manner and conversation that her allegation is absolutely groundless and arises from insane delusions'.

In August, Mr. Markwick, a refreshment house keeper of Whyclift [?Whyteleafe] and Purley, complained that the committee allowed refreshments to be supplied to visitors to the asylum, 'by which he has sustained . . . great loss'. The committee replied that tea, coffee, bread and butter were provided at the asylum at the repeated desire of the Visitors, many of whom had suffered great inconvenience from fatigue and exhaustion in walking the long distance from Caterham Junction [now Purley Station] and remaining in conversation with the patients; and while the Committee regret he should have sustained loss ... they are unable in view of the immense convenience such refreshments have been to Visitors to direct that they shall no longer be supplied.

Visitors were refused permission to visit when there was serious infection in the community, as when there was small pox in 1885 and scarlet fever in 1887.[45, 46] In August 1888, with dipheria in one of the asylum's Pumping House Cottages, the engineer thought it was caused by the earth closet being only 2 foot and ten inches from the sitting room door, the smell going into the sitting room. The earth closet was to be cleaned and disinfected daily but, in September, the committee decided that the disease did not result from its proximity to the scullery.[47]

Chapter 5: Overcrowding

In April 1885, with no empty beds, the visiting committee wished to clear the asylum

> as much as possible, of quiet and harmless cases, and that with this in view have today signed orders for the discharge of twelve patients on the grounds that they might be taken care of in a Workhouse provided they are put in the Infirmary and placed on a dietary as suggested by the Board . . . The Committee and Medical Superintendent have still under consideration the condition of several other patients whom they hope to dispose of in a similar way.[1]

It was decided, in May, to discharge ten patients to workhouses, provided 'they are placed on the dietary for the aged and infirm, or a dietary equally good'.[2] Two eventually went to Croydon Workhouse, its Guardians accepting them reluctantly.

Investigations began in 1886 to ensure that patients with sufficient means be transferred to private licensed houses, the first being Florence Madeline Bailey, admitted in April. Croydon Union were informed that she had an income of £85 a year.[3] The Clerk to the visiting committee wrote to the Union's Guardians that, as the Surrey Asylums were 'rapidly getting filled', they were anxious that only pauper lunatics should be in Cane Hill. On 13 May, she was discharged to her sister's care.[4]

In March 1887, a draft contract was drawn up with the Board of the Western Counties Idiot Asylum at Starcross near Exeter, to take children and young 'idiots' who could benefit from its training programme. In April, with beds for 480 males and 644 females, the greatest number occupied at any one time in the previous year was 474 male and 620 female beds.[5] However, on 1 January 1887, there was an increase of 118 in the total number of patients and, that summer, 76 were placed in other asylums and private licensed houses.[6] A letter was written to the Unions in South London and Croydon that no more patients could be admitted. Other Unions were instructed not to send patients unless they had checked that they could be accommodated. Gloucester Asylum could take 50 males and 30 females and, after September, 40 more females, charging 13s a week, and 14s for epileptics.

At the Late Midsummer Quarter Sessions in July 1887, the magistrates set up a committee to prepare plans and estimates to enlarge the asylum to take 2,000 patients, recognising they would need to retain 'a large proportion of quiet chronic cases', the Unions being unwilling to take them. On 5 July there were 2073 male and 2756 female pauper lunatics in Surrey, being 47 per cent male and 53 per cent female. A report from Dr. Moody and the County Surveyor, Mr. Howell, recommended against large wards, although it was cheaper: 'Except for the laundry block, we should prefer wards more like D with larger dayrooms and so planned that each ward may be worked as two separate wards of not more than 70-75 patients'.

The Commissioners approved the plans but suggested purchasing more land, and that the laundry ward (Block L) be moved to give a view from the corridor towards the wood rather than into the courtyard. In December, the plans and costings were:

<u>Female side</u>

Blocks H and K – 150 patients each at £70.5s per patient.

Block I – 96 patients at £78 per patient.

Block L – 100 patients at £81.10s per patient.

Building for 3 head attendants and 11 night nurses.

<u>Male side</u>

Block F – 150 patients at £81.10s per patient.

Block G – 80 patients at £83.15s per patient.

Block H – 150 patients at £75 per patient.

A large steam coal store, a small detached house for the steward, extension of boiler house, extra machines and gearing in the laundry, extra cooking apparatus, extra tanks for condensed water, a glass roof over scullery yard.

There would be additional attendants' cottages, extensions to cow sheds, the piggery and farm buildings, extra workshops, a cricket pavilion, seven airing court sheds, telephones, a weigh bridge at the pump house and tar-paving for the old airing courts.

Hearing of the plans, in March 1888, the London, Brighton and South Coast Railway offered to run a workmen's train at £1 a week to carry 200 men third class from East Croydon to Stoats Nest Station leaving at 5.35 a.m. and calling at South Croydon and Caterham Junction, now Purley Station. The return journey would be at 5.35 p.m. or 6.12 p.m., or another time could be decided on. The committee requested a station at Smitham Bottom, which the railway company would consider once its differences with the South Eastern Railway were settled. In December, 120 poles, hooping, barbed wire, and two gates were ordered, to construct a six foot high fence from the corner of Woodmansterne Road to a point south of the proposed new railway station.[7]

The South Eastern Railway's station opened at Coulsdon, near to the main lodge, in October 1889 and, in 1896, the suffix Cane Hill was added.[8]

Transferring Patients

In May 1888, General Sibley, chairman of the visiting committee, and Dr. Moody visited their patients at Gloucester and, in November, negotiations took place to transfer 5 male and 5 female idiots to Berrywood, Northampton's county asylum, where a new 'idiot ward' for children had opened, for five years at 14s a week, the contract being sent to the Commissioners for the Secretary of State's approval.

That same month, the Guardians of St. Olave's Union complained that their patients were transferred as far away as Gloucester and that Jane Riddell was detained there because of 'her proneness to immorality and drink which, alone, the Guardians think are not valid reasons for her admission': they were informed that the statutory power for discharge lay with the visiting committee and the medical superintendent.

The committee stated that they had endeavoured to send only patients who did not have visitors, but it had been impossible to adhere to this in every case. It was 'fully sensible of the hardship to many patients to be deprived of such visits, and it has therefore been the desire of the Committee in such transfers to cause as little pain as possible either to the patients or their friends [relatives]'.[9] In June 1889, there were 113 patients at Gloucester, 5 at Starcross and 4 at Berrywood.[10]

Dorking Union complained that discharged patients had to be readmitted almost immediately 'entailing great expense upon the ratepayers'. Its Guardians were informed that every care was taken in selecting patients to go out on trial leave and, in the majority of cases, patients kept well.[11]

Change

In the Spring of 1888, central government informed the Unions in Surrey that Cane Hill Asylum would be taken over by the London Asylums Committee for pauper lunatics from all the Unions in London. The Guardians of the Dorking, Godstone and Croydon Unions unsuccessfully petitioned against the decision and, in July, Surrey's magistrates decided not to go ahead with the proposed enlargement.[12]

At the same time, the Local Government Act of 1888 enabled Croydon to become a county borough in 1889, with its own Council, free of the county's jurisdiction, and responsible for providing for its pauper lunatics. In 1890, an agreement was reached between London County Council, Surrey County Council and Croydon Council to provide beds in Cane Hill for 80 male and 120 female patients sent by Croydon Council or the Guardians of Croydon Union, for five years with a covenant for either side to renew if required. These beds were retained until 1899.

Croydon Council formed a committee of lunacy visitors, all councillors and alderman, two of whom, with the approval of the London County Council, visited Cane Hill twice a year, alternating with Guardians. They would not take part in, or interfere in the management of the asylum, but could bring issues to their committee, who would liaise with Cane Hill's committee. Croydon Council paid 14s. a week for each pauper lunatic in Cane Hill. Rural unions in east Surrey, as well as parishes in the Croydon Union not part of the new county borough, such as Addington and Mitcham, now sent their pauper lunatics to Brookwood Asylum.

On 21 January 1891, there were 61 male and 89 female patients from Croydon in Cane Hill, 9 females at Gloucester Asylum and 3 idiots at Berrywood Asylum in Northampton, a total of 162 in asylums. Sarah E., at Gloucester, wanted to return to Croydon and 'was not likely to give trouble', but there was no space in the workhouse infirmary. It was suggested that she 'be handed to friends if, upon enquiry, they are found to be respectable', but none were found. She died in Gloucester Asylum in January 1893. Councillors commenced visiting Gloucester Asylum finding, in 1892, the patients 'appeared well cared for and kindly treated'. At Berrywood, patients were 'kindly treated and contented'.[13]

Gloucester

Patients transferred to other asylums could experience worse conditions than at Cane Hill. The Commissioners visited Gloucester in 1890, where 1,108 patients were 'properly dressed, quiet and well behaved', although nine were secluded 29 times, and four restrained in straitjackets to prevent self-injury, and for surgical reasons. With no 'daily extended exercise beyond the grounds', 225 patients were confined to airing courts, although staffing numbers were similar to those at Cane Hill. 87 staff were on duty during the day and 10 at night, but 46 had been employed less than two years and 19 less than six months.[14]

Visiting in February 1891, there was no use of seclusion, and restraint had reduced, but medical officers complained about 'an undue proportion of troublesome or dirty patients sent them from Cane Hill'. Bathrooms needed screens and water-closets were inadequate. Passages were very cold, and dormitories could only be heated by fires. Many could not be lit, because of the fire risk, since the rooms were 'visited at long intervals'. More amusements were needed on the wards, but 417 patients now walked beyond the grounds.[15]

Physical conditions continued to improve, although seclusion and mechanical restraint increased in 1892, including three females secluded for a total of 1,478 hours.[16] In February 1894, the Commissioners reported a maximum temperature of 55F, even with good fires. Dormitories were very cold, with rain driving in through windows. They believed that one patient, Mr. H.I., had a valid grievance in having had visitors every two weeks at Cane Hill. If so, he should be returned 'and some friendless patient sent in his place'.[17]

They consistently praised Western Counties Idiots Asylum and, in 1894, were pleased with the 'order and neatness' and the 'exemplary behaviour' of the children at tea, the institution being 'highly creditable to those having charge here'.[18]

Children

The authorities at Cane Hill and the Commissioners remained reluctant to admit children, despite attempts by Union Guardians. In August 1889, Alice Preece of 42 Laurel Grove, Penge, applied to Croydon's guardians for her daughter Marion to be admitted to the Union Infirmary, but they decided that she was more suitable for a reformatory. She was admitted to Grove Hall Asylum in Bow, a private licensed asylum but, in January 1890, its owner wrote to the Guardians that the Commissioners had directed him to request the Guardians to transfer her to the children's ward at Berrywood Asylum in Northampton.

On 11 February, Croydon's Guardians decided that Marian, aged 11, be moved from Grove Hall to Croydon Workhouse before going to Berrywood Asylum for 'special treatment as recommended by the Commissioners'. Probably because Berrywood would only accept an admission from an asylum, Marian was transferred from Grove Hall to Cane Hill on 24 February.

On 5 March, Dr Moody wrote to the Guardians that she exhibited no signs of lunacy, and he had informed the Commissioners to that effect within the statutory period of seven days. He would keep her under observation for a further fourteen days during which time she might have an 'epileptic attack' or display symptoms of insanity. If not, she would be discharged but, if she did, she would be transferred to Berrywood 'as I think it very inexpedient for a child of her tender years to be confined in an Asylum with adult patients'. Something happened for she was transferred there on 29 March.[19]

Despite Dr Moody's reply, Croydon's Guardians sent Henry Stacey and Joseph J. Ingram, both aged six, to Cane Hill in late 1890, with a view to their transfer to Berrywood or the Western Counties Idiot Asylum, Henry having been accepted at the latter when there was a vacancy. As no transfer were imminent, the committee at Cane Hill discharged them back to Croydon Workhouse on 30 March 1891 while the Clerk to the County of London Asylums Committee wrote to the Guardians requesting that directions be given not to admit 'children of such tender years'. The Guardians admitted them to the Workhouse Infirmary, where Joseph remained in the 1891 census.[20]

Guardians continued to visit, usually twice a year. Since at least 1888, Miss Ely and Miss Shanks, two Guardians from the Croydon Union, 'devoted a large amount of time and attention to visiting the female lunatics at Cane Hill'.[21] Dr Moody sent regular reports, a few of which survive, such as three presented at the Guardian's board meeting on 20 October 1891:

David Haynes [sic Haines] – Subject to Chronic delusional mania but otherwise in good health. [Admitted March 1890, transferred to Fisherton Asylum 1899].

Charles Johnson – Had improved but not yet fit for discharge but it is hope he will be at an early date. [Admitted July 1890, discharged 'recovered' 24 October 1891].

Clara Ramsdale – Had improved a great deal since admission but is still delusional and at times depressed. At present recovery is only partial and imperfect. [Admitted May 1891, discharged 'recovered' January 1892].[22]

Generally, Union Guardians wanted their pauper lunatics to be in asylums. In England and Wales, the number of pauper lunatics increased at a greater rate than the increase in the total population. In 1870, 61.8 per cent of pauper lunatics were in asylums, 23.5 per cent in workhouses, and 14.7 per cent received outdoor relief. In 1890, the proportion of pauper lunatics receiving outdoor relief had reduced to about 6 per cent, as more entered asylums.[23] On 1 January 1889, 82 per cent of Croydon's pauper lunatics were in asylums and licensed house, which had increased, on 1 January 1900, to 86.8 per cent in asylums and licensed houses, 11.6 per cent in the workhouse and 1.6 per cent who received out-relief.[24]

Magistrates sometimes refused to sign admission papers to admit pauper lunatics to Cane Hill. More often, it was the medical superintendent, through the asylum's committee, who discharged those considered to be sane on admission, and reported such events to the responsible Guardians and to the Commissioners in Lunacy. In June 1891, Dr Moody wrote to Croydon's Guardians about Oliver Goldsmith who was admitted twice and, on both occasions, recovered after a few days. The Guardians agreed and sent a copy of his letter to the Union's medical officer, informing him they were 'of the opinion he should not have been confined as a lunatic for removal to an asylum as he was evidently merely suffering from the effects of overdrinking'.[25]

Chapter 6: A time of change 1889 to 1899

On 4 April 1889, the visiting committee of the Surrey's magistrates, with General Sibley as chairman, formally handed over to the 'committee appointed by London County Council for the management of Cane Hill Asylum', which would be known as the 'sub-committee'. Only one former committee member remained, Mr Richard Strong, who became the new chairman. Its new members included Mr P.M. Martineau, chairman of the London County Asylums Committee (LCAC).

Five members attended their first meeting on 2 May, namely Mr Strong, Mr Martineau, Mr Nathaniel Robinson, the Hon. R. C. Grosvenor and Dr W.G. Bott. Their luncheon was carefully itemised, each paying 2s 2d. The ingredients, which cost a total of 10s 10d, were:

2 bottles of Claret at 1s 6d each	3s 0d
3 lbs. Bread at 1d each	3d
1¼ lb. Butter at 1s 2d each	1s 5½d
1 lb. Sugar at 2¼d	2¼d
5¼ lbs. Beef at 8½d a lb.	3s 8½d
4 lbs. Potatoes at ½d a lb.	2d
4 lbs. Vegetables at ½d a lb.	2d
1 bottle of Soda Water at 2d	2d
1 bottle of Apollo Water at 4½d	4½d
4 lbs. Rhubarb at ½d a lb.	2d
¼ lb. Rice	¼d
6 Eggs at 1d each	6d
2 pints Milk at 1s a gallon	3d

They met fortnightly, the accounts surviving until 18 July. From June onwards, they brought their own drink, two bottles of claret and one of sherry.[1]

In 1890, asylums in England and Wales contained an average of 802 patients.[2] Plans to enlarge the asylum, agreed by the Home Secretary, would go ahead to provide for about 2,000 patients.[3] With slightly more patients than the designated number of beds, staff in charge of patients living in the gardener's and gas work's cottages complained that bedrooms were too small for the numbers of patients occupying them, and ventilation needed to be improved. The Commissioners suggested a proper laboratory and museum: 'we doubt not that a full medical staff could prosecute medical and anatomical enquiry into the pathology of insanity, and so do something towards alleviating the misery of many'.

The wards were in 'excellent order', bright and cheerful with good ventilation, and amusements were frequent and varied'. There was now a cottage hospital. The Commissioners reported few complaints: although many patients appealed for discharge, they did not think any were unduly detained, suggesting that 'the most insane are the most forward'. By June, £900 transferred from Wandsworth Asylum, for a benevolent fund, had provided money for fifteen patients while on trial leave.[4]

The 1890 Lunacy Act, which defined a lunatic as 'an idiot or person of unsound mind', laid down detailed administrative and management procedures which tried to cover every contingency, with little attempt to develop new kinds of care for patients. Even if the Union made only a partial contribution for maintenance, the remainder being met by close relatives, the patient was labelled as a pauper lunatic, which meant that patients came from a wide range of social levels and occupations. After the first year in an asylum or workhouse, medical officers would review long stay patients every two years, and re-certify. There would be no new licensed houses, but county and borough asylums could include beds for private patients.

In May 1890, when the Commissioners visited, there were 464 male and 635 female patients, a total of 1099, with 603 admissions since their last visit. While 112 patients were discharged as 'recovered', 389 left as 'relieved' or 'not recovered', the majority to Brookwood Hospital as part of the re-organisation. With 118 deaths, including 39 with general paralysis, they considered Dr Moody's clerical workload very heavy, and recommended a third medical officer. Five patients on Female D Block had had typhoid, of which two died, the cause being traced to locally contaminated water which had been remedied and contained.[5] The following year, Cane Hill was 'in excellent order, but quite full'.

While the planned extensions were built, supervised by Mr C.H. Howell and anticipated in his original designs, the Secretary of State approved more attendants' cottages, cow-houses, new farmyards and piggeries, another nurses' residential block and an assistant medical officers' office, estimated at £10,500, and additions to workshops, more airing courts and minor improvements which would cost £2,950.[6] Twelve attendants' cottages would be built parallel to Woodmansterne Road, a continuation of the existing cottages, leaving the existing mound between them.[7]

With the increased numbers, Dr Moody's salary would be increased to £1,000 per annum from March 1892.[8] In 1891, Miss Louisa Collins, Chief Nurse, was appointed as Matron, at £100 per annum, including board, lodging and washing, rising to a maximum of £150.

Improvements continued: the band's worn out instruments would be replaced, fifty garden chairs were bought for the airing courts and portable baths with india-rubber tyred wheels for the infirmary wards.[9] As well as a cricket shed and five airing court shelters, they purchased a billiard table, nine bagatelle tables, four weighing chairs, five pianos, pictures and ornaments for the new wards.

The LCAC wanted increased security, but was it to keep patients in or people out? The sub-committee requested the LCAC to sanction the purchase of 2,008 yards of unclimbable iron fencing, with two double and two wicker gates for the Backwood where the cricket pitch was laid out, and three more double gates and one wicker gate.[10] A number of patients escaped and, in 1898, a wall in the builder's yard was raised by 18 inches after one escape.[11] However, in 1894, a large number of burberries planted along the drive were damaged, and pieces removed.[12] The following year, further 'great havoc' was caused to burberries and laurels planted alongside the drive in front of the buildings and in the cemetery.[13]

The new buildings were completed in 1892: Cane Hill could now accommodate 860 males and 1,140 females. Patients returned from other asylums including 190 patients from Lancaster in a special train of eleven saloon carriages, Dr Moody believing it to be the largest removal at one time yet attempted.[14] Eighty-six more came from Lancaster. On 24 March there were 1,306 beds and, on 7 April,

2,000 beds, with 1,411 patients.[15] However, in September 1893, there were already 2,024 beds, with 2,025 patients. Building was still not finished, including the extra storey of the Nurses' Block, 85 to 100 men being 'constantly employed besides those in the contractor's shop'. In December, it was decided to enlarge the two lodges, and to add a floor to that occupied by the back gate porter.[16]

Cane Hill would constantly be short of space. Throughout England and Wales, admission rates rose each year, the Commissioners reporting in 1892 that they included a large proportion of 'incurables' who would remain under care until they died. It was difficult to find accommodation for those who improved, but did not recover, who could be discharged if there were homes elsewhere, relatives generally being too poor to take them. The public's confidence in asylums had led to families agreeing to admit their 'incurables but above the status of paupers, their relatives reimbursing the cost of their maintenance'.[17]

With more patients, accommodation was needed for extra nurses, and Dr Moody planned to put 20 additional female patients in a former needleroom, and convert some coal cellars and the late cutting-room into nurses' rooms. The following year, he prepared to receive 100 additional patients, resulting in 2,222 patients whereas there should only have been 2,000.[18] They now had a large number of beds with 'wire-wave mattresses' instead of wooden laths.[19] In 1887, there were additional beds in already overcrowded wards. An outbreak of scarlet fever on the male side meant the immediate transfer of 13 women from the Cottage Hospital to sleep in dressing rooms attached to the bathrooms.[20]

The estate

In August 1892, Croydon District Highways Board complained of flood water pouring down the drive leading to the Brighton Road. The asylum's engineer reported, in October, that he would lay pipes to take the water to the nearest cultivated land, enlarge the existing catch pits, lay a moulded channel and construct a catch pit at the entrance gates.[21] In September 1894, the Board complained of 'the mass of water rushing out of the road leading up to the Cane Hill Asylum – it flooded the roads on the Lion Green and washed through the ground floors of the cottages there'. It suggested large catch pits, while their chairman, Mr Thomas Brooke of the nearby

Red Lion, welcomed a deputation from the asylum's sub-committee to their next meeting.

The asylum's sub-committee was probably more occupied by the news, in January 1894, that the London, Brighton and South Coast Railway planned a Bill in Parliament to purchase part of Cane Hill's estate adjoining the Brighton Road to build a new line from Purley to Earlswood. The sub-committee opposed the plan: it would be a danger to patients, disturb the main drive and other roads on the estate and necessitate finding other means to dispose of the drainage from the farm buildings. It insisted the cutting be covered in, and the area near to the railway securely enclosed to prevent patients reaching the railway. They suggested keeping the railway entirely outside the asylum's grounds, and diverting the High Road on to the asylum's estate to make a natural barrier between the railway and the estate, as was the case with the South Eastern Railway line.

In March, the railway company replied that it was unable to divert their line, or place it close to Coulsdon Railway Station on the east side, but proposed taking the whole line through the asylum's estate and covering it so 'that the railway will be practically in [a] tunnel, after which the ground may be returfed and planted 'as may be required by the [London County] Council'. The only alteration would be a few steps where the footpath from the railway station passed through the retaining wall. The company having made this offer, the sub-committee thought the LCC would have little chance of getting the Bill thrown out. Subject to the slopes on the western side of the covered way being made less steep, it agreed to the proposal, asking the Valuer to seek compensation.[22]

He reported in July 1895 that the railway would take just over one acre, destroying just over three acres of agriculture land including a belt of 1,452 trees which were just over 12 years old, and 8 large oaks. He suggested the LCC should claim £2,000, including the temporary occupation of just over 7 acres, and pay for two additional attendants while the land was occupied by the railway company, which was accepted by the railway company's surveyors. The sub-committee agreed to a new footpath with 17 steps, or a bridge from the station approach road, an unclimbable fence on either side of the footpath and a temporary fence at least 8 ft high.

The railway responded that it had no power to build a bridge, but would construct a 5 ft high fence on the south side of the new footpath to meet with the retaining wall fence, no fence being needed on the other side of the path. A two foot depth of soil would cover the girders over the 'covered way' where the track ran, with an 8 ft high brick wall at each end.[23]

In 1897, Dr Moody asked the Clerk to contact the Commissioner of Police to request a constable being stationed near to the asylum, because of 'the very rough element attracted to the vicinity of the asylum by the construction of two new railway lines and the number of gipsies and vagrants who haunt the neighbouring downs and roads'. The Commissioner replied that it was not possible.[24]

With a local railway station, large houses were built in the neighbourhood for commuters to London, and Smitham Bottom grew in size. In 1895, the sub-committee was relieved that Croydon Rural District Council [CRDC] declined the offer of a site for a parish cemetery close to the lower gates of the Asylum, adjoining the asylum's estate but recognised that some of Mr. Tucker's land at Rickman's Hill close to the estate would probably become building land. Thinking it might be purchased to become part of the asylum estate, they asked the Valuer to report on its value and the possibility of diverting the road separating it from the estate. Soon after, CRDC recommended land for building which belonged to Mr. Watney and adjoined the existing churchyard, which the asylum opposed.

Meanwhile the Valuer contacted Mr. Tucker's agent regarding a plot at the south-west corner of the estate. He thought Mr. Tucker would only agree to sell all the land, consisting of about 85 acres including the house, but might let 10 to 15 acres on the other side of Chipstead Road adjacent to the asylum's cemetery, and suggested that, if the sub-committee showed any anxiety in wanting to obtain it, Mr. Tucker would ask an exorbitant price. They accepted the Valuer's suggestion to leave it in his hands for 'a favourable opportunity'.

In 1897, news came that the CRDC would abolish cess pits close to the asylum and provide new sewers for about 40 houses on Lion Green, and for 28 cottages belonging to the asylum whose gardens were in Coulsdon. Six of the asylum's cottages were partly in Coulsdon and partly in Woodmansterne, and twenty wholly in Woodmansterne, but their owners could pay a rent for the use of the sewer equal to what they would pay had they been in CRDC.[25] The following year, water from the asylum's well was polluted by the cess pits.[26]

Both Surrey's magistrates and the South Eastern Railway Company had seen the advantage of a local station, used by the staff and those visitors who could afford it but suburban stations attracted commuters who wanted to live close to a station and to the country. Houses were built in Smitham Bottom, which would become known as Coulsdon, and shops opened. Cane Hill Asylum was no longer an isolated community.

Chapter 7: Staff and patients 1890-1900

Each year, the Commissioners made their two day visit, generally approving of what they saw. In 1890, Cane Hill's patients were 'quiet and well-behaved, the wards bright and cheerful, and considerable comfort prevailed'.[1] The following year, it was 'in excellent order, but quite full'.[2] Similar comments were made each year and, in 1899, they had 'high praise' for the condition of the Asylum. Patients were 'generally contented', describing themselves as 'being comfortable and kindly treated by the attendants and nurses'. The women's dress was 'bright and varied' while men had working clothes and a better suit for Sundays.[3] Year after year, there was no use of mechanical restraints or seclusion, while the use of strong clothing was rarely reported, apart from four females in 1894.

In 1890, of 112 attendants, 45 had been there less than a year, although 24 had considerable experience working in asylums. No charges of ill-treatment were brought to the Commissioners' attention, and they observed that attendants seemed on good terms with patients.[4]

Recruiting suitable staff was a continuing issue. It is not known if attempts were made to recruit locally: in the 1891 census, of 93 nurses and attendants living in the asylum, only eight were born within ten miles of the building. Seven were born in Ireland, five in Wales and ten in Scotland. Four, perhaps friends, were born in Aberdeen: William Morrice 30, James Murray 27, John Ross 28 and John Davis Stott 25, and Nellie Ross 20, perhaps John's sister. There were other siblings such as Sarah Liddamore 32 and Mary Ann Liddamore 28, born in Euston, Suffolk. Apart from two born abroad, of British origin, the remainder were born in all corners of England. Promotion could be swift: John Ross, appointed in May 1889 as a second class attendant, the lowest grade of attendant, became a deputy charge attendant in June 1892 and a charge attendant the following November.[5]

In 1895, 21 per cent of attendants had been at Cane Hill for less than a year: the Commissioners suggested that 'much needs to be done to give them a reasonable indulgence to induce them to remain'.[6] Dr Moody had questioned in 1892 whether there had been 'any happy results from the recent extension of holidays to the younger nurses'.[7] In 1896, there were 239 attendants, of which 60 had less than a year's service.[8] Turnover increased and, in 1899, 30 per cent of attendants had been there under a year, although almost the same percentage had been employed for over 5 years.[9]

In 1898 male second class attendants earned £29 a year, with an annual increment of £1 to a maximum of £35, while their female equivalents earned from £18 up to £24 a year, with the same wages and conditions as female laundry maids, the latter working up to 54 hours a week. Board, lodging, washing and uniforms were provided. Head male attendants, in charge of wards, earned up to £60 a year, and their female equivalents, £40, both having one day a week off and 21 days annual leave.

Ordinary attendants and nurses worked 14 hours a day, from 6.00 a.m. to 8.00 p.m. If required to work longer, the time was made up to them. While entitled to the equivalent of one day off a week, it might not mean one whole day off. From 1895, female attendants had special evening leave two evenings a week in the summer, from 8 p.m. to 9.30 p.m., until the end of August. Night staff worked from 8 p.m. to 6 a.m., with 3 nights off in 28. Attendants had 12 days leave in the first two years, and then 14 days a year.

Not just attendants and nurses lived on the estate. The 1891 census lists three medical officers, the steward and his family, the clerk, the dispenser, the cook, the estate bailiff, the fireman, the back door porter and his family, assistant storekeeper, butcher, hall porter, hall boy, mess man and mess maid, a kitchen maid, a scullery maid and scullery man, a laundry maid and laundry man, laundresses, housemaids, two sewerage labourers, two dairy women, three stablemen, and two servants. Dr Moody and his family had a cook and a servant, while Esther Johnson 80, a labourer's wife who was deaf, lived with them.

All were subject to many regulations, on and off duty. Attendants and nurses were regularly reprimanded for being drunk on hospital property, returning late from leave and, between 1889 and 1898, staff were disciplined for negligence on twenty-three occasions, seventeen being for allowing patients to escape, usually while in working parties. John Anderson would not have escaped had the farm bailiff carried out Dr Moody's instructions that two working parties stay together, and to place the portable W.C. close to the party and away from the hedge.[10] Alexander Munro, appointed a second class attendant in April 1884 and a deputy charge attendant in June, was discharged in January 1885 for being intoxicated having been sent to bring back an escaped patient. Likewise, Esther Ann Tupper, a charge nurse, and Fanny Robins, a deputy charge nurse were dismissed in 1887 for 'being intoxicated and misconducting' themselves when on duty at Gloucester, presumably escorting patients transferred there.

Staff were dismissed for unsatisfactory performance: Alfred James Brown, a messenger boy, stole letters and property, Alfred James Course, a house boy, 'performed his duties in a slovenly and neglected manner', while Emily Clara Tupper lent her keys to a patient who then escaped. However, James Donovan resigned in 1893 to join the police force.

When Nurse Fanny Hunt was pregnant by Attendant Stephen Joyce in 1893, he was called before the sub-committee where he admitted having 'seduced her' but would marry her the following month. He 'declined to say where the impropriety took place', and both were dismissed, but Joyce would have a testimonial if he produced the marriage certificate.

Maxwell Tripp and George Albert Horey, second class attendants were asked to resign on 28 December 1893, having been found on the female side of the asylum on Christmas Eve, while Frederick Edward Chapman, another second class attendant, was dismissed in 1889 for getting out of his window and leaving the asylum without permission, taking the mess boy with him, and using bad language in the local public house.[11]

Mr Thomas Brooke, landlord of the Red Lion Hotel, wrote to Dr. Moody in 1893 that, on Boxing Day, Charge Attendant John Ross came in drunk at 9. 30 p.m., having been to a wedding, and 'caused a bother' with another attendant. Mr. Brooke having never had any problem before with Ross, asked Dr Moody to 'give him a good talking to', after which he was sure it would not happen again. Ross had been given leave to sleep out that night, and returned with two black eyes. When interviewed, he denied being drunk but admitted to quarrelling with another attendant with whom he had a longstanding dispute. His wages were reduced to those he received as a second class attendant, the lowest grade, and he forfeited his good conduct money. Ross handed in his resignation, which was accepted.

Two male attendants, who took the wrong train and were absent without night leave, were dismissed. Another missed the return train from Ramsgate and was asked to resign.[12] However, a few years later in 1897, attendants and nurses who returned late or stayed out all night generally just forfeited their good conduct money.[13]

Attendant Martin Beadle, asleep on duty, claimed he was frequently kept awake by 'Excursionists' near his lodgings. He was cautioned, while Night Attendant Adams, found asleep on duty at 3.00 a.m., was fined 2s 6d and severely reprimanded.[14] Nurse Ross, perhaps John Ross's sister, slept at a discharged patient's home and handed in her resignation, but Dr Moody recommended she be allowed to withdraw it as it was her first offence and she was a satisfactory nurse. She was reprimanded and forfeited two days' leave.[15]

There was no formal training, and staff could be quickly promoted, especially as most male attendants remained at Cane Hill for a short time. Just four male attendants recruited in 1884 were there in 1899.[16] Dr Moody promised training for attendants and nurses when the asylum was enlarged and, in 1898, 20 attendants and 20 nurses passed the St. John Ambulance examination.[17] John Watson, who joined in 1884 and became a charge nurse in 1894, received his nursing certificate in 1901, and an additional £1 a year on top of his annual salary of £42.

However, late 1899 and 1900 and the Boer War saw 31 Reservists called up. A handful returned, including William Somerset in November 1901.[18]

Ill treatment of patients

On twenty-eight occasions in the 1890s, nursing staff were accused of ill treating patients, perhaps a consequence of the pressures of working in an overcrowded hospital without training. There was one day attendant to about ten patients, a ratio which continued into the 1900s when recorded incidents greatly reduced, by which time staff received training.

Seventeen of the incidents were observed by senior staff, generally a medical officer, matron or a head attendant, seven were complaints by patients, and four by relatives. Most involved male patients. All were investigated, leading to two dismissals and three staff asked to resign, the rest being financially penalised with two demoted. Dr Moody asked for prosecutions but the sub-committee, composed of magistrates, took no further action.

One involved Rose D. from Croydon, admitted from July 1898 to March 1899. When recommended for a month's trial leave in February, she complained of ill treatment and appeared before the sub-committee. She said she was treated kindly on three wards but, on B2, Nurses Pacey and Patrick twisted her arm on several occasions, while she was taken to the bathroom and put on the floor for washing her stockings in the lavatory.

Nurse Pacey was seen and denied ill treatment, having only given her 'a good scolding'. Another patient was interviewed, and claimed Nurse Pacey was kind to her, but Nurse Patrick had pulled her hair and boxed her ears. The medical officer reported that Rose D. 'was no doubt excitable and resistive before Christmas' while Nurse O'Brien said 'patient D. didn't go without stockings that day and was wearing locked boots'. The committee decided there was no evidence that Rose D. was ill treated by Nurse Pacey.[19]

If accusations came from just one patient, they were rarely accepted, unless supported by staff or other patients, as in 1892 when Patient Smith complained that, while helping to clean the dormitory before breakfast, Attendant Skeets hit him in the side, so that he fell on the bed and bruised his hip and leg. Skeets denied it, while Attendant Farmer, who in the ward, said he saw nothing, thinking it impossible that Skeets pushed a patient without him knowing. Head Attendant Slattery said that the patient complained to him but, as Smith spoke 'very indistinctively and was the habit of making complaints', he ignored it being unaware that Smith was bruised. However, Patient Parker said he saw Skeets hit Smith down on the bed. Skeets was immediately dismissed but, as the violence was slight, no further action was taken. As the sub-committee believed Farmer knew about the assault, confirmation of his appointment was withdrawn, and he served an extra three months' probation.[20]

This case may have made senior staff more pro-active. Later that year, Mr Slattery entered a ward and saw Attendants Tushey and Welch holding Charles Shephard, a 'weak-minded epileptic, occasionally bad tempered and spiteful', and repeatedly bumping him on the floor. Tushey hit him once in the back which two patients confirmed, although one of them did not think the attendants 'were very rough'. Both attendants were instantly dismissed and Dr Moody asked the sub-committee to prosecute them, but again they took no further action apart from informing the Commissioners in Lunacy.[21]

The following year, Matron saw Attendant Emily Grace Parks strike Patient Pearson with her open hand. Parks appeared before the sub-committee where she was fined 2s 6d, lost three month's good conduct money, and was censured.[22] In May 1896, Dr Moody heard screams from the ward adjoining his garden and, looking through the window, saw Nurse Ellen Ellis smacking a patient on the bare shoulder with her open hand. Ellis denied and then admitted it, and was fined 5s, forfeiting her good conduct money.[23] In 1899, no patients complained of harsh treatment, but the Commissioners prosecuted a nurse for ill treating a patient, the asylum's committee having declined to do so. She was fined 40s and costs.[24] There were, doubtless, many occasions when patients were roughly treated which were not observed or reported.

A murdered attendant

George Guy, a former criminal transferred from Colney Hatch Asylum on 11 September 1895 in exchange for another patient who would not eat because of delusions regarding the medical staff, had a diagnosis of chronic mania with delusions of persecution for more than five years. Five days later, while exercising in an airing court with about 100 other patients, supervised by three attendants, he suddenly climbed up the stackpipe on to the roof of the male infirmary and began stripping slates from the roof and throwing them in all directions. Although he had a history of suicidal tendencies, the medical officer had not considered him actively suicidal, and had not issued a red ticket to keep him under special supervision. He was on a ward with constant supervision day and night, and remained in the airing court rather than join a working party as he was considered dangerous: at Colney Hatch, he carried stones in his handkerchief and hit staff and patients with them.

The hospital's fire brigade brought ladders, and the fireman and some attendants climbed up, with slates being thrown at them incessantly. Attendant Edward Finch, aged 30, reached the patient on his own and received several blows on the head from a piece of wood which Guy had wrenched from the roof. The first blow knocked off

Finch's fire helmet, the others fracturing his skull. He died two days later, and Guy was eventually sent to Broadmoor, the inquest jury and Commissioners recommending more attendants during exercise.[25]

Food

In 1890, the patients' main complaint concerned the new diet with its lack of bread, while the Commissioners were concerned that all patients in London's asylums would have uniform clothing: 'We are sorry to hear this . . . the patients look very well in various garbs of different hues . . . [the effect] will be, we fear to in a great measure destroy the individuality of the patients and lessen their self-respect'.[26]

The proposal for uniform clothing was abandoned but patients still complained of insufficient food. In August 1890, the sub-committee commented that too large a quantity of bone was served to patients in E Ward but, in November 1891, they tasted the sick patients' beef-tea lunch and declared that it was 'first rate'.[27] In May 1892, the LCAC asked Cane Hill's sub-committee why the dietary scale, which was precisely laid down, was 'deviated from in the following respects':

> Luncheon – not issued to wards, but to working patients a lunch of bread and cheese or cake.
>
> Dinner – no milk issued to working patients. Currant dumplings issued 3rd Friday in lieu of fish, and Hot Pot on Wednesday in lieu of Roast Meat. The Sub-Committee had authorised extra bread is supplied to those who ask for it, and altered the rota to:
>
> Sunday – Preserved meat.
>
> Monday – Boiled beef and bacon.
>
> Tuesday – Irish stew.
>
> Wednesday – Hot Pot.
>
> Thursday – Roast Mutton or Pork.
>
> Friday – Fish.
>
> Saturday – Meat pies.
>
> Supper – not issued to the wards but to those who ask for it. Lime juice is given during the summer.

The sub-committee replied that the former sub-committee had, in February 1891, resolved 'That [the] uniform dietary scale be amended so that luncheon or supper is given only to working patients and at the discretion of the Medical Superintendent to other patients, that an alternative drink such as lime juice be allowed for working patients in lieu of milk, that the daily order of issue be left to the Medical Superintendent'.[28]

In November, William Brown's daughter complained of insufficient food and unkind treatment, asking if he was fit to come home. The sub-committee saw him, deciding he was 'full of delusions, with no reason for his complaints and that he was quite unfit for discharge'.[29]

From late 1892 onwards, the sub-committee praised the food which was of good quality, sufficient and well-cooked but, in August 1893, thought not enough attention was given to how it was served on the wards, some patients having 'an unfair ration of fat and bone'. In 1894 some patients complained about having fish, the Commissioners doubting 'if it is politic to give this dinner so often as weekly'. They commented on the tea: 'we think that some better method of tea-making than the present one of placing the tea in cloth bags and boiling it for twenty minutes or so should be adapted'.[30] More than one patient spoke to the Commissioners about the food in May 1895: "It's very nice, but there is not enough of it". They had ham and pork the previous day, and pea soup that day.[31] Meals were considered of good quality but 'if it could be arranged for patients to commence their dinners in sections rather than wait until all tables are served it would be an improvement'.[32] Cutlery, which was checked in and out, was probably handed to the patients after the food was all served.

The LCAC introduced a new diet to its asylums on 1 June 1895, the house committee observing that it gave satisfaction but, in July, over two weeks, 1,353 lbs. of bread were returned from Cane Hill's wards while the allowance of 6 ounces of unpeeled potatoes for each female patient's dinner was insufficient and would be increased to 8 ounces. In September, 3,342 lbs. of bread were returned from female wards in the previous four weeks: a check would be made with other asylums if this was excessive.[33] Visiting the male wards, the house committee commented that dinners in many wards were 'in excess of what the patients could eat although a complaint of starvation was made in the case of a patient who refused to clear his plate'.

In July 1896, a revised diet was introduced by the LCAC. The weekly menu, which could be varied at the discretion of the medical superintendent, was:

Sunday – pork, beef, mutton or bacon (roast or boiled).

Monday – ditto.

Tuesday – corned beef, 1 oz. of salad dressing or pickles for each patient.

Wednesday – meat pies.

Thursday – beef, mutton, pork or bacon (roast or boiled).

Friday – fish (fried or boiled) with melted butter fortnightly. Currant dumplings (made with dripping or suet), or suet pudding with jam or syrup on the alternate Friday.

Saturday – Irish stew (liquor of meat) thickened with 1 oz. dry vegetables, 6 oz. potatoes and 4 oz. green vegetables, with 4 oz. uncooked meat for each patient.

Each day, a man had 6 oz. bread and a ½ oz. of butter or margarine for breakfast. For dinner, he had 5 oz. of meat Sunday to Thursday, with 12 to 16 oz. of fish on Fridays, 9 oz. of unpeeled potatoes, 8 oz. of other vegetables, and 4 oz. of bread (5 oz. on Saturdays). Tea consisted of 5 oz. of bread, ½ oz. of margarine, butter or jam and 3 oz. of cake. Each female patient had slightly less.

Working patients had an additional luncheon, probably a mid-morning meal, with 3 oz. of bread, 1 oz. of cheese or jam and a ½ pint beverage. Every one had a pint of tea, coffee or cocoa at breakfast, and a pint of tea at teatime. Male working patients received 2 oz. of tobacco or 1 oz. of snuff weekly, and female working patients a half pint of tea every afternoon, or 2 oz. dry tea, 8 oz. sugar, with 14 oz. of milk weekly.

Each male patient had 15 oz. of bread a day, equivalent to just over half a modern large loaf weighing 28 ozs., and each female 12 oz., with an additional 3 oz. for each working patient. However, most probably had a better diet than they would have had in the outside world. Still true to the principles of moral treatment, patients should be well fed and healthy.

Patients' dinners were considered by the sub-committee to be 'excellent in quality and quantity' in April 1897.[34] In May, the Commissioners thought them good, but requested that some attendants and nurses be trained in the art of carving joints of meat.[35] Dr Moody reported that it was due to the knives being blunt, which would be remedied, and to the meat being boned. In June, with a scarcity of green vegetables, he directed the Steward to use fresh instead of tinned meat for helpless patients, there having been several cases of scurvy, until enough green vegetables were available. Fruit would be bought during the summer months at no more than 4d a lb for patients selected by Dr Moody, with no more than a ½ lb a week for each patient.[36]

No more complaints were recorded. In 1899, the house committee suggested hot plates on wards, while the serving of dinners could be improved on the male wards where dinners 'appeared to be of good quality and well served and satisfactory, with very little waste'.[37]

In 1894, staff complained about the food.[38] The following year, the LCAC produced a new weekly diet. Assistant medical officers, matrons and assistant matrons each received weekly 7 lbs of bread, a lb being equivalent to 16 ozs, 7 lbs of uncooked potatoes and other vegetables, 14 eggs, 10½ lbs of uncooked meat, 1½ lbs bacon, 1lb butter, ½ lb of various kinds of cheese, 7 lbs cooked fresh fish, 2 lbs uncooked dried fish, 8 oz tea, 8 oz coffee, 1½ lb sugar and 7 pints of milk.

Nurses, attendants and servants, who did the most physical work in the building, received less. Females received the least: 7 lbs of bread and 7 lbs of vegetables, but no eggs, and 4 lbs of uncooked meat, 1 lb bacon, ½ lb butter, ½ lb of fresh fish *or* dried fish, 3 oz tea, 3 oz coffee, 3½ pints of milk and 1 lb of jam. There was a choice of a ½ lb of standard cheese or an additional ½ lb of butter.

Increasingly, some members of staff broke rules when they thought they could, and the 1890s produced the largest number of reported incidents of abuse to patients. However, most were newly appointed and had no training, only learning by experience. Little was known about mental illness and, although treatments were tried, it was mainly a case of providing care until a person recovered, or looking after them long-term until death.

Chapter 8: The daily routine

Apart from remaining patients from the Croydon Union, patients now came from London Unions including Hackney, Kensington, Poplar, Paddington, Greenwich, Camberwell, Chelsea, Holborn, Shoreditch, the City of London, Lambeth, Wandsworth and Clapham, St. Olave's and St. Saviours. Their previous experience included knowledge of a wide range of occupations and professions. In the 1891 census, the men included a barrister, a medical man, a marine engineer, a civil engineer, a merchant, soldiers, a professor of music, a photographer, a police sergeant, a barge builder, a costermonger, a high walker and a French cook. The youngest, Horace Gentle aged 13½, was a schoolboy. Admitted from Camberwell Union in June 1890, and discharged as 'recovered' in October 1891, he was a bank clerk in the 1901 census. Among the women, there was an actress, a dancer and singer, dressmakers, needlewomen, milliners and servants, as well as housewives.

Some male patients had been labourers and there were some tailors and carpenters, but few had probably been agricultural workers. It was easier to replicate women's work. In 1890, with 1099 patients in the asylum (464 males and 635 females), the Commissioners were informed that 230 male patients worked on the land, 52 in workshops and 40 as ward workers while 100 women were ward workers, 72 worked in the laundry and 150 did knitting and sewing. Fewer women were employed than in previous years, and in a narrower range of tasks. No patients appeared to work in the offices or kitchen. By 1898, many women made items for a bazaar, proceeds going to a fund for recreational activities or to help patients on discharge, and making dresses for the new asylum at Bexley.[1]

As numbers increased in 1892, with about 2,000 patients in the asylum, it was decided to keep 140 pigs. Two cows were regularly killed for the asylum but, this time, five dry cows would be killed for consumption. Fifteen sheep, four cows in calf and 'a supply of bulls for the wards' would be purchased, and 850 yards of beech hedging (3,000 saplings) to provide shelter for the exposed parts of the kitchen garden. Thirty-three acres of meadow land, comprising five fields along the Chipstead Road, would be rented from Mr Tucker of Portnalls Farm at 18s an acre to replace fields at Hooley which were too far away and patients could not be employed there as it was dangerous, being close to the railway bridge and rails at Hooley House.[2]

In April 1893, there were 37 cows, a bull, 7 horses, pigs, 25 sheep and 113 fowls. Milk, eggs and meat were supplied to the asylum, while the fields produced mangolds, hay, roots and potatoes.[3] Most food was purchased, such as 974 lbs. of potatoes and 25 jars of jam, each weighing 14 lbs, in August 1893 following the increase to 2024 beds and 2025 patients.[4]

One patient, a trained bricklayer, was laying bricks on the estate.[5] In the gardens, thousands of bedding plants were grown and, in 1892, the sub-committee decided to make attendants' uniforms in the asylum, as well as boots and shoes. Twelve patients, good workmen employed in the shoemaker's shop, had made 219 pairs of boots and shoes in the previous three months, about half the required number, and repaired shoes. Dr Moody and the Steward recommended making more to provide full work for the patients 'who are tradesman and willing and able to work'. In addition, they did not want to increase the number of employed shoemakers as there was a scarcity of hospital accommodation, while local house rents were high and staff and their families did not want to live so far from shops and markets.

On reflection the sub-committee decided it was undesirable to make footwear and uniforms.[6] The Steward probably thought the asylum should be more self-sufficient: in 1893 he rejected some purchased items, namely uniforms, 12 pairs of men's nailed boots, 144 pairs of leather slippers and 24 pairs of carpet slippers.[7] In 1898, he reported that, to cope with the work in the kitchen, it was necessary to employ two male patients, but Dr Moody thought that this practice should not continue, and they advertised for a female cook and two scullery men.[8] Meanwhile, women worked in a new heated vegetable room, while workshops were extended and men worked in a new warmed wood chopping room.[9] In 1900, 71 per cent of men and 63 per cent of the females were 'usefully employed'.

There were risks: in 1899, G.S., a cabinet maker aged 35, admitted on 23 February with delusional insanity but no history of a suicidal tendency, improved quickly and it was thought he might soon be recommended for discharge. From 13 March, he worked 'steadily and well' in the carpenter's shop but, on 23 March, having sharpened the iron of his plane, a joiner saw him hammering it against his neck with a mallet. Although medical help arrived immediately, he died within seven minutes having severed his larynx, the anterior wall of the larynx, the external left jugular vein and the right superior thyroid artery. In the inquest, his wife reported that he tried to jump off a bridge in May 1898, but she had not told the asylum when he was admitted.[10]

In January 1896, the Asylums General Purposes Committee sent a memorandum that nurses and attendants could, after 5.00 p.m., 'utilize working patients for their own personal benefit'. The sub-committee thought it desirable, but restricted it to between 5.00 p.m. and 6.00 p.m. No payment should be permitted.[11] Two nurses were fined for leaving scissors with patients including Nurse Florence Jones who, in September, lent a pair to Sarah Girling, 'a dangerous epileptic', and gave her private work in prohibited hours. She was fined three months' good conduct money.[12]

Exercise and entertainment

In 1890 with about 1,100 patients, nearly 700 went to entertainments in the winter but in 1895, with double the number of patients, it was just 855.[13, 14] In 1900, with 2,210 patients, and an excess of 132, it had dropped further to 34.4 per cent or under 800.[15]

Besides the annual fete, and festivities at Christmas and the New Year, there were regular evening entertainments such as St. Cecilia's Hand Bell Ringers, the Nubian Minstrels, the Irving Amateur Dramatic Company and Mr Nelson Hardy, a ventriloquist.[16] There had been refreshments for those providing the entertainment but, from 1897, coffee and cakes were given to patients attending entertainments, perhaps an 'encouragement' to attend. Visiting days, since 1891, were on Sunday, Monday and Thursday afternoons, and all Bank Holidays.[17]

Whereas 700 patients, nearly three-quarters of the patients, attended Anglican services on Sundays and 450 during the week in 1890, just 844 went in 1895, but 150 out of almost 200 Roman

Catholic patients went to their service in the recreational hall, it being proposed to turn a room into a Roman Catholic chapel.[18] Four years later, services were held on the infirmary wards on each side, with about 50 males and 50 females attending.[19]

Patients were allowed beyond the estate: in 1885, John Dodds and Frederick Ffitch, second class attendants, were dismissed for going into a public house while on duty, each leaving his patient whom he was escorting outside.[20] In 1887, the Commissioners commented that Dr Moody had not yet instituted a recommended system of daily walks in the grounds beyond the airing courts although, with almost 1,100 patients, about 600 of both sexes were taken on weekly walks beyond the estate. Several were allowed parole, some within and others beyond the estate.[21] In 1890, 468 patients, mainly male, went out beyond the asylum's grounds. Another 45 men and 279 women went into the grounds about three times a week. All were accompanied, but 25 male and 8 female patients went out without staff. Twenty males and 20 females were confined to the airing courts.[22]

In 1894, many had 'extended walks' but 200 men and 400 women did not exercise beyond the airing courts or cricket field. A new walk in the grounds was recommended to provide longer walks so that only the feeble were confined to the airing courts.[23] The following year 965 patients now walked out beyond the grounds, while 355 only walked in the airing courts. There were drinking fountains in the airing courts and cricket field.[24]

In 1898, Mr Moorson Roberts wrote to Dr Moody asking that, when patients were out for exercise, they should not pass the new villas facing Fair Dean [Dene] Close. The Clerk replied that while the committee 'was desirous patients should be no cause of inconvenience etc, they are quite unable to give direction that they should not make use of public roads in the neighbourhood'.

Mr Roberts replied from Debenham in Suffolk, that the committee and Dr Moody misunderstood the objections raised by his tenants in the new villas, asking Dr Moody to 'instruct the attendants of these lunatics not to let the gangs under their charge walk close in front of the villas, near Fair Dean Down, particularly of a Sunday, but on the contrary, as you suggest, make use of the public roads in the neighbourhood'. The committee decided to take no further action.[25]

In 1900, with 2,210 patients, 61 per cent (over 1300) went weekly beyond the asylum or walked in the grounds beyond the airing courts, where 12.2 per cent (less than 300) stayed, because they were physically unable or unwilling to go further.[26]

Leisure was provided for on 'bright and cheerful wards', as in 1894, with new paintings, 'other decorative objects' and a liberal supply of plants. Books, games and other 'appliances for the amusement of the patients' were fairly well provided although some pianos appeared 'inferior instruments'.[27]

Treatment?

Little is known about medical interventions used to 'treat' patients' psychiatric symptoms, as case notes have not survived: it was not reported in the sub-committees and the Commissioners did not include it in their inspection although they commented favourably each year on nursing methods, particularly the lack of bed sores. Medical nurses and attendants were regularly called upon to treat physical illnesses, particularly those accompanying old age, general paralysis, and the prevention and treatment of infections, fevers and tuberculosis.

J.M.S., admitted in 1892 with melancholia and refusing to eat, was forcibly fed with a soft tube and funnel. She died in Cane Hill, the post mortem showing that food had entered the lungs, perhaps when vomiting.[28]

Year after year, there was no mechanical restraint or seclusion recorded. Commissioners only reported patients kept in strong clothing on the days when they were there: four women wore it in 1894 while they were there, and twelve in 1896, and reports of ill treatment mention the use of locked gloves and shoes.

Returning to the outside world

There were generally a handful of patients on trial. When the Commissioners visited in 1899, there were seven 'to whom allowances seem to be freely given'. Cane Hill's recovery rate was 39.24 per cent, compared with a national average of 38.9 per cent.[29]

Care was taken before discharge. In 1897, Alexander Turney's father applied for his discharge, which was refused as enquiries showed his accommodation to be unfavourable. When Charlotte Hardingham's husband applied for her discharge to his care and custody, he promised a special attendant and someone constantly with her. Once Mr. Sears had visited the house and considered the arrangements 'likely to be satisfactory', she was discharged home.[30] In 1895, Dr Moody instructed that Mary Ann Brown be supplied with a set of artificial teeth, the cost not to exceed £4.4s 0d, to aid her recovery.[31]

The Commissioners always commented that the least well patients asked for discharge. In 1892 Alice Bunn, first admitted in January 1886, wrote with such a request. Dr Moody reported to the sub-committee that

> The patient's mind is extremely unstable. She has little control over her temper or actions. Her condition varies. She is at times sullen and morose, at other times depressed. Sometimes she threatens to commit suicide, at others she is querulous and abusive. [She] Nurses imaginary grievances against people. Her family history is very bad. Her father and paternal grandfather were insane. Her statement that her brother offered her a home, is founded on a qualified offer he made to take her provided she was sufficiently well to leave the asylum recovered, but he would not undertake to ask for her discharge on his responsibility. On one occasion when she was discharged with his custody from Croydon Union, she attempted suicide with poison.
>
> She was discharged from this asylum on 8 July 1886, after a probationary period of one month.
>
> Eighteen days later she was readmitted, having threatened to drown herself, and actually having left home for 10 days. During this time she wandered about and was reported to have lived promiscuously with several men.
>
> I am of opinion she is insane, and a proper subject for detention in an asylum.

Dr Moody had written to her brother to ask him if he would take her out on his own responsibility but her brother's wife replied and refused to have her. The sub-committee sent a copy of her letter to the Home Secretary assuring him that, from time to time, it gave special attention to Alice's case.[32] She remained at Cane Hill until September 1899 when, with others from Croydon, she was transferred to Fisherton House.

In 1894, infirmary beds were blocked because of the 'great number of very aged patients' and it was necessary to rearrange the wards.[33] By 1899, many wards were overcrowded. Some died soon after admission, such as in 1899 when a man aged 79 was brought by road from Stepney Workhouse and died four days later from natural causes. The inquest jury decided he had not been in a fit state to be removed and that it accelerated his death.[34]

Both Dr Moody and the Commissioners would check that patients with means were not unnecessarily paid for by the Unions as pauper lunatics. In 1893, the Commissioners informed the committee that Sarah Stores, admitted by Whitechapel's Guardians, had an annual income of £120, suggesting her trustee transfer her to 'an Institution for lunatics' where 'she might derive further advantage from her means'. When a male patient from St. Pancras Union had £535 held in trust by his two brothers who did not want him transferred to a private asylum until compelled as they considered themselves 'responsible to account for the money', Cane Hill's Clerk instructed the Guardians to remove him.[35]

It would have been with relief that Croydon's patients moved to Fisherton House near Salisbury in September 1899, apart from a very few considered too frail to be transferred until they were fit, but these beds were soon taken by patients belonging to London Unions who had been in other asylums including 25 females from Fisherton House and 17 females from Claybury Asylum in Essex.[36] In April 1900, with capacity for 2,078 patients, there were 2,210, an excess of 132.[37]

Chapter 9: The new century 1900-1914

Following their visit to Cane Hill in June 1912, the Commissioners recorded that

> This Asylum continues to be efficiently administered and well maintained, and throughout bears evidence of being conducted with a view to the well-being and contentment of its inmates. The wards are comfortable and bright, papers books, periodicals and a variety of books are provided for the amusement and distraction of the patients, whom we found suitably clothed, tidy in person, and except in the matter of detention, generally satisfied with their surroundings.[1]

In 1905, the Guardians of St. Giles, Camberwell, Union formed a similar impression seeing their 182 patients, the bulk of whom seemed 'hopelessly chronic': 'the patients appear to be very comfortable, and we were very much struck with their quiet and orderly demeanour', but complained that the meat in the butcher's shop was of inferior quality and in a bad condition', the Steward responding that it was English meat and of good quality.[2]

The Commissioners in 1912 observed an excellent dinner of fried fish with two vegetables and bread, followed by rice pudding. There was criticism: the dinner and plates were not hot due to a 'general dislocation of water arrangements', while stiff gas brackets remained on the walls and unprotected towel rollers, both risks for suicidal patients who could hang themselves, while floor polish was still kept in open tins and locked in bookcase cupboards on two wards. They were impressed that steam jets in the kitchen yard sterilised milk churns, with improved means of filtering milk in the dairy.[3] Praise was not automatic, for they remained critical of poor conditions in many asylums.

Three years earlier, Dr Moody was knighted 'after twenty-five years successful administration' of Cane Hill. Congratulated by the sub-committee, he replied that 'My work here has been always most congenial'. He had a large number of letters from ex-nurses and attendants and patients 'all couched in the most kindly terms'.[4]

It was not without danger: in 1899, visiting patients placed at Fisherton House, he was attacked by a female patient who had secreted a knife.[5] After a long convalescence, he returned to work but, in 1901, was attacked at Cane Hill by Henry Watson, a 'troublesome, dangerous man with fixed delusions of persecution and a record of criminality. He struck Mr Moody who was talking to him, with so violent a blow on the face with his fist that he succeeded in fracturing the upper jaw on the left side'. The Commissioners approached the Home Office, and the patient was transferred to Broadmoor Hospital.[6]

The Secretary of State permitted Dr Moody to advise Croydon Borough on its building of Croydon Mental Hospital which opened in 1903. He told them of a narrow escape from patients at Cane Hill when he

> went into the laundry one day, and the patients therein suddenly came to the conclusion that he required to be boiled. "Let's put the doctor in the copper" suggested one of the loonies, and the idea was no sooner broached than they proceeded to carry it out.

Seeing assistance would not reach him in time, he

> resorted to stratagem, as all good Medical Superintendents have to do. The laundry ladies gathered around him and told him they were going to put him in the copper. "Oh, that will be fun" quietly remarked the doctor, "but, I say" (looking down at his boots), "I have a pair of new boots on, and it seems a pity to spoil them. Suppose I go and change them first". The women fell into the trap at once, promptly consented, and dismissed him from the injunction that he should not be long.[7]

On their annual visits, the Commissioners regularly reported that patients at Cane Hill were contented, quiet and orderly and, in 1906, 'a marked absence of noisy excitement'.[8] The previous year, they noted one bedsore, but had 'satisfactory assurance that careful attention is paid to the nursing of the sick, of which we saw many other indications'.[9]

The number of staff employed in the LCAC asylums rose from 1,070 in 1889 to 3,677 on 31 March 1905, with 446 employed at

Cane Hill, including those on the estate and farm.[10] In the 1901 census, of 72 single attendants resident in the asylum, only a handful were born in the London area: 1 was born in Ireland and 19 in Scotland (almost 24 per cent of the total) and, of 141 resident nurses, 24 were born in Ireland, 16 in Wales and 5 in Scotland (nearly 34 per cent of the total). Most of the medical officers were born in Ireland or Scotland. Until their closure, asylums and later psychiatric hospitals in the London area had difficulty recruiting local junior staff in a part of the country where better paid and more amenable jobs were available. Vacancies were advertised in areas with higher unemployment levels, in the hope young people would be attracted to the metropolis. By 1909, they advertised for nurses in the *Morning Post*, *Daily Chronicle*, *Lloyds*, *The Yorkshire Post* and *The Leeds Mercury*. From its early days, Cane Hill attracted senior staff from other asylums.

In 1909, Dr Moody requested an extra month's leave for a holiday in the USA. He told the sub-committee that, in twenty-six years as medical superintendent, apart from six months sick leave after the assault at Fisherton House, he had little sick leave and, for several years when first appointed, did not take his full leave 'in his desire for its welfare'. They recommended it to the LCAC, who granted two and a half months absence.[11]

By 1912, Cane Hill was particularly successful in retaining male attendants, with 85 per cent there for over five years, and only 7 per cent for less than a year. There was a greater turnover of female nurses, 36 per cent having been there for over 5 years and 20 per cent under a year, probably because married women were not employed.[12] In 1912, advertisements for nurses were placed not only in national papers, but in local papers in Croydon, West Sussex, East Anglia and South Wales.[13] Staff were encouraged to attend lectures on the care and treatment of patients which, held during working hours, were 'quite voluntary'.[14]

Discontent

From the 1890s, staff presented petitions for issues such as increased pay or altered hours, which were generally ignored. In 1908, the sub-committee agreed to staff in the workshops, who worked a 54 hour week, taking a half hour for lunch, so as to finish work a half hour earlier at 5.30 p.m. They had worked from 7.00 a.m. to 6.00 p.m.

Mondays to Fridays, finishing at 2.00 p.m. on Saturdays.[15]

In 1912, several attendants refused to take their wages on pay day because the money given in lieu of rations on leave days was short. A petition was signed by 31 men and 141 women, resident staff, who thought it unfair that they were compelled to be out of the asylum by 8.00 a.m. on leave days, or forfeited a money allowance given when away from the asylum. The sub-committee saw three men and three women – who said staff wanted a hour or two or more hours rest in the morning if they desired it, and be allowed to have the money allowance. The sub-committee agreed to an allowance of 5d if they did not have breakfast at 7.15 a.m. Dr Moody wanted to be able to compensate for the cost of meals on their weekly day's leave; he had not contemplated that staff would want to stay in the institution.

Those staff who declined their wages could apply again for them, money would be paid to those who did not have rations, and the sub-committee would get clarification from the LCAC.[16] Later that year, 27 attendants petitioned to start work later and, in June 1914, there were six petitions from staff groups about new scales of pay. The sub-committee could only refer these to the LCAC.[17]

Uniforms

Male attendants wore serge suits, while uniforms worn by female staff varied according to the grade and position. Head female attendants, in charge of wards, wore black serge dresses, those worn in winter being of a heavier weight, with collars and cuffs with black strings, a shawl, and a cap. In 1909, they adopted white knitted jackets instead of shawls.[18]

First class nurses, and the chief mess woman, in charge of the mess room, had a blue dress in estamene and two Galatea stripe dresses, a shawl, bonnet, collars and cuffs fastened with blue or black ribbon, washable caps with strings and bows tied in front, a hood in the same material as the striped dresses, an apron, and a belt with a sheaf and chain for scissors and a sliding hook and chain for keys.

Second class attendants, and the assistant mess woman, wore the same uniform but their caps had no strings, while laundry maids had twill dresses and a hood in a heavier, stronger material the same colour as the nurses' Galatea stripes, the same belt as the nurses, and a 'cross-over as required'. Female kitchen maids wore the same as laundry maids, but with collar and cuffs, and the housemaids a black estamene dress, two print dresses in the same material as the laundry maids', duck and muslin aprons, stand-up collars, cuffs, the same belt as nurses, and washable caps with no streamers in the 'Cane Hill Pattern'.[19] When issued with new uniforms, staff could keep the old clothing for themselves, apart from the female staff's shawls and hoods, and the men's brass buttons and overcoats.[20]

In 1905, when Bexley Asylum's sub-committee recommended that female staff wear washable dresses and 'Sister Dora' for nurses, Dr Moody wanted to keep estamene as it was warm and comfortable for winter wear, especially out of doors, where as much as possible of the time of many nurses is spent . . . Nurses here dressed in it are neat, tidy and clean, I can understand the desirability of a washing material for Nurses in a general hospital . . . but in an ordinary Asylum ward where patients are in the proportion of about 50 to 4 or 5 nurses I cannot realise any gain from having the few Nurses thus dressed, when the patients are clothed in woollen and other materials and which they have to wear for months . . . the laundry facilities at this Asylum are already taxed to the upmost, and that it would be impossible to undertake more washing than is now done.[21]

Large shawls were provided for patients to wear in the grounds and airing courts. The LCAC proposed in 1912 that shawls for female patients and nurses be replaced by capes made in the workrooms, as were nurses' caps and aprons. Caps would be replaced when condemned rather than annually. Dr Moody replied that shawls had been used for patients 'for very long times past'. He was informed they were better for both nurses and patients, the shawl being a better wrap giving the nurse 'the greatest freedom in handling her patients'. Were capes adopted, he preferred dark blue, as red 'is over-conspicuous when walking on the public roads.[22]

In 1914, probably with economy in mind, he recommended that head nurses had three washable dresses instead of two black serge dresses, the stock of serge to be used as mourning dresses for the patients. An extra 150 yards of gingham would be required. Nurses and mess women would have three Galatea dresses instead of two Galatea and one estamene, saving £60 a year. One hundred female patients were employed in the needleroom making and repairing clothing and linen.[23]

Little else is known of the patients' clothing, but the male patients' underwear was modified in 1903; seven-eights of the patients wore socks, which were encouraged rather than long cotton hose. Most wore flannel drawers, but those who did not could still wear 'stockings'.[24] In 1912, they agreed to adopt the same materials for underclothing as the other asylums, but Dr Moody was thought grandrill shirting too heavy for men's day shirts in warmer weather, preferring to keep to Oxford shirting, which was agreed to by the sub-committee.[25]

Staffing issues

Some staff were injured in attacks by patients, and several patients accused staff of ill treatment but, apart from a handful between 1900 and 1903, and one in 1913, where accusations were pursued, the others were considered unfounded, and the number of complaints was lower than in the 1890s. When one male patient was found with a severely bruised leg and another with a severe bruise on his buttock, the former, a 'fairly sensible' patient, accused an attendant of hitting them, who was asked to resign because of his generally unsatisfactory conduct. In another case, Matron saw Nurse Shorter put a wash leather, used for ward cleaning, into a noisy patient's mouth. The nurse, previously 'kind and attentive', was asked to resign but remained at Cane Hill after two members of the sub-committee suggested a severe reprimand instead.[26] In 1910, 'many patients bore testimony to the kindness of those in charge of them', while some patients complained that the Guardians of their Union had not visited since 1904.[27] The Commissioners noted, in 1912, that Guardians visited infrequently, particularly those of the Poplar Union.[28]

Despite the regulations laid down by the LCAC, each year male and female staff were severely reprimanded or dismissed for misconduct, often for repeatedly returning drunk, and for missing trains and returning late from leave. Some let patients escape on more than one occasion. The sub-committee now listed the names of all sick staff in the minutes, often with details of illnesses and the length of time off work, including regular influenza epidemics when forty or so staff were ill.

Young unmarried men and women in their twenties worked and lived close together, albeit on separate sides of the building. The LCAC did not employ married female staff, while unmarried men had to obtain permission from the asylum's authorities before they could marry. John A. Thornton was not permitted to marry in 1899, as there were no vacancies for married staff.[29] But, there were secret liaisons.

When in 1901, second class nurse Jane Ferrier Campbell gave birth to a still born child, having secretly married Attendant George Bell, both were dismissed.[30] In 1904, Nurse Elizabeth Nichols Dorrell was found 'advanced in pregnancy by Bertram Charles Marshall'. They were 'walking out together', Dr Moody having seen them a few months before after which he had cautioned Marshall 'as she had become hysterical and from a good Nurse to an indifferent one'. She resigned and Marshall was asked to resign.

Two exceptions had been made in 1900 when a number of staff, who were reservists, were 'called to the colours' to fight in the Boer War, resulting in a shortage of male staff. When a nurse informed Dr Moody that she had married by special licence as her husband, a former attendant, was leaving to fight in South Africa, she was allowed to remain, and the sub-committee sent a memo to the LCAC asking them to reconsider the regulation. Head Mess Room Attendant Horace Potterton and Nurse Selina Curtis were allowed to marry, and she continued in her present position, with lodging found for them in the asylum, but would have to leave if she became pregnant. It was stressed that it was not a precedent.[31]

In 1909, the LCAC increased the proportion of male attendants allowed to marry and live outside the asylum. Dr Moody considered that, if ten men were added to the married establishment of 75 attendants, their rooms could be adapted, at £5 a room, for use by patients. Cane Hill was two men over the married establishment, with 28 married men living in cottages on the estate, who all appeared settled, while five more men had applied for permission to marry. The full establishment of attendants was 130 men, of which a minimum of 42 slept adjacent to each dormitory in case of an emergency at night. It left 13 who did not require to be resident, and he suggested that the number of married staff could be increased provided the money was available, each married man receiving £20 in lieu of lodging and washing. He suggested the vacated rooms be used by married attendants as dressing rooms, who relied on single attendants allowing them to use their rooms for cleaning themselves, shaving, etc.[32]

The sub-committee appear more tolerant than the LCAC,

probably because of difficulties in recruitment. When second class attendant George Cusack married without permission in 1912, he was admonished but allowed to remain, the sub-committee having no objection to his wife, formerly a laundry maid at Cane Hill, being employed as a temporary laundry maid. That same year, second class attendant Ransom renewed his application to marry and be allowed to reside in the asylum's accommodation, but there were three in front of him on the waiting list. He was informed that, if he elected to marry, he would remain but would not receive the privileges granted to married men until he reached the top of the waiting list.

Staff sickness

Names of sick staff were presented at sub-committee meetings and show regular influenza epidemics. Resident staff were treated in the asylum when they became ill.

Some were injured at work. Workmen fell off ladders, while attendants and nurses were hit by patients. Charge attendant George Williams was hit on the back of the head by a patient with a 'shove-halfpenny' board while playing cards with other patients. Dr Moody reported that the board was broken but Williams 'showed not the slightest blow or even had a headache'. Others were less fortunate. When Hannah Richardson escaped thorough a window and over the airing court wall, she was returned safely the next day having gone to her brother's home in Norwood. Meanwhile, nurse Alice King, while finding what clothes she wore, fell from the shelves on to which she climbed and had concussion of the brain. She was improving rapidly, but Dr Moody 'did not think it advisable to worry her for details of the escape'.[33]

In cases of long term sickness, sick pay was paid for up to a year but, if it appeared a member of staff would not improve, they were dismissed. There was a particular care for those with tuberculosis, perhaps because they could have contracted it from patients. Attendant J. McKeohan had consumption and was on extended sick leave. When he died in 1904, he was buried in the asylum's cemetery, his funeral expenses being paid for, up to £5 and his widow given £10 from the Tea Fund.[34]

In September 1912, Dr Moody obtained a bed for Nurse Julia Gaffney at Mount Vernon Hospital for Consumptives where she had two admissions, and did light duties at Cane Hill in between the two. When discharged the second time, she went to Ireland where her sister 'found her very weak'. Dr Moody's opinion was that she would not be able to return to nursing. In April 1913, the sub-committee granted her 5s a week until September, when she would have had twelve month's sick leave, and dismissed her.

Charge Nurse Helen Henderson, aged 52, had joined in 1886 and was one month off twenty-six years service at Cane Hill and in charge of L female ward where 24 pieces of crockery were broken in one week and another 71 items were concealed in the ward. It became known because bowls were being used instead of cups. When interviewed, she said she acted that way because 'the medical superintendent would have been so cross with me'. Dr Moody thought she should be retired as she showed 'signs of mental enfeeblement and incapacity'. She was examined by the LCAC's deputy medical officer of health who found her 'quite unfitted for her post', concluding it 'was probably the result of a large number of years spent in dealing with insane people'. If she resigned, she would receive a pension.[35]

The sub-committee and senior staff were responsible to the LCAC, having to abide by the regulations and to account for the administration and funding of the asylum and to seek permission for much of the day to day running. Usually the sub-committee supported Dr Moody's proposals, but not always. These pressures probably told on the Clerk and Steward.

In 1907, Mr Ralph, the Clerk, who began at Brookwood Asylum in 1875, and came to Cane Hill with Dr Moody, resigned because of failing health. A letter from his doctor, told of 'repeated nervous breakdowns and that his nerve power was now so reduced that he was totally unable to cope with the duties of his position. He received a pension of £191.3s 4d a year. Later that year Mr Smith, the Steward had rheumatic problems, facial paralysis and a nervous breakdown. Given a month's rest from work, he returned to work for four more years.[36]

Chapter 10: Law and Disorder

Despite regulations and supervision, thefts became frequent. Bertram Charles Marshall does not appear to have left for, in 1906, patients accused him of asking them for tobacco and cigarette papers, and suspected him of taking tobacco from their pockets after they had gone to bed. When two patients were interviewed, Marshall denied taking tobacco but admitted asking for and receiving cigarette papers from patients, and was again asked to resign.

Although all parcels were to be checked before leaving the estate, items were still smuggled out. In 1904 a kitchen maid told Dr Moody that she saw two scullery men taking about three lbs of raw mutton and bacon issued for boiling, and that Cook knew about it. The two men were dismissed, the cook was asked to resign, and two kitchen maids resigned. It was decided to have only female staff in the kitchen as men and women 'do not agree', there having been friction in Cook's absence, while it was 'undesirable' to have male staff close to female patients. In 1906, 2 lbs of best end of neck of lamb disappeared from the butcher's shop where it had been prepared for Matron's dinner, until the cook said Matron wanted beef instead. No one knew who took it.[1]

The previous year, when soap was regularly stolen, private detectives were employed to check out three laundry men. They questioned their neighbours but could not find any evidence. Soon after, when Inspector Baker, in charge of the male attendants, found sugar, patients' tobacco and other items went missing on Monday nights in G1 male ward, the Chairman saw one of the staff, suspected having made a duplicate key, and warned him to 'act more wisely in future'.[2]

In 1903, Attendant Charles Allen left a parcel with Inspector Baker, claiming it contained clothing, to be sealed and for Allen to obtain a pass before he took it out of the estate. Baker, being suspicious, found it contained a rug made by a patient in the tailor's shop and sold to Allen by Attendant William A. Newman. Another rug was found in Newman's room on F1 ward, made by another patient, who said he had made about thirteen rugs from cuttings in the tailor's shop, including six or seven for Attendant Thomas Burton. Five canvas bed-slips were found missing, one rug having been made from one of them.

Allen was asked to resign and three other attendants were dismissed, including Burton who refused to leave his cottage. Returning his uniform, he could not find his lamp, belt, whistle and chain. Willing to pay 6s. 6d for them, he could not find another house but was told to leave in a week. Baker, despite having discovered and reported the parcel, was severely reprimanded and his salary reduced from £110 to £100 with no increment for two years. The Steward was severely censured for not marking all articles in the asylum, and the master tailor instructed only to give out items with permission from the Steward.[3]

In 1908, the new Clerk, Thomas Mynott, aged 29 and promoted in 1907 from being first assistant clerk, asked for special leave on the day of the sub-committee's meeting, having received a telegram that his invalid wife was seriously ill. As it was not the first time he absented himself on Committee Day, the Clerk of the LCCAC investigated the accounts and found £216.10s. 0d missing. When Mynott appeared before Croydon County Bench on 15 June, he was allowed bail. Pleading guilty, saying he had a delicate wife and lived above his means, he was imprisoned for four months with hard labour.

When an additional £21.3s. 6d was found missing, an enquiry took place during which Mr. Taverner, a former clerk dismissed for taking absence without leave, said Mynott began betting when appointed to Cane Hill and was addicted. Another clerk said Mynott, 'a silent man, rarely entered into conversation other than of a business character', but often gave clerks extra leave if they worked late, and was frequently absent himself. Mynott had assured Dr Moody three years before that no betting went on, but staff from the office went to the Derby and the Oaks.[4]

Thefts continued: in 1912, when certain staff stole small quantities of farm produce, the potato and fruit stores were kept locked. Then, Mr. Fish, the farm bailiff, discovered second class attendant Yandle, some distance away from the patients with whom he was working, bending down close to the main drive and putting grass over a bag. Fish examined the bag and found it contained potatoes. Yandle begged him not to report it because of his wife and children.

He said the bag was not his, and that he had left his gang to relieve himself, and looked into it out of curiosity. Because of his previous good conduct, he was severely reprimanded.[5] From 1906, the Inspector of Stores visited Cane Hill one day a month to check all condemned items. Everything worn out, damaged or broken had to be presented as in May, when he did not consider an apron, bonnet, three counterpanes and one shirt worn out, while breakages seemed high on the male side with 96 on F2 and 91 on G2 in four weeks.[6] He consistently suspected the losses of clothing, bedding and other materials to be due to theft, suggesting striped material be used for all items and clothing, which Dr Moody refused to do. For his part Dr Moody suspected that, while some staff were dishonest if they had the chance, more articles were destroyed on the wards than admitted, while patients in the laundry secreted towels so they could have one entirely for their own personal use, old articles were torn in the laundry, and items were put down the WC. They recovered items at sewerage outlets but unrecognisable rags passed through the drainage although Cane Hill had its own sewerage farm.

Dr Moody was probably becoming irritated by this interference. Approval had to be constantly sought from the LCAC. When the Inspector of Stores suggested re-footing stockings, Dr Moody responded 'I have no doubt that after some practice useful articles will be produced', and when, from 117 condemned dresses, the Inspector recommended that six of the skirts might make petticoats. Dr Moody thought this inadvisable as, when stocktaking, they and dresses would be the same colour, and suggested using them as dress linings.[7]

Thefts from outside

While the main building and airing court gates were securely locked, the rest of the estate was as open as any farm and park, with fencing and some hedging on its boundary. There was an unclimbable fence alongside the footpath from the station, as the new path dropped steeply and there might be accidents in the dark. At least one field, where hundreds of young cabbage plants were grown, was surrounded by an iron fence. In 1900, a wire fence was erected from the corner of the cricket field to the Brighton Road, with wire and an unclimbable fence around the steward's house at Posterns.[8]

Most patients only left the building as part of a working or walking party. The majority of patients who escaped got away when in a working party, most not being recaptured, although police were informed and went to their homes. If not found within two weeks, they were discharged. Some were caught because they met off-duty attendants outside the estate or on the station platform. Dr Moody complained several times that visitors left money and knives with patients, although instructed not to do so.

The back gate keeper, Mr Muir, and his wife, lived in the back lodge in Portnalls Road where both were employed to check all vehicles in and out. All workmen and artisans used that entrance while visitors and all other staff used the front main gate, where the lodge had been occupied by the clerk of works and was empty in 1904. He had been responsible for closing the gates at night, lighting the lamp and extinguishing it. Since then, unlike other asylums, it remained open. Staff returned their keys to the hall porter in the entrance hall of the main building, used by all staff, apart from artisans and workmen, as well as patients, visitors and relieving officers.

A gate opening onto Woodmansterne Road, used by farm traffic, was closed in 1904, and a new gate made close to the back of the lodge, with a new road constructed using patients' labour with metal picked off the fields. That year, the LCAC insisted Bundy clocks be introduced, and all staff checked in and out. Dr Moody accepted its use at the back gate, but was reluctant to have it introduced in the entrance hall where up to 50 married staff left at 8.00 p.m. and up to 70 resident staff came in at 10.00 p.m. He lived on the south side of the front block of the asylum and complained that, with the proximity of his house to the hall and corridor 'every entry of the Clock when a gong dongs would be heard in my house and I fear the noise would become intolerable and get on one's nerves'.[9]

More problems arose two years later when it was realised that medical officers were unable to hand their keys to a gate porter, and the regulations prevented the hall porter handling keys for the female side of the asylum. It was decided medical officers would hand them to the female 'corresponding officer'.[10] By 1913, there was again a gate keeper, Mr Windebank, at the front East Lodge.

The back gate had a Bundy clock but was open from 6.00 a.m. to 6.00 p.m. Stockmen began work at 5.30 a.m., the three carters and the early stoker at 5.30 a.m. while the late stoker started at 8.15

p.m. and the assistant gardeners did late duties in cold weather.[11]

Most thefts were of fowls from the farm, as in 1901 when six were taken and two found with their necks wrung. Thieves were rarely caught but, this time, small pieces of cloth were found on a fence and near the hen houses. The police arrested a man called Curtis wearing a torn coat, and found the pieces fitted. He pleaded guilty, appearing in court in Croydon the next day where, because he could not provide bail, he was remanded to Holloway Prison.[12] In 1905, fifteen yards of growing Eldorado and Southern Star potatoes were taken from the kitchen garden, despite locked gates and unclimbable fencing.[13]

Twice, berberis shrubs planted on either side of the main drive were stolen and others damaged. On one occasion, one of the staff, coming to work, saw three men with a light horse and cart at the 'cinder gate path' at 5.45 a.m. and questioned them, accepting their story that they were removing ivy left there the previous evening.[14]

Thefts could be more audacious: in 1905 two men with a cart stripped lead off the roof of the new water meter house. Stopped by police, they pleaded guilty, each receiving one month's hard labour. The following year, seven canaries disappeared from the aviary on Male A1 ward. The window opened directly onto the road connecting the front and the back of the building, and a footstep was found in the flower bed below.[15]

The Rules

In 1904, the LCAC published its General Rules, laying down the responsibilities for each asylum's sub-committee and its officers. The sub-committee, which comprised at least seven members, with the chairman and vice-chairman of the LCAC as ex-officio members, appointed, suspended or dismissed all staff apart from the medical superintendent whom they could only suspend, as he was appointed and dismissed by the LCAC. The sub-committee had to prepare an annual estimate of expenditure showing rents, taxes and insurance, the cost of the maintenance of pauper lunatics chargeable to the County of London, repairs, additions, alterations and improvements not exceeding £400, as well as those not exceeding a total of £1,000 for each work which were other than those providing increased accommodation, which was seen as inevitable.

The medical superintendent was to be resident, with responsibility for the direction of all 'the medical and surgical treatment of the patients, and their management, exercise, amusements, employments and medical classification, subject to the regulations of the Asylum, and the orders of the Sub-Committee'. He should not 'practice out of the Asylum nor be employed professionally in any way unconnected with his office' except, at the request of the Secretary of State, the Solicitor to the Treasury or the Commissioners in Lunacy, to visit and examine the medical condition of any person charged with a capital offence. He could not absent himself for more than one night without the permission of the chairman of the sub-committee, or three nights without the permission of the sub-committee.

He should visit the wards as often as practicable, and ensure every ward and patient was visited at least twice a day by an assistant medical officer, who ordered the necessary diets for sick patients. He was to occasionally visit wards and bedrooms at 'uncertain times' during the night, accompanied by the matron, female head night attendant or another female officer when visiting female wards. He, or an assistant medical officer, was to be present at 'the celebration of Divine Worship in the Asylum on Sundays'.

Matron supervised female patients, ward nurses, female domestic servants, and the laundry and work rooms: 'She shall endeavour in every way to promote the interest and happiness of the patients, and the welfare of all committed to her charge'.

The Clerk of the Asylum maintained all the books and accounts, preparing a financial statement for each meeting of the sub-committee, and listing and returning all property found on a patient on admission, except for wedding rings, to the patient's parish or Union. When a patient was permitted trial leave, the Clerk was to give written or printed instructions to the patient's relatives that, in the case of a relapse, the patient was to be immediately brought back to the asylum. At the end of the trial period, the patient must either appear before the sub-committee, or a medical certificate be sent to the medical superintendent certifying that the patient's detention was no longer necessary.

Male and female patients were to be kept in separate wards. Only medical officers, the chaplain, the engineer and workmen doing necessary duties could enter female wards. Females could only enter male wards if the medical superintendent deemed it necessary for a nurse or servant to do so. Excepting single rooms, no ward for male patients should contain less than three beds, and all patients should sleep in single beds. During the day, patients of both sexes were to be employed

> as much as practicable, especially out of doors, the men in gardening, husbandry and handicrafts; the women in occupations suited to their ability; and as a principle in treatment, endeavours should be continually used to occupy and employ the minds and bodies of the patients, to induce them to take extended exercise in the open air, and to promote happiness and cheerfulness amongst them. Such patients as the Medical Superintendent may direct shall, in such numbers and at such times as he may think fit, be allowed under proper supervision to take walks or excursions beyond the grounds of the Asylum . . . Workshops and tools shall be provided and artizans and others be encouraged to follow their particular callings, and to learn shoemaking, tailoring and other common and useful trades; and needlework, laundry work, and other suitable employment shall be provided for the women.

Books, newspapers and publications were to be regularly circulated through the wards, and 'various means of amusements' be available to the patients, which they should be encouraged to participate in frequently. Airing courts were to be accessible every day when the weather was favourable.

If a patient needed to be 'secluded', the compulsory isolation of a patient in a single room between 7 a.m. and 7 p.m. by closing its door, it was to be recorded and reported to the sub-committee. Since the opening of Cane Hill, it was rarely recorded but, in 1900, Mr McDougell, a member of the sub-committee visited a female ward and found 'an acutely maniacal female patient' in a single room. The door was unlocked but three nurses were standing with their backs against it. Mr McDougell 'believed it was an instruction at this Asylum, in order to avoid reporting cases of patients secluded, that the doors of single rooms were not to be locked'.

As Dr Moody was on sick leave, the sub-committee informed the acting medical superintendent that a door 'secured by manual force is as much secluded as if that door was locked', and asked to consider whether steps taken to avoid reporting cases of seclusion were justifiable. Dr Moody always instructed that seclusion was 'undesirable'.[16]

There were always padded rooms on wards, but their use was not generally recorded in sub-committee meetings. The books in which their use was recorded have not survived. However, in 1900, Robert Ward, a feeble, restless man aged 78, admitted on 14 June, was found on 22 June to have three fractured ribs, having been kept in a padded cell since admission to prevent any such occurrence. With a diseased heart and lungs, he was not expected to live long.[17]

Each year the Commissioners formally stated that 'mechanical means of bodily restraint' were not used at Cane Hill, but they very occasionally mentioned seeing strong dresses worn, which were included, under the 1890 Lunacy Act, in a list of permitted instruments and appliances which restrained or impeded the free movement of the body or any limbs, namely:

1. A jacket or dress made of strong linen, or a similar material, laced or buttoned down the back with long sleeves with closed ends which may have tapes for tying across the back when the arms have been folded across the chest, namely a 'strait-jacket'.

2. Gloves without fingers, fastened at the wrists so that the wearer could not remove them, made of linen, leather or some strong material, perhaps padded.

3. Sheets or towels tied to the sides or ends of a bed or to other objects.

4. Some other means sanctioned by the Board of Control. (Locked shoes were still used at Cane Hill into the 1960s).

Other methods which could be used, and were not considered as mechanical means of bodily support, were:

1. The continuous bath, but a cover was not to be used unless the aperture for the patient's head was large enough for his body to pass through.

2. The wet and dry pack, not using any straps or ligatures. The patient should be released for 'necessary purposes at periods not exceeding two hours'.

3 Splints, bandages, etc., when used for surgical purposes, fractures or local injuries.

4 Gloves removable by the patient.

5 Sheets or towels used for artificial feeding and held, not tied or fastened.

6 Trays or rails fastened to front of chairs used by idiot children, cripples or aged infirm patients to prevent them falling out but, in the case of adults, able to be opened by the patient.[18]

Chapter 11: Progress and development

There was £17,497.8s 9½d in the Building and Repair Fund in 1900, most of which came from charging Croydon Borough £2.2s a week for each of its patients remaining in Cane Hill, being too frail to be transferred elsewhere. The sub-committee expected to make a profit of about £2,500.[1]

In 1904-5 the net expenditure on maintenance at Cane Hill was £62,563.14s 9½d, with no capital expenditure.[2] Until 1910-11, the expenditure on maintenance gradually fell and, that financial year, capital expenditure was £781.6s 4½d. The weekly maintenance cost per patient gradually reduced and was 10s 0¾d that year.

In 1908, the LCAC's General Purposes and Finance Committee observed that, of the older asylums, Cane Hill had the highest weekly expenditure of 10s 8.48d per patient.[3] Economies were made including, in 1909, selling old books and forms over three years old.[4] The asylum would make a loss for five of the six years from 1 April 1907 to 31 March 1913.

Year ending 31 March	Loss/profit	Total
1908	Loss	£907
1909	Profit	£245
1910	Loss	£1,751
1911	Loss	£3,906
1912	Loss	£3,973
Up to 9 December 1912	Loss	£2,480

Cane Hill received £3,500 as assistance for the year ending 31 March 1912. In February 1913, it was estimated that the deficit on 31 March 1913 would be £4,000, and it would have to ask for £4,500. At that meeting, Sir James asked for four weeks special leave because he 'was feeling the strain of an arduous year's work', to enable him to recuperate. He was authorised four weeks' leave the previous year but couldn't take it because of the steward's illness, the appointment of a replacement, and many changes in the medical staff. Staff were now well established and the administration working well. He completed thirty years as medical superintendent on 31 January. A week later, a surplus of £4,500 from Hanwell Asylum was transferred to Cane Hill.[5]

The buildings were over twenty years old and needed to be upgraded and modernised. In 1900, Dr Moody wanted a verandah built out from the upper infirmary dormitory of A Female Block to provide a change of scene and air for patients who could not be taken downstairs.[6] Once completed, similar balconies were built onto other wards. From 1902 onwards, 160 incandescent gas burners were introduced instead of ordinary gas burners, chiefly in bathrooms, lavatories and dormitories to improve lighting.

In 1902, it was decided to replace horsehair in twelve beds and pillows with coir fibre as an experiment.[7] Coir became hard and matted and had to be remade, whereas horse hair showed no signs of wear and tear and had 'improved elasticity'. It was cheaper to retain 'hair mattresses'.[8] When, in 1904, Dr Moody asked to replace linoleum in older wards, which had been down for 21 years, he was instructed to patch it.[9] In 1907, there were insufficient pillow cases to enable a clean one weekly on the female side. When Dr Moody said that the Commissioners would want it, the sub-committee agreed to purchase 823 more.[10]

In 1905, Male H2 ward was painted and wall-papered, and twelve additional painters taken on to paint the outside of the buildings. To save money, valves on water pipes to the farm buildings were shut off at night, reducing the quantity to the outbuildings from 4,000 to 1,000 gallons. Gas consumption had increased, so all gas to the kitchen was metered to check how much was used for cooking.[11]

From 1908, the bakery opened from 7.00 a.m. to 5.30 p.m. Mondays to Saturdays, closing at 1.00 p.m. on Sundays. The kitchens were open from 6.00 a.m. to 8.00 p.m., all cooking being done in the main kitchen, with no separate facilities for cooking meals for senior staff unlike many other asylums.[12] Men and women would eat separately for many years, as would medical staff, officers, the various grades of ward staff, and servants. Workman and artisans had to provide their own meals.

Major modernisation took place in 1907-8 to build a subway to take steam and hot water pipes. In July 1908, 170 feet was completed and the remaining 30 feet under the ironing room was being excavated.[13] In late 1909, 8-10 men, working continuously, began constructing a new heating subway. By January 1910, 16 men and 21 patients were excavating the subways.[14]

For some years, the sub-committee regularly complained when steam wagons bringing coal damaged the back gates and stores' entrance, but they accepted the inevitability of modern transport. In 1909, it was agreed to house Dr Cribb's motor car, charging him £2 a year. They applied to the Commissioners for permission to build a motor shed of corrugated iron with a brick footing, a pit and a petrol store outside No. 3 male airing court using patients' labour to do the bricklaying, stating that patients' labour would be 'utilised wherever possible'. When the Commissioners did not support the proposal, the sub-committee used part of a cart shed in the farm buildings, where a wagonette was stored, with a concrete floor for the wagonette, and a pair of folding doors.[15]

In 1900, following a suggestion by the chaplain as captain of the cricket eleven, Dr Moody suggested planting trees 30 feet apart around the cricket. Patients would help the staff by digging holes.[16] Portugal Laurel was planted in 1903, following a suggestion from the Steward, along the south side of the path from the drive to the railway station.[17] When many berberis plants on either side of the drive were stolen and damaged soon after, and in 1908, it is likely that Portugal laurel was also planted there.[18] In 1906, 10,500 young saplings were purchased, to be nursed for two years before planting three short lengths of hedging along two sides of the paddock at the cricket field, from the ash yard near the piggeries to the Farm Road and to complete the hedge on the main drive between the Garden House path and Farm Road.[19] It was decided, in 1908, to extend the boundary hedging on Chipstead Road from Oaks Wood to Postern Villa, where the Steward lived.[20]

Mr Bond, of The Coulsdon House and Estate Agency, wrote in 1911 to complain about the sharp bend at the corner of the Cane Hill estate by the junction of Brighton Road with Lion Green Road. Drivers often had to stop dead because vehicles could not be seen until the corner was turned, and children played there on their way to and from school. It was agreed that the sub-committee would give up the land to remove the bend, Croydon Rural District Council (CRDC) doing the work.[21]

Patient Labour

The London County Asylums Department, formerly the LCAC, and those who ran its asylums continued to see the use of patient labour as therapeutic, but also as a means of saving money. Male patients played an valuable role in keeping the farm and estate going, while those with skills were placed in workshops.

Male patients were regularly employed to pick up flints which were then sold, as in 1899 when 20 yards were offered at 4s 6d a yard, other flints at 4s a yard and the remainder at 2s 6d.[22] In 1908, 100 yards of flints were available for sale.[23] In June 1909, Dr Moody requested a crushing machine costing £25, there being a large accumulation of bones needing to be crushed for manure. The sub-committee refused him, and told him to arrange for a party of patients to break the bones with hammer and anvils.[24] The hospital was heating by coal. On one occasion, a patient strained himself lifting an iron cover off the coal shoot in the back yard.[25]

The shoemaker's shop became able to keep the asylum fully supplied with boots and shoes.[26] In 1908, patients working in the upholster's shop were generally 'quiet old dements' i.e. long term patients with schizophrenia.

That year, patient labour was used for the joinery work when improving attendants' cottages. The engineer engaged W. Balcomb, a bricklayer recently an in-patient at Cane Hill. Some patients cleaned bedsteads and painted the cricket pavilion. Patients helped with cleaning in the cowsheds, but the bailiff didn't 'know a patient he could trust to milk'.

In 1909, when attendants' rooms in D block were converted in single rooms for patients, the shutters were made by patients. A large frame holding a mirror, made by patients, was fixed on the wall between the dormitory and nurses room on C ward, while patients in the fitters shop made castings for reading slopes for Claybury Asylum, using 56 lbs of old brass which came from Claybury to be melted down at Cane Hill.[27]

Attendants' Cottages

In December 1900, there were 26 cases of infectious diseases in the previous 13 months in the twelve St. Dunstans Cottages or Old Attendants' cottages, occupied by attendants. These were two blocks of six four-roomed 'two up two down' cottages each with an earth closet immediately adjoining the back room, which would be replaced by a proper WC as soon as new sewers were completed. The back room contained the kitchen range, sink and waste pipe and, when doing the laundry, the room was damp, with the steam pervading the whole house. Other cottages already had sculleries, and the plan was to build separate sculleries and wash rooms but the LCAC were deterred by the considerable expense.

The engineer thought the infection was caused by earth closets and slop cess pits, and reported that five tenants kept fowls close to the houses. They were instructed to remove them to the end of the back garden. An application was made to CRDC to connect the drains to the public sewer. In 1901 earth closets in the Chaplain's House at Glencairn were replaced by 'water closets with flushing systems' as the house was near to drains.[28]

In 1902, the Committee of Ladies of the Coulsdon Nursing Association offered to nurse attendant's families in Asylum Cottages and Maybank Cottages, in Woodmansterne parish where no nursing arrangements existed. Attendants would pay 5s a year and 5s a week during sickness. The total fee during sickness would be 15s and 10s to cover the nurses' travelling expenses, an extra payment for infectious diseases and a service beyond 6 weeks. 20 of the 33 intended to join. Miss Tucker would act as 'Committee lady' and liaise on Dr Moody's behalf. For the present, any extra fees would be paid out of the Tea Fund.[29]

In 1900, three attendants living in the 'half cottages' asked for them to be converted into larger cottages, three of them being empty. A combined scullery and wash house for each cottage would cost £750, but no action would be taken at present.[30] However, the sub-committee accepted Dr Moody's suggestion to covert the old tramway embankment, about 65 yards long, between the old and new blocks of attendants cottages, into gardens for the half cottages.[31]

Four years later, the attendants asked Dr Moody to reconsider making eight sets of half cottages into four whole cottages, and to convert the first floors of the old cottages from two to three rooms as parents wanted to separate the bedrooms of children of each sex. The engineer reported back that the four cottages, with five rooms and a scullery, would take four married attendants.

The Steward complained of inadequate accommodation, asking

for his house to be enlarged, having three bedrooms for a family of seven. His wife was an invalid and the children frequently sick. They could only sleep separately from their parents by having boys and girls sleeping in the same room. His request was accepted, and the engineer drew up plans.

In 1906, the sub-committee agreed to lay on gas at the twelve Dunstan's Cottages.[32] In 1908, it was decided to add sculleries at a cost of £29 per scullery if built in pairs.[33]

Fire fighting

In 1903, following a fire at Colney Hatch Asylum in February, there was a review of the situation at Cane Hill. An extra man was employed to keep one of the pumping engines going all the time to maintain as large a reserve as possible of water in the Tower Tank, and a constant supply to outbuildings, and the farm and garden houses. The Tower Tank had a capacity of 34,000 galloons which was considered insufficient, and a new tank was proposed with a 50,000 gallon capacity which would deal with the outbreak of a fire.

If the fire grew larger, the well was the only means of supply, but with only 7,000 gallons for a limited period. There were also two rain water tanks below the laundry drying ground. It was decided to connect to the East Surrey Water Company's (ESWC) mains 'without delay', to provide additional ladders and to connect the cottage hospital, garden and farm houses to the fire alarm system. The ESWC's supply, from Alderstead Reservoir, would be softened before delivery.[34] The asylum had maintained a 'lime pump' to provide a water softening plant.[35] On 25 July, the ESWC completed laying pipes to connect with the asylum's system. Testing the system in September, when 4,000 gallons were used between 5.00 p.m. and 6 a.m., it was decided that all-night pumping would no longer be needed, with a saving of £68 a year.

The fire alarm was a steam hooter and two bells, one in the fireman's quarters and the other in the back lodge gate, with twelve points in the corridors from which an alarm could be given. There were already bells on wards in case of emergencies. Fire doors and exits were proposed, but a suggested second fireman, who could also flush drains and yards and be relief hall porter, was postponed. Dr Moody suggested an Artisans Fire Brigade, which would be available during the day when wards were most denuded of attendants. CRDC was asked to provide fire hydrants for the attendants' cottages.[36] This was agreed by the Local Government Board in 1904.[37]

Unwelcome developments

Once more, in 1901, there was threat of a railway. The London and Brighton Electric Railway intended to build an electric railway from London to Brighton through the estate, with a tunnel entering near the pumping station at a depth of 90 feet and passing directly over the bottom of the well, which was also 90 feet deep. It would then go under the farm buildings at a depth of 195 feet, the piggeries at 210 feet and leave the estate near to the cinder path. If it went ahead, the asylum would need another water source, as making the tunnel might cut some fissures feeding the well and interfere with the direction of the source of the water supply. The Parliamentary Committee was requested to oppose, and the project did not go ahead.[38]

Another threat came in 1903 with the Sutton District Water Bill, brought to Parliament by the Sutton Water Company who wanted to extract water in Chipstead Valley Road, close to the asylum's well. Advised that they might not have a strong case, the LCC made an agreement with the Company whereby, if water was abstracted and the well was affected, the Company would give the LCC a supply not exceeding 100,000 gallons a day at the same price it cost the LCC to raise water from the well.[39] In 1906, they heard that Croydon Borough was to take a Bill to Parliament to sink a large well at Wallington, two and a half miles away. Again, they wondered about the effect on the water supply.[40]

Mr Thomas Trish, who ran 'The Stores' in Smitham Bottom, applied in 1902 for an off-licence which the magistrates said they could not refuse.[41] It was then successfully opposed by both Cane Hill and the landlord of the Red Lion until 1904 when two hundred residents signed a petition in favour. The sub-committee had to accept that the local population had greatly increased when, despite their objection and that of the Red Lion's landlord, he was granted a licence provided 'beer was not sold in less than six Imperial pint bottles at any time'. He could not sell on Sundays or Bank Holidays.[42] In 1908, Mr Trish, and Mr John G. Kirby, a chemist in Brighton Road, were refused licences to sell four types of medicated wine.[43]

Water and Sewerage

Both before and after World War One, Cane Hill's medical superintendents were proud that sewerage from the main building went to the asylum's sewerage farm, to be prepared for use as manure on the farm, especially to grow fruit and vegetables.

However, the disposal of sewerage would take up much of the sub-committee's time. In 1899, the local sanitary authority questioned the emptying of cess pits. The asylum needed to employ four men and two horses overnight from 11.00 p.m. until mid-day at a cost of 24s 10d. a week.[44]

In 1905, surface water from Woodmansterne Road and surrounding land collected by the cottages and ran onto and damaged asylum property. The sub-committee undertook the work on the estate, and Croydon RDC agreed to kerb and metal the footpath and provide an outlet for surface water, the costs shared between the two authorities.[45]

In 1908, a letter was received from CRDC who were trying to arrange with Croydon Borough for the drainage to go into Croydon Borough's sewers, and would ensure all cess pits were impervious to soaking away. Because of proceedings between the two in the High Court, CRDC was unable to extend its drainage areas. The foreman engineer's house was the only one on the estate with a cesspool: a new cesspool would be constructed and lined. That same year, Croydon Borough obtained a judgement against CRDC for arrears claimed by the Borough in respect of the disposal of sewerage in Coulsdon and other parishes from 1901 to September 1905.[46]

In late 1909, the asylum's engineer reported that the contents of cesspools of houses opposite to the asylum's cottages were being emptied into gravel pits contiguous with the asylum, as CRDC had not yet connected the houses with the main sewer. He feared the asylum's water supply would be contaminated. The CRDC replied that he was mistaken, and it probably came from the asylum's sewerage farm but the engineer insisted he was correct, having several times seen a sewerage van in the meadow next to and north-east of the asylum's cemetery, his attention being attracted by the foul smell, while the chemist reported that the water from the well was less satisfactory than it had been.[47]

The Clerk of CRDC still believed in early 1910 that cesspits were not polluting the well, but assured the sub-committee he would ensure the contractor carried out work in 'a reasonable and careful manner' and that any leaks would be promptly made good. Soon after, S. Ayling, an attendant complained that he had suffered for some time from overflowing cesspools and constant flooding of his water closet and yard gullies. He refused to pay his rent until the nuisance stopped.

The drainage of the twenty-four attendants' cottages emptied into cesspools at the end of the terrace and, when full, blocked the drain. The sink gullies overflowed down the passage and sewerage flowed into the main road. Cane Hill's clerk was advised to contact CRDC but, if it re-occured, would contact the Local Government Board which governed the finances of both asylums and local authorities.[48] In 1911, despite contacting the Board, no agreement could be reached until Croydon Borough and CRDC reached a further agreement in their ongoing dispute.

The ESWC applied in 1912 to extend the limits of its supply. A Bill passed through Parliament, strongly opposed by Croydon Borough, while the sub-committee feared that boring at Purley might lessen the yield of water in Cane Hill's well. The dispute between Croydon Borough and CRDC was eventually settled by the establishment of Coulsdon and Purley Urban District Council (C&PUDC). Surrey County Council agreed to include eighteen cottages in the new C&PUDC, while Croydon Borough were willing to remedy the problems of house in Woodmansterne parish in about twelve months, although it would take the proposed C&PUDC about six years to abolish the cesspits.[49]

In 1909, the local police sergeant had brought a military census form to be completed, to detail the number of horses, carts, etc. available in an emergency.[50] In 1914, the First World War began, with lasting effects for the asylums and delays in maintaining and improving the estate.

Chapter 12: The patients' lot

Between 1869 and 1906, the estimated population of England and Wales increased by 55.5 per cent, while the total of insane patients rose by 153 per cent. There were 10,472 admissions in 1869 and 21,812 in 1906, an increase of 108.2 per cent. In 1906, 33 per cent were discharged as recovered within two years of admission in England and Wales, and 48.5 per cent of deaths were within two years of admission. In the years 1901 to 1905, a quarter of patients in asylums were under 35, and nearly an eighth over the age of 65. In 1905, in England and Wales, senile dementia accounted for 38.4 per cent of first admissions.[1]

However, this was not so at Cane Hill in 1909, where the earliest surviving medical register, recording details of female admissions, begins in 1907.[2] Two years later, in 1909, it recorded the admission of 116 females and their diagnoses: only one was diagnosed with senile dementia, only four of the admissions being over the age of sixty-five. Fifty-one females had a diagnosis of mania, and forty-nine of melancholia (See Figure 3).

Figure 3 Diagnoses of female patients admitted to Cane Hill Asylum in 1909 (Extracted from CA, CAN/2/3/2).

Diagnosis	Patients
Melancholia	33
Chronic melancholia	14
Recurrent melancholia	2
Mania	31
Chronic mania	13
Recurrent mania	7
Confusional insanity	7
Acute delirium	1
General paralysis of the insane	3

Insanity with the grosser brain lesions	1
Imbecility	5
Imbecility with epilepsy	2
Dementia	1
Non-systematised delusional insanity	1
Insanity with epilepsy	5
Total	116

The general health of most of the women was described as fair or poor, with that of a few being moderate. For most, it was their first admission, and was within a month of the onset of symptoms. The aetiological factors leading to admission were recorded (see Figure 4).

Figure 3 Aetiological factors leading to admissions of females to Cane Hill Asylum in 1909. (Extracted from CA, CAN/2/3/2).

Aetiological Factors	Patients
Prolonged mental stress	24
Unknown	23
Alcohol	14
Heredity	12
Epilepsy	7
Privation	7
Puerperal	4
Syphilis	4
Bodily illness	3
Lesion of brain	3
Sudden mental stress	2
Influenza	2
Pregnancy	1
Congenital syphilis – imbecility	1
General paralysis of the insane	1
Masturbation	1
Renal and vesical system	1
Climacteric [menopausal]	1
Anaemia	1
Lactation	1
Total	116

Most were discharged within eighteen months, and mainly within three to four months. Some became long stay patients, such as Esther Troy, aged 29, who had a one year history of symptoms. The aetiological factor in her case was 'lactation' with anaemia, her physical health being moderate. She was diagnosed with 'confusional insanity', probably having a post-puerperal psychosis.

Even after several years, discharge was possible. Mary Ann Flude, an unmarried dressmaker, aged 51, was admitted on 23 December 1909. The aetiological factor was prolonged mental stress, a secondary factor being 'climacteric', and her general health was moderate. Diagnosed with chronic melancholia, like so many, she gradually came out of depression and was discharged as 'recovered' in February 1917, and would have had to restart her life.

Overcrowding meant fifty patients were moved to Winson Green Asylum, near Birmingham, in 1901.[3] In July 1903, twenty females went to Fisherton House, but their saloon carriage was not attached to the arranged train at Waterloo, so they arrived three hours late at Salisbury.[4] In 1904, there were 2,138 patients in Cane Hill. Patients were transferred to Fisherton House and to Hollymoor Asylum in 1906.[5,6] In June 1907, there were 2,109 patients, and vacancies so that London County patients were transferred to Cane Hill from another asylum.[7]

In 1912, the hospital remained overcrowded with 2,195 patients (959 males and 1,236 females), with an excess of seventeen males and thirty-seven females, despite space being made for nineteen more beds. In 1900, there were only five private patients, which had increased to fifty-five in 1912, five of whom were 'criminals'. Two female criminal lunatics were admitted in 1911, one in 1912 and another in 1914, the latter being later discharged, all diagnosed with mania, and with 'alcohol' as the reason for admission. A charge was made of 9s 11d a week for pauper lunatics from the London Unions, and from 9s 11d to 16s 11d a week for private patients.

For those with no supportive family, it was easier to be admitted than discharged for the asylum's sub-committee, on the recommendation of the medical superintendent, insisted on being assured that a patient would be discharged to a place where relatives or others who would provide the necessary supervision. From an early stage, patients from Cane Hill were discharged to the care of the Mental Health Aftercare Association who provided hostel care and found employment.

It meant that many remained in asylums. Agnes Goom was admitted a few months after the birth of her son James Henry who, in 1903, was tenant of 'The Edinburgh Castle', a public house in Park Crescent Mews, Marylebone. He thought her dead until his father's death, when he saw his father's papers, and now wanted her to be discharged to live with him. The sub-committee were informed that she was lucid, and quickly ascertained that her husband had left debts and, as she had no separate estate, she could not be charged as a private patient. When her son's story was confirmed by his father's sister, Agnes was discharged to his care.[8]

Being a private patient brought no advantages as they were treated exactly the same as those maintained by the Unions, but they or their close relatives had to pay. In 1908, in a list of five private patients, all wore asylum clothing, but one was provided with 'private outer clothing'.[9]

Patients were helped in family crises and escorted to see sick relatives. In 1904, Southwark Infirmary wrote that Mrs Bissidine's child was on the danger list with measles. It had died by the time she visited, and she saw the body, but it meant going into isolation on her return to Cane Hill.[10]

Patients were helped to re-establish themselves on discharge. In 1902, a friend of Dr Moody offered employment to Neil Cotton, a patient, provided he be discharged at once. Not waiting until the sub-committee meeting, Dr Moody obtained the signatures of two members, so that Cotton was discharged and working.[11] In 1909, when Ethel White was discharged, the Mental Aftercare Association would find 'a situation for her' but as she had no suitable clothing, an outfit was purchased at £1.14s 10d.[12] Inpatients could be helped: in 1904, when Clara Haywood asked Dr Moody for a new wig as she was ashamed of her very dilapidated one, the sub-committee allowed him to purchase one.[13]

In 1904, a female patient had paid weekly instalments on a Singer Sewing Machine before her admission. Dr Moody arranged for it and a box of clothing to be brought to Cane Hill, the sub-committee refunding him for 2s 2d he paid for its carriage, as the agent wanted to repossess the machine. As she was making good progress towards recovery, Dr Moody was willing to see the agent to arrange for her to continue payments when discharged.[14]

In 1909, when Maria Bradshaw 33, a widow and servant, was

admitted, she was buying a pair of dentures, worth £5.5s, in instalments. Dr Moody's opinion was they 'would be highly beneficial for her health and comfort', but the dentist would not hand them over until the money was paid. As she had savings, Dr Moody asked the sub-committee if she could sign a form to withdraw £1. Although she was rambling and irrational, she was lucid but, on the day, was too excited to sign any document as she relapsed. No more is known but, hopefully, she signed it later.

That same year, Dr Moody suggested that the Chief Commissioner of Police should send a former patient for him to examine as to his fitness to hold a licence to drive a taxi-cab. He had examined and recommended him, but had not yet heard the result of the application for a licence.[15]

The Asylums Committee instructed that efforts be made to repatriate foreign patients, following the Aliens Act of 1905. In 1907 a man from Utrecht, admitted with mania, was visited by his parents. His father applied to the Home Secretary for a warrant for his son's discharge, and paid all the expenses for two attendants to accompany him to Rotterdam. Later that year, the Guardians of Westminster Workhouse attempted to deport Franz Jannes, an Austrian waiter admitted to Cane Hill, once a magistrate had issued a certificate to the Home Secretary recommending it. Dr Moody described him as being in a very advanced state of general paralysis, and doubted he would be fit to be taken out of the country. He appears to have remained in Cane Hill.[16] On the other hand, Ramasammy Samoo, a convalescent patient from Madras, wanted to return to India, which Dr Moody thought was in the patient's best interest, and the Clerk wrote to Lord Onslow to see 'if any arrangement existed to enable it'.

Dr Moody questioned the admission of frail patients sent by the medical officers of workhouse infirmaries, who often died soon after admission. When Mary Ann Brown aged 68 was admitted in 1900 in 'a very critical state' from Plumstead Infirmary, Dr Moody complained that she should not have been brought so far, having been in the infirmary since 1898. In reply, the workhouse's medical superintendent did not consider that she had bronchitis. Agreeing that a long journey was inadvisable, he had 'no control over the distances these cases are sent'.[17]

In 1903, after two patients were admitted needed infirmary care, Dr Moody wrote to the Clerk of the LCAC that there was only accommodation allocated on each side for 100 elderly and infirm patients, but they had far above this number so that many infirm people were on unsuitable wards where they could not be properly nursed, and were liable to be injured by 'more robust fellow patients'.

Charles McLeish, admitted from Lambeth Infirmary on 4 December 1903, died three days later. He was brought by cab to Charing Cross, then a train to Coulsdon and a cab to Cane Hill. The temperature was 50F, and he was accompanied by a man representing the relieving officer. Very feeble, he was put in bed immediately but did not rally. The coroner's jury recorded that 'greater care should be exercised in the removal of patients from the Infirmary to the Asylum'. On 11 December, Mary Ann Chamberlain was brought from the same infirmary in 'a recumbent position, in a properly equipped ambulance. Her condition was very precarious, but by assiduous care she has been pulled through'.[18]

Later, the workhouse infirmary's 'attendant on lunatics' denied having told the relieving officer that McLeish was fit to travel by train. He had been accompanied by two attendants, one of whom left at Croydon having 'evening employment to go to'. The Guardians apologised, stating that, in future, the medical officer would decide the means of travel, and that the attendant who brought him would not be employed again to 'remove lunatics from this parish'.[19]

Daily Life

The number of patients able to leave the main building gradually reduced until, in 1912, 28 per cent (just over 600) walked beyond the estate, 41 per cent outside the airing courts but within the estate, and 4 per cent (about 90), who were confused, were confined to wards and airing courts although able to walk.[20]

However, this was a higher proportion of patients going beyond the estate than the other nine asylums belonging to the LCC, the next highest being Claybury with 14 per cent, and only 3 per cent at the Manor and 2 per cent at Hanwell. At Banstead, only 10 per cent went beyond the estate, while 45 per cent walked only in the estate beyond the airing courts and 35 per cent were confined to airing courts. Apart from Bexley, the other asylums kept more patients in airing courts than happened at Cane Hill.[21]

The decline in the number of patients walking beyond the estate may have been influenced by the incident in 1907 when a female patient in a walking party tried to get in front of a motor car. Dr Moody said the possibility was a 'source of anxiety' to him regarding walking parties although it was the first time a suicide attempt was made, and the patient was not known to have suicidal tendencies.[22]

On Sundays, 41 per cent went to morning Anglican services and the same percentage to the evening service, a much higher percentage than in the other London asylums. Similarly, apart from Bexley where 61 per cent went to weekly entertainments and Horton where 50 per cent went, 41 per cent went in Cane Hill, a higher percentage than in the remaining six hospitals. There were a large number of simple games 'to engage the attention of the patients, and a large variety of books scattered throughout day rooms', but the Commissioners thought there might be more bound illustrated periodicals, noting that book cases were not always unlocked.[23]

In 1902, the LCAC had decided evening papers, and 'papers of which the *Sporting Times* and *Referee* are typical or magazines which are purely literary', were unnecessary. Local papers were at the discretion of the sub-committees, but weekly foreign papers should be provided where there were foreign patients, and certain technical papers for hospital officers.[24]

Winters were cold, and open fires were still used in some wards until the 1930s, but steam was gradually introduced to provide hot water and heated radiators on wards. In 1911, tin hot water bottles were used on wards. Made in the tin workshop, they rusted and were liable to leak and scald. Earthernware bottles were suggested but, as the medical superintendent thought the tin bottles were usually satisfactory, no change was made.[25]

Sir J.G. Tollemache Sinclair donated a gramophone and records in 1905, for the patients' amusement, provided it was only for an hour a day. The gift was accepted, its use being left to Dr Moody's discretion. A further offer from Sir Tollemache was declined because of the restrictions, and there were already two gramophones.[26] A few years before, Dr Moody was refused permission to have a cinematograph but he was given permission for a demonstration in 1907.[27] Nothing appears to have happened until late 1913, when 258 patients petitioned for 'cinematograph entertainments'. The following February, while the LCAC's Engineer sought quotes for two performances in each winter quarter at ten asylums, using an eleven by nine foot screen, the sub-committee accepted Messrs. Pathé Freres quote of £4. 10s for a two hour performance.[28]

Coffee and cake was provided to patients attending entertainments.[29] Staff participated as, on one occasion in 1901, when a nurse injured her knee dancing with a patient. To celebrate the Coronation of Edward VII, one shilling a head was allowed at each London asylum for each staff and patient, but no visitors were allowed to any function.[30] When people visited patients they paid 1d for tea, ½d for a slice of bread and butter and 1d for a slice of cake. The money went into the Tea Fund. The annual fete in June was a major event with swings and a roundabout: in 1909 it was considered a very great success with 1615 patients, 238 staff and 31 visitors attending, a total of 1884. The previous Whit Monday, 755 people visited patients.[31]

Fewer patients went beyond the estate, but more were employed, with 69 per cent of males and 59 per cent of females in 1912. 371 men worked on the farm and in the gardens, 284 women did sewing and 96 women worked in the laundry. Life was routine and disciplined. Attendant Henry George Baker was reported by the Steward for 'idly gossiping' with a patient.[32]

From an early date, four working male patients lodged at the Well Cottage, near Lion Green Road, twelve males at the Farm and twelve at the Garden House, each supervised by a member of the estate staff and his wife rather than attendants. Some wards in the main building were unlocked, allowing patients to walk in the corridors.[33] In 1912, permission was obtained from the Home Secretary to adapt Posterns House, formerly occupied by the Steward, for fourteen female patients.

Daily Food

At meal times, tables were 'neatly laid and everything conducted in a decorous manner. In as many wards as possible, the patients are seated at table and, grace having been said, their portions are placed before each immediately it is served from the dish'. It was impossible on some wards as 'the attendants cannot serve meals and look after their charges. The most that can be done is to have the plates as warm as possible, to apportion the dinners rapidly, then seat the patients so they eat under the careful supervision of the attendants'. In the winter, each ward scullery had a fire in a range which heated water. Plates were heated by placing them in hot water. The sub-committee considered steam heaters, but thought them too expensive.[34]

In 1906, the sub-committee were informed that Cane Hill's meat consumption was 21,453 lbs per 1,000 patients. The lowest was 16,991 lbs per 100 patients at Banstead, but they omitted 25,338 lbs of rabbit, suet and lard. Dr Moody and the Steward suggested an identical return for all the asylums. The sub-committee stopped using tinned meat in 1905, usually given to patients in the summer, unless it was produced in Britain or the British colonies, and substituted it with boiled frozen mutton. As mutton cost more than tinned meat, instead of Irish stew, the patients had pea soup and bread and butter pudding twice a week, to keep the butcher's bill down. It would continue as Dr Moody had personally interviewed 'a large majority' of the patients who preferred soup and puddings. Fish was stopped from July to September.

In the six months ending September 1905, the patients' meat was reduced from 160,726 lbs to 146,797 lbs.[35] In June 1907, meat and Canadian bacon given to patients was down by 2,066 stones that year and, as well as soup and pudding twice a week, the sub-committee anticipated larger supplies of beef and pork from the farm.[36]

In December 1908, it was decided to serve fish on alternate weeks on male and female sides. The following year, the sub-committee noted a great amount of fish was wasted as it was unpopular with the patients. When Dr Moody proposed corned beef instead, the sub-committee suggested half the usual quantity of fish with blancmange and 1 oz. of jam for the second course. Dr Moody reported back that it was a great success. Instructed to inspect fish frying apparatus at other hospitals, he visited Claybury and saw fish fried in dripping which was 'vastly superior to that prepared by us here, and like that specially cooked for E, F and J [male wards] and so highly appreciated by the patients. I believe it desirable to have a fish frier'.[37]

Farm produce

With its own sewerage farm, the hospital's sewerage was spread on the fields. A wide variety of vegetables were grown on the estate, but they often ran out in the summer, and patients were given rhubarb instead. In July 1908, they began to order in fruit. That autumn, both staff and patients 'much enjoyed' bananas, each person being issued with three a week. It was an experiment from which Dr Moody believed people had benefited.[38] In June 1909, the LCAC agreed to a ½lb of fruit weekly for each patient during the summer and autumn, but not to exceed 4d a lb.[39] One hundred loganberry plants were bought in 1913.

In 1912, a drought in May caused the strawberry crop to fail while 60 lbs of beetroot were unfit for consumption, and there was an additional shortage of 56 lbs as beetroot had shrunk. Plums were bought, but some were very unripe: they were stewed using 1½ cwt of sugar. Another long spell of dry weather in July 1913 meant that broad beans were almost a failure, while lettuces and salad items were very short but, a year later, they sent 20 cwt of white broccoli to Claybury Asylum.[40]

Dairy cattle were kept to provide milk, dry cows being slaughtered and used in the asylum. Tuberculosis frequently occurred and infected cattle were buried. There was a bull, so that calves were breed. In 1912, Mr. Wheeler a neighbouring cow keeper sent a cow, without permission, to be serviced by the bull. The Clerk wrote to him, and he paid a fee, but the practice would be prohibited in the future. Cows and calves were regularly bought from a farmer in Norfolk and transported by train. In 1912, six cows arrived, delayed 36 hours because of floods. They were milked and fed at Stratford Station and, although the Great Eastern Railway Company kept the milk, it charged 4s for feeding which the Clerk disputed.[41]

There was always a large piggery, buying in pigs and using waste from the asylum to provide most of their food. By November 1907, more bacon was used at Cane Hill than any other asylum. The sub-committee decided that, although it had become dearer to provide and swine fever occurred periodically which meant many were slaughtered, boiled bacon was very popular and there was very little wastage. At the same time, a fixed recipe was issued for ginger ale syrup at all asylums.

As it was no longer compulsory to have a 'baked beef dinner' twice a week, a cheaper dinner was proposed. The sub-committee responded that, because of the poor soil, no profit was made from the farm. Because of the smallness of the wards, they could not see how the proportion of staff to patients could be reduced, but they hoped to centralise the hot water supply which would save about 10 tons of coal a week.[42] In 1909, the cost of the Christmas festivities rose to £120 because it would have to be English killed sides of beef instead of New Zealand.

In 1908, female servants complained that 4 lbs of meat a week was insufficient while male staff complained of not enough vegetables. Their comments were forwarded to the LCAC's General Purposes and Finances Sub-committee as the amount of food given to each person was decided centrally.

On 18 December 1909, a report appeared in the *Purley, Caterham and Oxted Gazette* that male staff received insufficient food; the sub-committee decided not to comment or act on it.[43] There were no further comments in the sub-committee's minutes until December 1913 when some male attendants refused to eat blancmange and jam at dinner as it was a cold dish. The remainder of the attendants, who ate it, joined them and left the mess room. In January 1914 a nurse, dismissed for being insubordinate to the assistant matron, threatened to consult her solicitors and wrote complaining of the food supplied to the nurses being frequently unfit to eat: she was among those who had to buy their own food 'in order to keep up my strength and enable me to properly discharge my duties ... my refusal to leave the kitchen was a protest'.[44]

Bad teeth were believed to contribute to ill health: in 1905, second class nurse Ellen Arthur was dismissed a few days after beginning at the asylum as she had 'extremely defective teeth. As this condition had, in other staff, led to 'unsatisfactory health', Dr Moody did not 'consider her fit for service'.[45] In 1907, after a local dentist repaired two patients' dentures, there were plans to look to a contract with a local dentist to look after staff and patients' teeth.[46]

Active 'treatment'

Little is known of treatment methods but, on 12 September 1898, Charlie Chaplin's mother Hannah was admitted from Lambeth Infirmary. Their Lunacy Examination Book recorded that she was 'very strange in manner', sometimes abusive and noisy and, other times, she used 'endearing terms'. She was repeatedly kept in a padded room because of sudden violence, as when she threw a mug at another patient, and shouted, sang and talked incoherently. On the day she was admitted to Cane Hill, she was depressed and crying, dazed and unable to give any reliable information, saying that she was sent on a mission by the Lord, and wanted to get out of the world. She had dermatitis which led to an erroneous diagnosis of syphilis, not observed in 1903 or 1905.

Hannah Chaplin, discharged from Cane Hill in November 1898, was readmitted from Lambeth Infirmary in May 1903 with a 'psychotic breakdown'. When her two sons visited her at Cane Hill, she was very pale and deeply depressed. Discharged in January 1904, she was readmitted on 18 March 1905 for 7½ years.[47] When the brothers visited her in Cane Hill, she had been in an 'obstreperous phase' and confined in a padded room. 'In order to calm her down, the attendants had been giving her shock treatments in the form of ice-cold showers and her face was blue. The two brothers paid to send her to Peckham House, a private Institution, where the care would be less callous'.[48]

Florence Chapman, admitted 12 June 1907 with mania, and still restless and noisy eleven days later, was prescribed 'hot baths with cold affusions to the head' each day for a week. There was no change and, on 7 July, she was 'ordered to have a cold shower bath, repeated the next day'. At about 8.30 a.m., she was put in a bath 'but the water had scarcely touched her when she was seen to collapse'. Immediately lifted out of the bath, she breathed for a few minutes and swallowed brandy but died about 8.35 a.m. Dr Moody reported that the treatment was used in numerous instances in the past thirty years, but it was the first time this had happened.[49]

Towards the end of the nineteenth century, there was an increasingly tendency to assume a link between syphilis and psychotic symptoms which would later be labelled as schizophrenia. In 1913, the commissioners reported that post mortems from the LCAC's asylums in the previous five years revealed 33.5 per cent of males and 8.7 per cent of females died from general paralysis. A considerable number of the women were 'euphemistically described as of "no occupation"', being prostitutes.[50] The Commissioners claimed that between 1900 and 1911, over 70 per cent of asylum patients suffered from general paralysis but, in 1974, Thomas Szasz wrote that hospital statistics showed that between 20 and 30 per cent of patients had syphilitic paralysis.[51]

At Cane Hill, in 1904, the Commissioners reported a 'large number of patients with general paralysis'. 21 per cent of deaths were from general paralysis, while 16.8 per cent died of organic brain disease, 13.7 per cent of tuberculosis, 12.7 per cent of pneumonia and bronchitis and 4.1 per pent of dysentery. Only two died from senile decay. When they visited in October, 33 patients had influenza, and 29 had dysentery which peaked in 1904 before gradually reducing until, in 1912, only two had dysentery, although four had scabies.[52]

Since the 1870s, the psychiatric world had become increasingly interested in eugenics. Believing mentally unfit people should be treated as soon as possible, and discouraged from breeding, led to more admissions. At neighbouring Croydon Mental Hospital, its medical superintendent, Dr Pasmore wrote that 'If our feeble-minded and mental undesirables were prevented from propagating their species, a large number of the Asylums in this country could be closed'.[53] Dr Moody's opinion is not known.

In 1912, Dr. Frederick Mott, Director of the pathological laboratory of the London County Asylums and an eminent neurologist who would be knighted for his work, reported his survey of 3,485 cases where two or more in a family were insane. His research strengthened his belief that mental illnesses were inherited, and the necessity of 'segregating congenital imbeciles now that nature by man's aid does not kill them off as formerly'. He wrote that 'one of the great arguments advanced for sterilization has been that recurrent cases of insanity breed lunatics in the intervals of readmission to the asylums', but concluded that 'there are a large number of off spring which do not become insane and these would be cut off if life segregation or sterilization were adopted'.[54]

Chapter 13: World War One and its consequences

Men from Cane Hill soon enlisted, with Sir James's permission, many having been in the Army's Reserve. In August 1914, soon after war began, thirteen attendants and two labourers were 'called to the Colours', most going to the Army or Fleet Reserve. Miss Lakeman, an assistant matron, became a nurse in the Territorial Army.

They were probably assured they could return to their jobs after the war while, if they had dependants, usually a wife, but sometimes a mother, received the man's half pay. Retired staff, including workmen and artisans, resumed work as temporary staff while the war lasted. Some lived in, while their families remained at home; advice was sought about their married allowance.[1] J. Wilkinson aged 43, a stableman at Cane Hill since 1909, became a temporary attendant, with a salary of £41 a year plus lodging, washing and uniform. If he attended lectures and gained a certificate, he would get an increase in his pay.[2]

With vacancies, some permanent staff were encouraged to remain, such as second attendant Richard Yandle with more than seven years service at Cane Hill, of which the last two were satisfactory. He was authorised, from 1 August 1914, during 'continuance of good behaviour', to wear one service stripe on his uniform which entitled him to a special allowance of £2.10s a year in addition to his pay. Night Attendant A. A. Harris, having completed ten years, received a second stripe and a further £2.10s.[3]

Dr Frederick Morres, appointed in September 1914 as a second assistant medical officer, volunteered in 1915 and joined the Royal Army Medical Corps. As Captain Morres, he served on a hospital ship for five months, and in France for three years and a month. His place was taken the same day by a locum tenens, at £6.6s 0d a week plus £90 per annum in lieu of emoluments less, when he ate them, 6d for breakfast, 9d for lunch and 1s for dinner.

Nurses, who had to resign when they married, were allowed to return temporarily, on the salary received when they left. Nurses and others were allowed to marry and be reappointed as temporary nurses while all new and probationary nurses were informed that they may have to nurse male patients. During the war, nurses would work permanently on male wards.[4]

However, in May 1915, Sir James could not employ a female locum tenens dispenser as the Home Secretary ruled that dispensers must be qualified men. Having stressed the urgency, he was permitted to employ a highly recommended unqualified man.[5]

In March and June 1915, as some asylums became military war hospitals, 121 male patients and 148 females were transferred to Cane Hill from Horton Hospital, in July 1916, 46 men from the Epileptic Colony and, in July and August, 72 women from the Manor Asylum.

Jemima Cockman, admitted to Horton in 1911, was discharged from Cane Hill as recovered in 1917, but only five out of 169 returned to Horton in 1919, almost all the rest having died, mainly of heart and lung disease and some of senile decay. In 1915, one died of acute dysentery and cardiac disease and another of acute dysentery and heart failure. Two died of typhoid fever in 1917. Of those from the Manor, 18 men and 26 women died, but most remained in Cane Hill in 1919.[6] In 1917, when the Board of Control visited Cane Hill, there were 2,408 patients.[7]

Further change

As staff at Cane Hill adjusted to the changes brought by war, they and the patients were shocked by the death of Sir James Moody on 20 September 1915 aged sixty-two, having been confined to his bed for a week. His funeral was held in the chapel and he was buried in the asylum's cemetery where his widow erected a headstone, having thanked the sub-committee for allowing his burial there 'next his life's work'. Lady Moody was allowed to remain in the house they had occupied until 31 December, and to purchase goods from the Stores. She received a gratuity of £229.4s 10d under the Asylum Officers Superannuation Act of 1909 but, stating that she had limited means, she asked to remain beyond the end of the year. She would not be charged rent, but paid rates, etc., agreeing to leave when the property was needed, which occurred in August 1916.[8] After the war, in 1919, a brass memorial plaque costing £18, was erected in the chapel in his memory.[9] Lady Moody who erected a memorial cross over his grave in 1920 would be buried with Sir James, following her death in June 1934.[10]

Dr Edward Salterne Littlejohn, who came from Horton Hospital in 1912 to be second assistant medical officer at Cane Hill, took over as acting medical superintendent until September 1918 when he joined the Army. Dr W.I. Donaldson replaced him as acting medical superintendent, before his retirement, until Dr Samuel Charles Elgee became medical superintendent in September 1919.[11] Born in Ireland, Dr. Elgee was formerly medical superintendent at Colney Hatch Asylum which had been a war hospital, as a result of which he was given the rank of lieutenant colonel and awarded the O.B.E. After the war, most of the medical officers had served, and retained their service titles, particularly as captains, as shown in local trade directories: whether they used them in the hospital is not known. Continuity at Cane Hill was provided by other senior staff who had been there for some years before the war, and remained in the late 1920s, including William Henry Henson, Clerk to the asylum, William Sennett, the house steward and Miss Beatrice Milne, matron, formerly assistant matron to Miss K. Broomhall.

2,687 attendants enlisted prior to the operation of the Military Service Acts in early 1916. That year, the Commissioners of the Board of Control, who replaced the Commissioners in Lunacy, reported that there were still about 5,289 male attendants of military age. Applications were received from asylums to recommend about 2,000 exemptions, and recommendations made for 922 permanent and 601 temporary exemptions.

The Acts stated that attendants in institutions for lunatics could be exempted from military service, but the Board of Control refrained from recommending those under the age of thirty, while those between thirty and thirty-five years old were temporarily exempted to allow time to find substitutes for them in the asylums, and those between thirty-five and forty-one years old were only exempted when they seemed indispensable to the institutions. All those exempted had to remain as attendants working with lunatics. The hope was that 'the set-back will only be of a temporary character, and that it will be best shortened by the prompt release for the service of their country of the maximum number who are likely to make efficient sailors and soldiers'.[12]

In February 1916, the 'Military Representative' in Croydon

agreed with Dr Littlejohn that, as attendants were in reserved occupations, 'no steps should be taken to call up the men concerned' but this had little affect as, the following month, Cane Hill was 'very short' of attendants due to sickness, vacancies, and a further eight single men were to be called up within two weeks. Of the remaining men of military age, the Board of Control had only granted six exemptions so that the hospital would soon be 'very seriously short of staff'. William Ford, an assistant stockman, had been called up in February. With the possibility of no stockmen in the near future, an unsuccessful application was made to the War Office for his release.

A re-arranged rota of attendants' weekly leave was introduced, permanent staff having their half day off stopped, to which they agreed as they were paid instead, and Block B, two wards with about 100 male patients, was closed during the day, freeing eight day attendants and providing thirteen additional day attendants. The chaplain, the Rev. John Crawford, due to retire, was retained annually until 1919 when he finally retired.[13] In October, Dr. Thienpoint, an assistant medical officer, was himself off sick due to a 'neurasthenic attack'. More retired staff returned, such as Mr W. Geary, who recommenced as a temporary shoemaker.[14]

That same month, Croydon Fire Brigade offered assistance if required, as the asylum's fire brigade was inadequate due to the age and physical condition of its members, two bombs having dropped two miles away in August, but Croydon's Brigade would check whether they could come if a Zeppelin raid was on.

In June 1916, an application was made for Mr Bedford, the senior assistant clerk to be transferred back from Horton War Hospital for four weeks to enable the steward to have his annual leave. Horton refused as his temporary exemption had been granted on the grounds that he was indispensable there.[15] Sir James had already his own female clerk for some years, but more female staff were employed in the offices: when Mrs French, a temporary clerk left in January 1917, they had great difficulty filling her post. Miss Mabel Owen, aged 15½ years was employed at 22s a week and Mrs Taylor at 25s, both with free dinners provided. There was a great pressure of work in the offices, three hundred hours of overtime having been worked since the previous sub-committee meeting.[16] In 1918, when one nurse left, a female farm worker was employed in her place.[17]

Restrictions

As soon as the war began, Sir James directed Mr Fish, the farm bailiff, to buy fifteen cows and eighty sheep and, after consultation with the chairman, another eighty sheep, made possible because Mr. Tucker allowed them to graze on part of the Portnalls estate before 8 November, the date that the LCC was due to take possession of the estate.

By the end of August 1914, there were already difficulties in obtaining food. In September, 66 lbs of preserved beef was issued to make up the patients' dinners and 42 lbs of bacon for staff breakfasts. To continue the same diet, staff paid 4d for breakfast and 11d for dinner instead of 3d and 1s, as only one egg a day was available, and it seemed better to have it at breakfast. In December, fish could not be obtained on two days, and roast mutton was served to the patients instead, costing an additional £10.9s 2d. Mr Fish had to work more land with fewer skilled workers. In July 1915, thirty-four pigs died, because the new pig man was inexperienced.

Sir James announced that association football had ended and, in January 1915, their eleven footballs, one inflator and two lacing needles were given to the troops. That same month, the chairman consented to a request from the officer commanding 250 men who were guarding the nearby railway, that they could bath in the asylum.

In May, when the LCAC wanted to reduce the quality of currant cake given to patients all the year round, and seed cake at winter entertainments, Sir James recommended it be kept at the present standard and, when the cost of supper exceeded 4d a head, he instructed that the ration should not be reduced, and to check with other asylums.

Meanwhile, in April, over fifty nurses and the band, conducted by Dr Sykes with the organist, Mr Hiscox, presented a 'very charming revue, at considerable expense to themselves'. They were anxious to repeat it to friends outside the asylum who were willing to pay for tickets, and the sub-committee agreed to a subscription concert on 1 May which raised £18.16s 10d for the Tea Fund and £15 for the Cane Hill Asylum Staff War Distress Committee.[18]

In December 1915, the sub-committee agreed that more male patients would wear corduroy suits rather than tweed, with calico and canvas linings, and cotton 'drawers' instead of flannel for summer wear. Women would use shawls instead of capes or coats and, for female staff, no more estamene would be issued after stocks were used up, with cotton aprons were used instead of linen.

Supplies of floor polish were reduced, as were the number of items laundered, to save on soap and soda. No new furniture would be made, while what had been made would be covered with cheaper calico. There would be no new carpets, apart from the infirmary if necessary, no curtain valances and only new curtains 'if absolutely necessary'. No condemned carpets, lino or blinds could be taken out of use until confirmed by the Inspector of Stores, while condemned garments, blankets, counterpanes and socks would be sewn into squares to make scouring clothes.

Margarine or dripping would be used instead of lard, with Scotch broth substituted for beef tea, the amount of new milk in milk puddings reduced by a third, and egg substitute introduced. A ½ lb of the 1½ lbs of bacon provided to male attendants and servants would be of a cheaper quality.

In February 1916, staff complained that the butter was rancid, and were given dripping instead, there being no other butter to give them. 'Certain agitators' led by two nurses, complained about the food, and a petition signed by 78 attendants and 89 female staff requested the abolition of Irish Stew and mutton hotpot, and an increase in the quality and quantity of food.

Three male and three female staff attended the following sub-committee meeting, men and women appearing separately. The men complained of insufficient food, with beef, bread and coffee not being good, while very little fat was served with meat, and vegetables were not always 'nicely cleaned' and sometimes not well cooked. They would prefer cheese for supper rather than jam for tea. Female staff, stating food had been inferior for some time, were glad that Irish Stew and mutton hotpot were not longer served, but would like brown gravy with the joints. They had little to complain about now a light supper had been introduced. The sub-committee agreed to all the suggestions, except an increase in the quantity of bread. At the same meeting, it was noted that 154 surplus eggs were sold locally and to Bexley Asylum.

In June, staff complained of the monotonous diet, asking to bring in their own piece of cake and make a cup of tea or cocoa for themselves. They would prefer a money allowance instead of rations because of prevailing high prices: the sub-committee sent their request to the LCAC.[19]

The sub-committee agreed, in November, to provide light refreshments at the four or so staff dances held each year, but complaints continued and, in January 1917, they agreed to meet with the Asylum Workers' Union when staff complained about having brown bread. Dr. Littlejohn was instructed to issue standard white bread 'now recognised by the Government'. In January 1918, there was an attempt to issue a supper ration to nurses, but it was impossible because of the limited allowances, while male attendants, who still received larger portions than female staff, refused to eat a trial dinner of Scotch pickled herrings, and were given cold roast beef.[20]

Only 3,770 lbs out of 4,020 lbs of fish could be supplied from 10 to 31 January. Meat was served instead while staff were given bloaters at one breakfast, which proved too salty. With further food restrictions, visitors could have no more than one cup of tea and piece of cake.

Farming and Food

In February 1918, 20 acres of neighbouring farmland was rented from Mrs Chapman for grazing, at 1s an acre, an agreement which would continue for some years. That same month, a local resident complained about the felling of 100 oaks and 2 ash trees in Oaks Wood north of the main buildings, and requested that a screen of trees be left along Portnalls Road, to which the sub-committee agreed.

Land was already rented from Mr Moule of Tollers Farm where 25 acres were ploughed up, and 15 heifers were moved to the recreation field. The chairman ordered that no cows be slaughtered, but reared for consumption in the hospital, and 45 pigs were bought. Four tons of potatoes were purchased from the local food committee to make bread. They continued to rent land from Mrs Chapman and Mr Moule for many years after the war.

Dr Littlejohn had to inform the local committee of all non-resident staff supplied with sugar, and to check if they had 'sugar cards' to prevent them getting double rations. Non-resident staff petitioned to be able to purchase meat rations at the hospital on leave days, but the sub-committee had no power to accede to this. Open trolleys were used to transport meals from the kitchen to the wards, but food was pilfered before it reached the wards. In the past, extra stores were issued but, with strict rationing, it was imperative to prevent theft and so an experimental open trolley was converted into a closed one, and the theft of food greatly diminished. The Board of Trade ordered that gas consumption be reduced by one sixth, which affected the main kitchen, and stopped cooking on the wards.

There was enough food for, in March, surplus stocks were transferred to other asylums. 3,690 eggs had been preserved, of which just 86 were unfit for consumption. One dairy cow would be killed weekly as they became dry, and ten surplus pigs were killed for bacon, the remainder going to other asylums or for sale. Grazing was extended at Tollers Farm and the farm bailiff looked for more grazing land as all grazing land at Cane Hill was needed for the milking herd. Corporal W. Walker, a former member of staff, was loaned from the Army for farm work.

Because of 'climatic change and insect pests', the first sowing of cauliflowers, broccoli and Brussels sprouts failed in May. In July, resident female nurses petitioned to be able to register outside the hospital to purchase bacon, a request taken to the local food committee, but the outcome is not known. On 14 July, a violent hailstorm severely damaged all the crops: cabbage, cauliflowers, Brussels sprouts, peas, broad beans, onions, beetroot, carrots, parsnips, marrows, cucumbers and salads, and fodder for the cattle. The runner beans might yield half a crop, the potatoes were almost stripped of foliage, while mangolds were bruised and their leaves cut off. At least 20,000 cabbages needed to be planted at once, plants being available locally. Fortunately, Mr Moule at Tollers Farm rented out more land which the hospital used for potatoes which were undamaged. Part of the oats on Mrs. Chapman's land were a good crop but had suffered badly.

About 2,000 panes of glass were broken, and many slates, with considerable damage to roads, as gullies became choked with branches and leaves from trees, so that water flowed down the hill and scoured channels in the surface. They were unable to engage extra men to repair the damage.

War ended in November 1918 but shortages and complaints continued: in December, male attendants found the soup inadequate, and were given fish instead. In March 1919, severe frost meant that about two acres of Spring cabbage and seed beds were destroyed.

60,000 cabbage plants would be ordered. In four weeks, 4,409 eggs were produced on the farm. 11,725 eggs had been pickled, of which 578 were unfit for human consumption but 200 could be boiled down to feed to the chickens. Fortunately, hot cross buns could still be served to patients and staff on Good Friday, which continued through the war.[21]

Staff complained about pay and working conditions, as in 1916 when charge and second charge attendants asked to be paid as 'special charge attendants'. The request was forwarded to the LCAC, the attendants' argument being that the proportion of 'special wards' at Cane Hill was higher than any other London asylum, being 10 out of 16 male wards and 16 out of 19 female wards, indicating it had a greater proportion of difficult patients. The sub-committee felt it inopportune at the present time, but Dr Littlejohn suggested that 'specially troublesome' patients in non-special wards be moved to special wards.

In January 1918, eleven night attendants petitioned for three night's leave in two weeks, in lieu of one night weekly which they thought 'hardly seemed equitable', comparing themselves with staff at Bexley and Long Grove, but the sub-committee reminded them that they worked less than those at the other two asylums, and that day attendants worked longer hours.[22] In November, as the war ended, staff petitioned against moving the start of day duty from 6.00 a.m. to 7.00 a.m. to save 600 tons of coal a year.[23] Dr Littlejohn may have been relieved to leave the grumbles of complaints of staff behind him in his decision to transfer to the Army?

Essential Works

Maintenance continued on the estate although Edward Charles Moore, who succeeded his father Edward J. Moore as foreman engineer in August 1914, would be called up in March 1917.[24]

As war began, tenders were accepted to enlarge the nurses' block but there was an immediate and considerable increase in the price of lead, glass and wood, and nothing would happen until after the war. In twenty-four wards, plans were made to replace upright incandescent gas burners by inverted burners, to save gas but the cost of replacement increased too much, and was put on hold until the war ended.[25]

Two new hot water boilers were ordered in March 1915. In May 1918, a permit was eventually granted by the Ministry of Munitions to allow them to be made and, in June, the two condemned boilers were eventually removed. One new boiler arrived in October 1918, to be installed for the following winter, and the second in December. Installed in June 1919, it was ready for use in October.[26] In January 1918, 'practically all the building was infested with rats, particularly the stores, and laundry while the kitchen was 'very bad'. Using heating conduits in the corridors, they had the run of the whole building, the wood cutting shed and the coal depot.

With high prices for sand and gravel, in August 1917, the engineer searched the estate for a gravel pit: some tons had been excavated from behind the pumping station and it was thought a large quantity might lie in the wood close to the back road.[27] It is not known if they were successful, but Oaks Wood was cut down, with complaints from local residents, the sub-committee agreeing to keep a screen of trees bordering the road. In November 1918, three days after the war ended, a great quantity of chalk needed to be removed as soon as possible, perhaps excavated while digging graves in the cemetery. It was suggested that the Army might need it at Kenley Aerodrome.[28]

The War ends

Eighty-six men employed at Cane Hill either enlisted, or called up from 1916 onwards. Many were now tired of war. In February 1918, two former attendants asked Dr Littlejohn to request their release. He supported Head Night Attendant Peter Russell, aged fifty-six, as 'especially now that it seems likely that more of our young men will have to go', but refused Attendant E.E. Boniface, aged thirty.[29] In June 1918, the attendants requested a Roll of Honour in a conspicuous place.[30]

Eight lost their lives, including Alfred Warren, a farm and general labourer, who joined the King's Royal Rifles and died of his wounds in St. George's Hospital, London, in 1916. Lance Corporal Henty, the mortuary attendant with twenty-one years service, served with the National Reserve and lost both feet in July 1915, being hit by a train in Kent. He was at Merstham Military Emergency Hospital when its female Commandant requested financial help from the sub-committee towards the provision of his artificial limbs at Roehampton Military Hospital: the sub-committee agreed to contribute if the government's grant was insufficient. That month, second class attendant James Duke, another recruit, lost the use of his arms and Harry Charles Rice, in the National Reserve, died of an aneurism of the heart. Buried in Cane Hill's cemetery, he received a military funeral. A handful of recruited men were found to be unfit, including second attendant Walter John Horne who had flat feet, and they returned to an overcrowded asylum under pressure.[31, 32]

Edward Charles Moore died of influenza in hospital in France on 29 November 1918.[33] In May 1919 his widow, who remained in North Lodge, was informed she could remain there rent free until her husband's position was filled, when she would be given a month's notice.[34]

As for J. Wilkinson, he may have been one of those less militant temporary attendants. In early 1918, he was invited to join the permanent staff, provided he presented himself for the examination of the Medico-Psychological Association but it was found that 'his mental abilities are such that all question of passing examinations is hopeless, but he is quite a valuable attendant'.

In February 1919, the first nine men returned to their former jobs following demobilisation, and temporary male attendants were gradual dismissed or returned to their former positions in the asylum.[35] As the war passed into history, attitudes would change. Notably, asylums were now called 'mental hospitals' and pauper lunatics were 'rate-aided patients'.

Chapter 14: War and asylum

Arthur Henry Dore was probably the first service man to be admitted, on 20 March 1915, and transferred to Powick Mental Hospital, Worcestershire, in 1923. Others followed with a home and settlement in London. Edward Fox, of Tyers Street in the Lambeth Union, and Percy Orchard from the Camberwell Union, were transferred from Napsbury War Hospital, in peace time an asylum in Hertfordshire, on 28 January 1916. Most suffered from shell-shock, now known as post-traumatic stress disorder.

Percy Orchard was discharged as recovered in June 1916 and Edward Fox in September. Other admissions included Frederick Charles Casbolt, John Carey and Edward Reardon, all transferred from No. 2 Eastern General Hospital in Hove, who were discharged as recovered, Carey in 1917, Casbolt and Reardon in 1918, but the majority remained at Cane Hill and died there in the following decades, many in the 1930s.[1] They included several German Quakers, who left Germany before the war and fought rather than go to internment camps. Samuel Schoolenart died in Cane Hill and was buried in December 1918 while others remained there. Some were discharged after decades, ending their days in residential homes.[2]

In October 1917, a memorandum came from the Ministry of Pensions that discharged soldiers and sailors be classified as 'Service Patients' from 10 October. Service men, admitted as pauper lunatics would, on the day they were classified as 'Service Patients', be treated as private patients, with better conditions. On 1 November, Robert Thomas was temporarily transferred as from 10 October, perhaps because of his failing health for he died on 5 December. From then on, men were transferred on the day they were admitted, or soon after.

There was heavy rain in the winter of 1916 and, in February, the Bourne River had risen for several weeks and was above the ground opposite the front entrance. The water in the well rose from 41 feet 6 inches to 47 feet 6 inches and, for a few weeks, it was difficult to dig graves in the chalk. In addition, there was sickness and vacancies among staff.³ In January 1917, Dr. Littlejohn suggested that, whereas graves were dug to a depth of 16 feet 6 inches, with the first 6 feet boarded up, they should be dug to 20 feet, saving about two and a half days labour each week. In late summer 1917, about twelve large elms at Portnalls were cut down to make coffins.⁴

Robert Thomas was probably the first service patient buried in Cane Hill's cemetery. On 13 December 1917, he was the first of six buried in Special Grave 420, a communal grave. Up to the end of 1920, six were buried in grave 441, six in grave 443 and at least one in grave 459. There were at least twenty-eight funerals up to the end of 1920, but probably more in later years as only one funeral book, covering this short period, survives.⁵ In August 1918, asylums were instructed that service patients were not to be buried in ground set apart in asylum cemeteries, other cemeteries or parish churchyards 'for the burial of pauper patients lying in the asylum'.

In the meantime, on 1 February 1918, the London County Asylums and Mental Deficiency Department (LCA&MDD) wrote to ask on what authority the asylum purchased two coffins for service patients 'and why so high a price as £3. 5s was paid'. Dr Littlejohn replied that their relatives

> were quite unable to arrange for a private funeral as the £4 allowed would not cover the cost and they could not afford to pay the additional amount required. Therefore, estimates had been obtained from a local undertaker for special coffins. As the sum of £4 allowed for the burial of Service Patients is refunded by the Ministry of Pensions, a coffin was selected at a cost of £3. 5s which the sum of 6s estimated for grave digging made the total cost £3. 11s for each funeral . . . ⁶

By May 1918, coffins were made at Cane Hill but it was impossible to buy the usual metal fittings. They made handles and split pins at the hospital but, if the difficulty continued, would have to dispense with handles and attach batons to the base of the coffin. Failing a supply of nameplates, thin wood would be used. The cost of the ordinary funeral, charged to the Guardians, would be the same at Banstead, Bexley and Cane Hill hospitals: 16s 6d for the coffin and 8s 6d for the incidentals, a total of £1. 5s. Service patients buried in the hospital cemetery would have a better coffin, making the charge for a funeral £1. 15s.⁷

In August, the Ministry of Pensions instructed that funerals for patients dying in asylums which were not arranged by their families, should be special but not elaborate, with a contract made with a local undertaker to provide a coffin, shroud, hearse and bearers, and to conduct the service.[8] Ralph Henry Hutchison's family may have made special arrangements for, in 1918, the sub-committee noted that a special coffin was ordered for his funeral in December. In April 1919, 300 coffins had been made in the previous year using elm from the Portnalls estate, with enough for another hundred.[9]

In June 1919, funeral expenses for a service patient dying in a borough or county asylum were increased from £4 to £7. 10s. The Ministry of Pensions instructed 'that only one mourning coach may be provided, and this *only where necessary and usual*'.[10]

At Cane Hill, in May 1920, the additional cost of fittings on coffins for service patients meant an increase to £2. 8s, not including 'upkeep of the cemetery, wages of nurses acting as bearers, etc.'.[11] The War Pensions Office in High Street, Purley, wrote in September 1921 that, if relatives wished to make private arrangements for a funeral, a grant of £7. 10s was available, or the actual amount, whichever was the less, may be paid by the medical superintendent and reclaimed from the Ministry of Pensions. The Clerk wrote to the LCA&MDD that the estimated cost of a service patient's funeral in the hospital cemetery was currently £2. 8s.

In late November 1918, the London County Asylums were informed that the headquarters of Eastern Command would provide firing parties and bearers, with a gun carriage when available, at no charge. Seven such funerals are recorded in 1919 and 1920. When Frederick Taylor was buried at 2.30 p.m., although not classified as a service patient, and George James Morris at 3.15 p.m. on 8 March 1920, there was a firing party, bearers and a trumpeter for both funerals. After 1920, most were buried in local authority cemeteries, particularly at Streatham Park and at Bandon Hill in Mitcham. As the years passed, there was little difference between service and rate-aided, formerly known as pauper, funerals. In 1930, John Price aged 28, a boy entrant to the newly formed wartime RAF, was buried in a public common grave. This must have been queried as, beside the entry, someone wrote in pencil: 'Ministry phoned usual practice "Common Grave".[12]

Alexander McKenzie was a photographer working out of a

studio off the Charing Cross Road, before serving in the Northumberland Fusiliers. Discharged on medical grounds in August 1917, he died in Cane Hill in March 1918, leaving a wife and seven children. The family was ashamed to have a father in an asylum, but his wife walked and hitched lifts from Kennington to visit him. The family was left in dire circumstances, and some of his younger children spent time in a 'children's poor house' in West Norwood.[13]

It was still common for servicemen who died in the years immediately following the war to have a Commonwealth War Graves Commission monument, but there is no record of any being erected in Cane Hill's cemetery, neither do their names appear in their 'Debt of Honour'.[14] The LCA&MDD wrote in December 1921 that the Ministry of Pensions had no objection to the body of a service patient being buried in the hospital cemetery, provided the patient had no relatives or the relatives did not wish to make their own arrangements for burial elsewhere,

> and provided the burial took place under circumstances which would give no ground for the suggestion that the deceased had a "pauper funeral". I understand, too, that where (as at Cane Hill) a suitable coffin could be made in the institution for less than an undertaker would charge no objection would be offered to this.

In January 1922, there were 110 service patients in Cane Hill and, in May 1924, 9 ex-service patients remained who were formerly known as 'non-attributable' service patients who had been temporarily accepted as service patients until it could be proved that their insanity resulted from war service.[15] These would have included Frederick Taylor who died in 1920. That year, one psychiatrist suggested that 'a very large proportion of the soldiers who manifested psychic disturbances were really potential psychopaths before they entered upon military service . . . now that the war is over they are burdens to the community, and unfortunately likely to continue as such'.[16] There was uproar in 1922 when a decision was made to regrade 'non-attributables', of whom there were about 800 in England and Wales, as paupers. They were reviewed, the Ministry of Pensions acknowledging mistakes in about 150 cases, the remaining being classed as 'ex-service patients': they would receive funeral expenses but none of the other benefits of service patients, and no allowances for their dependants.[17] Many ex-service men returned home to their families before symptoms were identified such as Edward Connington, with six children born between 1912 and 1922, admitted in 1923.[18]

Some service patients in Cane Hill had physical disabilities as well resulting from the war. Edward Babot attended Roehampton Military Hospital four times in 1922 to have artificial legs fitted, with expenses paid by the Ministry of Pensions.[19]

In 1925, one hundred service patients remained in Cane Hill, eighty-five of whom received a grant of 2s 6d a week or the equivalent in kind, and eleven ex-service patients.[20] From 1921 onwards, a few service patients were considered able to handle 2s 6d a week themselves, at the discretion of the medical superintendent. In 1949, six war pensioners from the First World War were patients, and ten 'other ranks' war pensioners from the same war in July 1970, some probably admitted as they grew old.[21]

In September 1922, the Mental Hospitals Department (formerly the LCA&MDD), wrote to Cane Hill that the Ministry of Pensions had been informed that mental hospitals had no facility for storing private clothing and 'that £3. 10s having regard to present values is an entirely inadequate sum to allow as a maximum to be spent on a private complete set of clothing for a man about to leave a mental hospital'. The Ministry of Pensions gave an extra grant to service patients of 3s. 9d a week (£9. 15s a year) to provide better clothing than the ordinary hospital clothing, with a further sum of £3. 15s, which they felt was sufficient. In October 1922, Dr Clarke wrote from Cane Hill that only about £1 per patient per year was spent on clothing.[22]

They wore different clothing. In 1928, Dr Elgee reported to the sub-committee that service patients at Colney Hatch, Hanwell and West Park hospitals wore 'tweed suits made from a material of a pattern distinct from that used for rate-aided patients instead of the khaki-serge used at the other hospitals'. There was no regulation compelling the use of khaki-serge, and it was decided at Cane Hill to use different tweed to that worn by rate-aided patients.[23]

Working Patients

In September 1915, there were 636 male and 439 female working patients. From the early years of asylums, there was an encouragement, or enticement, to work as those men who did received tobacco and the women extra morning and afternoon tea.[24] Perhaps because of the war and staffing shortages, patients worked in many departments.

Males

Assisting in Grounds, Gardens, Farms, etc.	333
Helpers in wards	126
Assisting in Hall	12
Assisting in Corridors	8
Assisting in Messrooms	2
Assisting in Stores	13
Assisting in Vegetable Room	34
Coal Carriers	12
Assisting Baker	13
Assisting Upholsterer	19
Assisting Tailor	14
Assisting Shoemaker	13
Assisting Carpenter	4
Assisting Painters	14
Assisting Bricklayers	6
Assisting Tinsmith	2
Assisting Engineers	1
Assisting Gashouse	2
Assisting Fireman	2
Assisting Stables	2
Assisting Plumber	1

Females

Ward and Villa Workers	86
Needleroom	110
Laundry	90
Kitchen	12
Messrooms	9
Corridors	25

Nurses Quarters.. 3
Officers Quarters 7
Knitters.. 21
Light work.. 66

In November 1916, elderly female patients worked in the vegetable room.

The previous month, it was decided not to plan entertainments for the patients in the winter, as dances were more popular and cheaper.[25]

Wartime conditions in London's Asylums

The Board of Control did not publish detailed reports on individual asylums for 1914 to 1916. The following year, there were 2,408 patients at Cane Hill, comprising 1,058 males and 1,359 females, There were 21 male and 34 female private patients, including service patients and two male and two female criminal lunatics.

While there was an average increase of 2,251 patients in England and Wales for the ten years ending 31 December 1914, there were decreases of 3,278, 3,159 and 8,188 for the years from 1915 to 1917, mainly due to the 'abnormal number of deaths' among patients in institutions for the insane in 1917 and 1918. Between 3,000 and 4,000 mental and nervous cases were in military hospitals 'who will probably eventually be certified as insane' and admitted to mental hospitals, the name now used instead of 'lunatic asylums'.[26]

Patients continued to be admitted and discharged as in peacetime, but men with mental health difficulties were called up to fight as, unlike physical disabilities, it was not a reason to be unconsidered unfit. Patients, generally females, occasionally complained of ill treatment. Allegations were investigated and nothing found to substantiate them. In 1914, Sir James complained that two girls aged 14 and 15 had been admitted, who were too young to be with adults. He was asked to report at the following meeting, but no more appears and they were probably discharged.[27]

People continued to have trial leave, such as Mrs A.L. Charlesworth, a private patient, in February 1915. At Cane Hill, they did not know that her husband had left her in lodgings in Ramsgate. Dr Littlejohn, informed of her relapse, brought her back, in a motor car. She said she had a 'hysterical attack' due to indigestion, having had brandy, oysters and bitter beer. On the return journey, she was 'excited', but 'quiet and well-behaved' once back in Cane Hill.[28]

The Board of Control ascribed the increased death rate in asylums mainly to the unavoidable reduction in the quantity and quality of the food, particularly flour, supplied to patients. A significant lack of food was reported at several hospitals, but no mention has been found at Cane Hill. Its staff complained about the food, but no similar complaints appeared from its patients; probably, it was mainly a lack of variety with other less popular foods being substituted. Despite crop losses due to bad weather, in 1918, surplus crops were supplied to other asylums.

In February 1919, Lt Col. Frederick Mott visited service patients at Hanwell Asylum, where several complained of insufficient food. They received about 2,200 calories a day, whereas 3,145 calories were recommended by the Army Council for patients in military hospitals, but he was informed that it was entirely adequate 'for chronic cases, such as most of the Service Patients are'.[29] The medical superintendent of Long Grove, in August 1918, criticised new austerity measures imposed by the Board of Control, leading to 'a 'grossly unjust' distribution of jam and cheese': 'staff, private patients and service patients received more than worker patients on whom the asylum economy depended'.[30] In 1918, the Commissioners reported that patients had suffered from starvation at Bexley Asylum.

Cane Hill's acting medical superintendent, Dr Donaldson, responded to the report by stating that every service patient had been seen. None complained about the food, apart from one who gave a negative reply to nearly all questions. He considered the daily allowance at Cane Hill of 2,599 calories sufficient for chronic unemployed patients, while those went out to work had an extra 369 calories. Many patients were putting on weight.

His view was that 'if service patients are to be treated from a philanthropic point of view and treated similarly to those in a military Neurasthenic Hospital, they are receiving this . . . but I do not understand why they are to be treated differently to the ordinary hospital patient . . . if service patients are to have extra food, they will need to be treated in a ward by themselves, otherwise there will be great discontent amongst other patients'. It would be very difficult to do that because of the varying mental conditions of the service patients.[31]

Infections and epidemics

The Commissioners concluded that, even if the diet was normal, the death rate increased because of other reasons including inadequate staffing, overcrowding and communicable diseases.[32]

Patients admitted during the war were of a poorer physical condition and of a greater age, as few men between the ages of 18 to 41 were certified and admitted to asylums, unless physically unfit for military service. Senile cases formerly kept in workhouses were often transferred to asylums as workhouses either closed or were short-staffed, while the increased demand for female labour in factories meant that 'weaklings could no longer be looked after in their own homes'. They recognised that some patients may have died soon after admission as a result of being removed from a familiar environment and from their relatives.

In the asylum, there were less staff, frequent changes of staffing and many substitute temporary staff were untrained. A loss of fit young men led to 'a reduction in cleanliness, little whitewashing, painting and papering, less washing and polishing of floors', while 'unskilled temporary staff failed to recognise sickness and debility in the early stages'. There was 'less personal attention than would have been the case in expert hands'. There was overcrowding, as at Cane Hill, which might have been combined with bad ventilation due to 'masking windows, etc. by curtains' which probably occurred at Cane Hill as Kenley Aerodrome was about a mile away. It was difficult to segregate sick and infectious patients, together with a lack of personal cleanliness, insufficient care and wrong methods of dealing with foul linen.

The transfer of patients from one asylum to another led to certain diseases and epidemics in asylums not previously affected.[33] Having had no cases since 1900, Cane Hill experienced typhoid fever from 1915 onwards when there were ninety cases that year on the male wards, including an attendant, and five deaths. In 1916, it affected seventeen male patients with one death and, in 1917, appeared on the female side. Eleven males and thirteen female patients, and two nurses, caught it, with two deaths and, in 1918, outbreaks were mainly on the female side.

Typhoid usually has an incubation period of ten to fifteen days with an insidious onset, the patient showing a gradually increasing fever, usually with abdominal pain and diarrhoea. Crops of rose coloured spots may appear from the eighth day onwards, usually limited to the abdomen, flanks and back, and frequently delirium at night, generally consisting of muttering. In some cases, ulcers appear in the small intestine in the third week, which may lead to haemorrhages and perforation.

The patient was left helpless, unable to turn himself in bed. It required careful nursing, with bed-baths once or twice a day, with careful disposal of excreta. Patients needed plenty of water, their main diet being milk, with some liberally salted beef tea if there was no diarrhoea. As the morning temperature reduced, boiled bread and milk or thin oat-flour porridge was introduced, and then steamed fish and, a few days later, chicken. With a shortage of skilled staff and good food, together with overcrowding, good nursing was challenging. The infection was mainly spread through dust, dried stools on bed sheets, flies, soiled bed-linen, blankets and clothes, and the excretions of carriers who have or had typhoid fever, the bacillus being able to retain its 'vitality' for a considerable period in the earth.[34]

Dr Littlejohn could not find a definite cause although 'the fact our sewerage is disposed of on the land has always been a source of anxiety to us – all patients employed there have been made to wash and disinfect in lysol, 2 p.c. on re-entering the building . . . the same for staff in ward kitchens and patients handling food.[35] He thought personal infection important and found it difficult to understand if it came from outside, as it was limited to a particular group of wards: regarding the patients, 'nearly all will not or cannot work' and had 'sunk to a state of helplessness'. He stressed the need for great care in personal and general cleanliness on the wards, including the handling of food and soiled bed linen, and contact with the land and sewerage.[36]

The outbreak in 1918 was thought to have passed to the female side through imperfectly disinfected clothing sent to the needleroom for repairs. That year, Cane Hill was the worst affected asylum in England and Wales with 22 males and 57 females, a total of 79 affected patients, and 6 staff. Two male and nine female patients died. Cornwall's asylum was next with 35 affected and 11 deaths.[37]

In 1919, there were twenty-nine notifications of infection, and four deaths, but the type of infection is not known. Although many staff at Cane Hill had Spanish influenza, it was not among asylums with the highest number of deaths from influenza.[38] Two female nurses were buried in the cemetery in 1918, namely Margaret Jane Morris, aged 20, in June and Kate Dalton, aged 22, in November. A number of staff would develop tuberculosis, probably the result of poor health following influenza.[39]

Outbreaks of typhoid fever continued. In late 1920, with cases on a male ward, it was decided that it may be caused by the sanitary conditions. The existing water closets, with valves that flushed when the patient rose from the seat, would be replaced with flushing cisterns, and cumbersome wooden seats by light seats. Urinals were to be reduced from four to two on each floor, and the enclosed iron waste pipe common to all the lavatory basins replaced by an independent pipe from each lavatory which would discharge over an open channel. Waste water from baths would discharge into open channels at the outer wall, with a reduction from three to two baths on each floor. An ongoing programme began to improve ventilation by replacing small windows in the sanitary annexes by larger sash windows.[40]

In 1922, having been free for some time, ten female patients developed typhoid. Two died, while bacteriological examinations found four 'carriers' who were isolated and kept under permanent observation.[41]

PHOTOGRAPHS OF CANE HILL
by kind permission of Croydon Local Studies Library and Archive Service

The main drive and entrance about 1905 or 1909

Aerial view

Female wards from the recreational ground, showing the wards built in 1891-2. About 1905

Male wards. Unclimbable fencing surrounded the kitchen garden to prevent theft by staff and the locals

Glencairn. The chaplain's house and, from the 1920s, home to the medical superintendant

The Chapel, with seating for 800 people

Ward gallery, about 1905

Building department with Edward James Moore, centre front, chief engineer from the asylum's opening to his retirement in 1914

The Football Team, 1926-7

The Building Staff Social Club's third annual outing in 1939, taken in front of the hospital

The Athletic Section of the Sports and Social Club in 1951

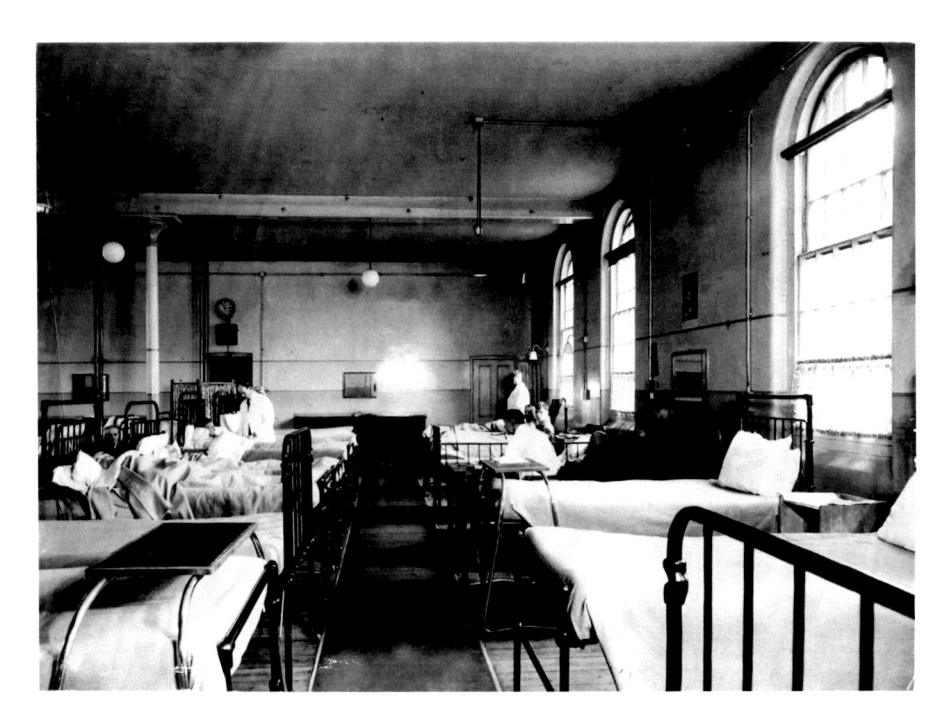

A dormitory, 1950s

A day room, 1950s

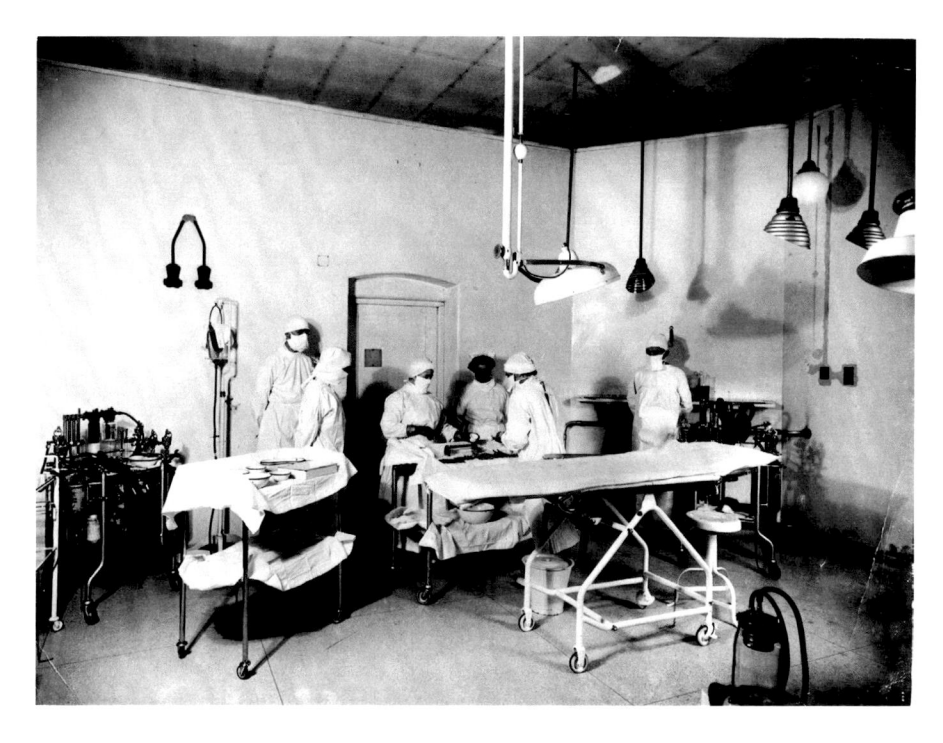

The Operating Theatre, about 1950

The Hospital Fête in June 1950

A male patient filling a mattress, about 1950

Patients peeling potatoes, about 1950

Queen's Ward gallery, probably in the 1960s

Princess Marina leaving in 1961 with Mr Geere, chairman of the HMC, *after one of her visits*

The staff social club about 1965 with Lorna Challis in centre front and Bill Armstrong back far right.

The nurses' prizegiving ceremony in 1973

Staff Nurse Doreen Groom, Cane Hill c 1940

Chapter 15: Portnalls

In 1899, a local estate agent offered to sell nearby land where staff cottages could be built, but the sub-committee decided not to buy. A few months later, with a lack of space in the main building, Dr Moody was authorised to allow fourteen single men to live out of the Asylum, and be paid a lodging allowance of £15 a year, and wages twice monthly.[1]

Joseph Tucker owned land to the west of Portnalls Road and, in 1901, contacted the sub-committee regarding three fields which they had recently rented from him. He was negotiating their sale for building land, but suggested the asylum grow cash crops there, paying a fair rent, providing he took back the fields as soon as he sold them. The sub-committee did not approve of his suggestion but decided to be open to negotiation.[2] They maintained a working relationship with him, as in 1908 when he offered a crop of about twenty loads clover, provided its carters cut and carted it away.[3] In early 1910, Mr Tucker offered to sell the asylum a half acre adjoining its cemetery, but Dr Moody thought the cemetery ample for the asylum's needs for at least twenty years, and the offer was refused.[4]

The land north of Cane Hill had been steadily sold off to build, in the main, substantial houses. Mr. Tucker looked to sell more land and, in 1913, approached Cane Hill Asylum offering part of the Portnalls estate. In October 1913, the LCAD's Engineer presented his report describing Portnalls House as a substantial rectangular brick building with a basement, ground and first floors and rooms in the attic. It had a morning room, dining room, billiards room, drawing room, library, boudoir, servants' hall, kitchen and scullery on the ground floor. A conservatory and greenhouse 'in fair repair' were built onto it. With a frontage about 110 feet long, and 48 feet deep, the house would be suitable for about forty-eight quiet, convalescent patients with five staff.

Other buildings on that part of the estate included the Old Manor House, built in 1602, with walls of lath and rough cast, and about sixteen rooms, with ceilings about eight feet high. In a bad state of repair, it was 'of no value' and would be demolished. The brick stables were in a fair condition with stalls for four horses, loose boxes for three, a coach house, harness room and four living rooms. The greenhouse built against it was 'of no value'. A large wooden cowshed with twelve double stalls and a tiled roof, with an adjacent shed, in a 'bad state of repair', could be used as a milking shed.

Stoney Cottages, built in 1799 of flints with brickwork above, and tiled roofs, at the junction of Hollyme Oak Road and Brighton Road, were a row of three 'two up two down' cottages, with rooms about ten foot square with low ceilings. 'Not up to the Committee's standard for cottages', they were damp as rain drove through the walls and roof while their privies were in sheds, with all waste water thrown on the gardens. The entrance lodge on Hollyme Oak Road, built in red brick on one floor about 1875, had four rooms.

It is not known how much land was offered, but its value was £150 an acre, and £4,000 was asked for the buildings. The Engineer recommended its purchase while, in January 1914, the LCAD's Finance (Loans and Estimates) Committee was in no doubt that, if they did not buy it, it would be sold for housing which would 'necessitate expense for enclosing the asylum's estate . . . a sufficient reason to justify the purchase', but they suggested the price was too high.

In March, two Commissioners recommended its purchase to the Secretary of State 'on the understanding that, if the Committee wished to provide for a large number of patients there, the buildings might become another institution under its own medical superintendent. In June, the LCC authorised the purchase, with an expenditure of no more than £15,000 for the estate and, in October, about £2,300 was given for renovations and alterations for patients. It considered using it for the asylum, mentally defective people or for wounded soldiers. In November, the LCAD agreed to add an extra 23 rooms to the nurses' block in the main building.[5] In November 1914, the sale was completed. The four tenants, including two asylum employees, could remain in the cottages with their 'primitive sanitary arrangements'.

Due to vacate the property on 18 December, the Tuckers auctioned its contents off three days earlier. That day asylum staff, there on duty as special constables, saw two men stealing holly. They escaped, leaving their pony and cart behind. One man was known and, in January 1915, the LCC prosecuted Alfred Pritchard, 35, a butcher of Old Town, Croydon, who pleaded guilty to breaking off fifty branches of holly in the garden at Portnalls, and was fined 5s with 5s 6d costs and 5s for damage.

A road to Portnalls, 150 yards long and 12 feet wide, would gradually be made as chalk and flints accumulated, using patient labour to reduce the cost from £715 to £200. It had a fairly good hedge but, where thin and unsatisfactory, a five foot high inclimbable fence would be erected, used standardly at Cane Hill, whereas other London asylums used 6 foot 6 inch high closely boarded oak. The main entrance to the house would be moved from the north to the south side. The sub-committee would ask the LCAD for £4,155 to adapt and equip the building. Temporary attendant William New and his wife became caretakers from 21 December, while the Tuckers' former gardener, James Turner, was paid £1 from the Tea Fund for his assistance before the Tuckers left.

At Stoney Cottages, the chairman suggested sculleries with a third bedroom above, and wood block floors on the ground floor. At Portnalls, the stables and cowshed should remain, but other outhouses would be demolished, providing hardcore for two new roads to Portnalls. The large Dutch barn had blown down in high winds in January. However, with capital expenditure restricted from April 1915, little would happen until the war ended.

Miss Edith Tucker wrote in May requesting to purchase the materials in the Old Manor House, together with its pathway, and an old cart shed at the rear of the large stable, as she wanted to rebuild the house to the same design elsewhere on the Portnalls estate. They still owned land to the west of Portnalls Road, and two fields south of Hollyme Oak Road.

The sub-committee agreed to sell it to her for £100 provided she demolished it and cleared the debris.[6] The sub-committee thought it a 'bad bargain' for her, although she had been professionally advised. In May 1916, Miss Annie C. Tucker's contractors had failed to remove it, when she asked for permission to remove the stumps of old yew trees formerly in the garden, about 220 yards of turf and to substitute slates for tiles, which she was supposed to leave there. She asked to leave corrugated iron sheets and two wooden partitions behind, and be absolved from making good a breach in the wall made by her contractor removing materials.[7] In February 1916, a new road was proposed across the meadow from the asylum to Portnalls House, where chimneys had been repointed and cowsheds repaired. In March, the engineer reported that Portnalls House, called the Manor House, had been waterproofed. Dilapidated greenhouses at its stables were demolished but, in April, progress was delayed by bad weather. The conservatory roof had been repaired, and a damp area of the west end wall, but a severe storm on 28 March had slightly damaged outbuildings.

Her brother, Mr. Horace Tucker, still owned 'Portnalls Farm' and, in May 1917, asked to lay a pipe from the asylum's stables to his tenant's farm buildings. It was agreed, and to allow him 'a reasonable quantity' provided Mr. Tucker arranged it with the East Surrey Water Company, and was responsible for any failure of supply, the water being charged to him.

On 16 July 1918 a storm, with hailstones 2½ inches big, broke about 2,000 panes of glass in the hospital and the greenhouses, but Portnalls was spared. With a replacement cost of £260 for the glass, it was decided to leave further work on Portnalls until the following Spring.[8]

Mr. Joseph Tucker had died, and land developers wrote in March 1919, offering to sell land adjacent to the cemetery, as they were laying out the surrounding land for building. Again, the sub-committee declined the offer.

With additional land, the livestock on the asylum's farm had doubled, although there was still twenty-eight staff as in 1912-4.[9] In 1920, patients were repainting iron fencing when, in May, it was decided to use Portnalls for fifty 'quiet chronic' female patients and five staff but, the Asylums Officer at the LCAD decided that renovations would cost about £10,800, which could not be justified with the eleventh mental hospital being completed. It would continue to be used for storing furniture. Meanwhile, there was pressure on beds as 29 female patients returned from Fisherton House.[10]

In 1921, no capital expenditure was authorised in mental hospitals unless 'essential for promoting the health of the patients and the staff'.[11] Plans were made to adapt Portnalls, at a cost of £1,890, to accommodate 39 male patients.[12] The sub-committee suggested central heating but the Board of Control preferred open fires or radiators, to expedite the scheme.[13] That same year, more land was purchased at a cost of £938.[14]

In 1922, about two hundred tons of chalk from the cemetery, and about one hundred tons of broken bricks and hard core, perhaps the remains of demolition at Portnalls, were sent to the eleventh mental hospital.[15] Boilers and radiators were installed at Portnalls, and gas for lighting and cooking. In 1922, 39 male working patients moved in, including twelve from Garden House. Hot water was provided for domestic purposes and occasional bathing, but they would usually bath in the main building. Mrs Collis, cook at Garden House, and her husband, one of the cowman, would live in and cook for staff and patients. Mr Collis, who was not involved with the patients, was paid £1.15s 10d including 12s 6d a week board, and his wife £1.7s a week plus board, lodging, laundry and uniform. The question of continuing high wages to domestic staff, which was under consideration, and she had no promise that even the present wages could be continued.[16]

Chapter 16: Attitudes in the 1920s

In 1923, when new more detailed regulations were published, little had changed, except that medical superintendents no longer needed permission to be away overnight, while Matron made her occasional night visits to female wards 'at uncertain times' without the medical superintendent.[1]

Head day nurses, both male and female, were to be on each ward daily at a set time 'to see that the nurses are at their duties and zealous in the discharge of them', and should visit their wards frequently each day. Duties included seeing that food was sufficient and served properly, and that everywhere was clean and ventilated. Patients were to be properly and neatly dressed, and helpless patients washed and bathed, 'taking special care that no roughness is used towards them', with particular attention paid to the state of their hair and nails.

They were to endeavour 'to become acquainted with the habits, trades or pursuits of the patients, in order to assist in keeping them usefully employed' and visit patients when they were exercising, to ensure nurses supervised them properly. Daily, at least one head nurse visited patients employed outside and in workshops, giving necessary supervision, encouraged sports and recreation among the patients, and visited wards in the evening, encouraging games and amusements between patients and nurses. 'They shall, by example and precept, endeavour to cultivate amongst the nurses a respect for their calling and courtesy and kindliness of manner in dealing with the patients', endeavouring to prevent 'upon all occasions any coarse language or truculent conduct on the part of the patients'.

The day nurse in charge of a ward was 'to bear in mind that upon his supervision and example depend the tone of the ward and the happiness and welfare of its inmates'. Duties included being 'most scrupulous as to the cleanliness and ventilation of the ward and the cleanliness of the patients' and their personal hygiene, particularly mouths and teeth. Reports were not to be completed until patients had gone to bed. At handover, in the morning and evening, the day head nurse and the night nurse were to go around the dormitories and single rooms together. If a patient's condition made it necessary for them to be placed in a single room, the nurse in charge of the ward was to inform the head nurse immediately.

Probationer nurses were to attend lectures, and study in order to acquire a recognised diploma of proficiency in mental nursing to become staff nurses, and be retained in the service. They and other ward staff cleaned out the dormitories as soon as the patients were up and dressed as 'the upmost cleanliness and tidiness must be observed in every part of the ward; everything is to be kept in the appointed place'.

They were expected to communicate freely to their superior officers any matter or occurrence affecting the welfare of the patients or the institution. Those working with patients were expected to participate in the activity and, when in the recreation grounds, not to talk and walk together, but supervise the patients properly. After every meal, knives and forks were to be collected and handed to the nurse in charge of the ward, who checked that the number was correct before patients were permitted to leave their tables. If any were missing, it was to be reported immediately to the inspector or matron. Knives and forks were to be cleaned immediately and locked up 'in the proper box'. No patient should use a carving knife or fork.

Each nurse had a whistle to use, only in an emergency, if a patient showed a threatening demeanour, violence, etc., and must heed all patients' complaints and report them. 'Under provocation of any kind, the nurse must be calm and forbearing'. Any nurse guilty of striking or ill-using or wilfully neglecting a patient was liable to suspension, and would be dealt with under the 1890 Lunacy Act. If convicted, the fine was between £2 and £20. Nurses who appropriated patients' food, 'sick extras', or any other allowance would be suspended, and there was no smoking on duty, unless allowed by the medical superintendent.[2]

The National Asylums Workers Union and others objected to employing female nurses in male wards in asylums, although the Board of Control believed that 'in a large number of cases it is marked by markedly beneficial results, it is regarded with favour by the nurses who undertake it'.[3]

Mental Nursing

A contemporary nursing text book suggested that, from the start, a mental nurse should 'consciously realise that every symptom ... results from a disease of the brain' and she should aim to 'remove the popular reproach of the disease, embittering as it does all the real sadness to relatives and to patient when he recovers, as well as adding many special difficulties to its treatment'.

To become a really first-class mental nurse the following qualifications are necessary: Good health, an equable temper, youth, power of observation, intelligence, kindness of heart, unselfishness, great patience, a pleasant manner, tact, large firmness and power of insistence, average strength, great staying power, coolness, force of character, and an instinctive knowledge of human nature.

The author described the need of

> a special knack ... of observing the mental changes that occur in them for better or worse, and a subtle power over the patients by word, look and manner. Persons with this faculty get on with mental patients from the first; they are not afraid of them, they have an innate tolerance for the disagreeableness of many of the insane, they have a soothing manner, and instinctively know the weak points of their cases. Commonly they do not get hurt by obstreperous patients, and they get them to do things with ease which others fail in doing ... the person who gets on well with children, ruling them firmly yet gaining their confidence and liking, is the one who is most likely to get on with those who suffer from mental illnesses, great or small ... Do not be tempted to use your power over your patient dictatorially or selfishly, but justly and for his good only ... To ill-treat or neglect an insane person is a far worse offence than to do so to a sane person, who can complain.

Classifying mental disorders

Mental illnesses were now divided into the following categories:

Mental Classification:

1   Melancholia

2   Mania

3   Dementia

4   Monomania or delusional insanity

5   Volitional or impulsive insanity

6   Stupor

<u>Bodily or Clinical Classification, the most important being:</u>

1   General paralysis

2   Ordinary paralytic insanity

3   Epileptic insanity

4   Alcoholic insanity

5   Insanities connected with pregnancy, childbirth and nursing

6   Insanities of the times of life, including adolescent insanity and the climacteric (menopausal)

7   Senile insanity

8   Idiocy and congenital imbecility

The nurse's main role with patients who had melancholia was close observation, as more than half of the cases would recover. For those with mania, 'a curable disease', it was 'walking in the open air "to let off steam" and to produce sleep, careful and constant feeding to keep up the strength'. It was observed that when cases of melancholia and mania did not recover, patients passed into dementia and were liable to become excited at times, in which case treatment consisted 'largely in keeping up the bodily health – a fat dement is less troublesome than a lean one – correcting the habits, and keeping the patient occupied in some simple way or other'.

Most of those with adolescent insanity were said to recover 'under proper treatment which consists of much walking and work in the fresh air, quantities of milk, bread and butter, fruit, vegetables, and a minimum of animal food. Close habits to prevent masturbation is necessary'. Women experiencing the climacteric (menopause) needed 'cheerful nursing, a change to sea or mountain air, good food, a little employment and amusement, with patience and quiet' and 'not allowing, or controlling, morbid thoughts and feelings', much of which was not available at Cane Hill.

The treatment of those with senile insanity (senile dementia) consisted of 'watching, soothing, giving food and sedatives'. 'Imbeciles' were still admitted to Cane Hill: nurses were to treat them by endeavouring 'to develop the body and muscles by feeding, suitable trades, simple games, and regulated exercise, in giving plenty of good simple food, in fresh air combined with warmth, and by a simple and special education through the senses' for 'some can even be made useful members of society'.[4]

Treatments

The principles of moral treatment were still used so that, in her work 'the nursing and treatment in many cases consist largely in systematically arranging conditions of life, hours, diet, occupation, amusements, exercise, and other conditions that will antagonise and counteract the mental symptoms present, and so act as mental medicines'.

Hydrotherapy, using warm baths, was an important part of the treatment of many forms of mental illness:

> Patients suffering from various kinds of motor excitement are frequently treated by prolonged bathing. The temperature of the water is maintained at a constant temperature (98°-105° F.), and the patient lies in it half an hour the first day, one hour the second, two hours the third and so on, up to six hours or more. The time is then gradually reduced. The cold shower bath, the wet pack, and the vapour bath are also sometimes prescribed.[5]

Cold shower baths had not been used at Cane Hill for many years and, in 1921, were removed from the general bathrooms at Cane Hill.[6] 'Continuous baths', devised at Bexley Hospital in 1918, had by 1924 become the most favoured form of treatment, used in twenty-five hospitals including Cane Hill. Special treatment baths, close to dormitories, ensured a continuous flow of water at a prescribed temperature.[7] However, in 1928, the commissioners noted that the continuous baths at Cane Hill were 'not greatly used', a pity, because they were inconveniently sited.[8]

In 1924, the London County Mental Hospital Committee (LCMHC) announced that 'considerable emphasis is placed on the physical treatment of patients as a preliminary to the application to them of psycho-therapeutic measures'.[9] Dr. George Austen Lilly, later medical superintendent at Cane Hill, was appointed as fourth assistant medical officer in 1919 and, soon after, did a short course in psychology at Cambridge. Soon after, Drs. Pearn, Lilly and McCowan took courses in Psychological Medicine at the Maudsley Hospital, and Dr. Lilly sat the first part of the examination in Psychological Medicine.[10]

Abundant fresh and exercise had long been recognised as valuable in treatment, as well as rest in bed for 'active and acute mental symptoms'. Now, the opinion was that this latter treatment was best if experienced in the open air: 'Open air treatment' at night, 'a material aid to healthy metabolism, is a powerful tranquillizer and a valuable corrective in cases of insomnia'.

New verandahs were built, as at Cane Hill, with glazed roofs but entirely open in front.[11] At Cane Hill they also appear to have been used for the treatment of tuberculosis, as verandas was built at the Cottage Hospital, as well as on female wards A1 and B1 together with an extension to the verandah on J1, a female ward.

Soon after Dr Elgee arrived, he noted that the surgical equipment was very deficient, and up to £100 worth of essential stock was purchased from War Office stock at Horton Mental Hospital.[12] A part-time dentist was employed, and a small number of patients were given dentures, perhaps to help them to on discharge from hospital.

The LCMHC announced, in 1923, that there should be a clinical laboratory at each large mental hospital. Cane Hill and Colney Heath Hospitals were to report on the expenditure, and Dr Elgee to confer with Sir Frederick Mott. Soon after, designs for the proposed laboratory were drawn up. In November, Dr Elgee informed the sub-committee that he desired to experiment with a new treatment for general paralysis by inoculating patients with malaria. He had sent two males to Hanwell for the day, to be inoculated with malarial blood.[13]

Wagner Jauregg of Vienna recommended the use of malarial therapy in 1917: he inoculated nine patients with general paralysis, six of whom improved greatly with three, five years later, able to work with no signs of the disease. Patients were either bitten by mosquitoes or inoculated with blood from a person with malaria. It produced a fever with a high temperature and, after a course of treatment, a marked improvement in mental and physical symptoms. Even in 1961, it was written that 'the results obtained through malarial treatment have been remarkable', and there was not yet evidence that penicillin would entirely supersede malaria treatment.[14]

In February 1924, the Ministry of Health asked Dr Elgee to collaborate in the new treatment, one of their laboratory assistants coming to Cane Hill for a few days to experiment: 'to convey the infection directly by means of mosquito bites, i.e. by nature's method of blood transfusion'. A male staff nurse was seconded from Cane Hill to the Maudsley Hospital from January, to train as a laboratory attendant.[15] Dr Elgee was allowed to buy six mosquito nets to surround patients undergoing malarial treatment for general paralysis as warmer weather was coming and there might be a danger of patients not receiving the treatment being affected by mosquito bites.

Frames for the nets were fitted to asbestos partitions on male G ward' verandah and in two single rooms on female J ward but, in August, it was decided female cases would only be treated at Horton and Claybury Hospitals. Two males would be treated at each of four hospitals: Bexley, Cane Hill, Claybury and Colney Hatch with patients transferred to these hospitals to 'undergo this special treatment'.[16]

In 1924, there were plans to install electricity at Cane Hill, and to install x-ray apparatus.[17] Ultra-violet radiation, or 'actino-therapy', and 'light baths' were believed 'to ameliorate cases of neurasthenia'.[18] In 1928, ultra-violet radiation was said to be of considerable value as a general tonic in the treatment of the insane, with striking results: debilitated patients, who refused food, began to eat ravenously and make considerable weight gain while 'melancholics of the stuperose type definitely improve'. Agitated melancholics were observed to be made worse, while some with 'hebephrenic seclusiveness change to catatonic excitement'.[19] From 1925, a female masseuse was employed three days a week and, although it was too soon to report on the effective of her treatment, there was no doubt that it would be of great value.[20]

The Board of Control encouraged an absence of a sense of restraint: 'we desire to see it restricted to those who really need it', and specific wards for recent admissions and those who would probably recover within a reasonable period, and other wards for those with protracted mental illnesses, with the able bodied in separate wards from the sick and infirm.[21] In the mid-1920s, female and male admission wards were opened at Cane Hill.

Medication

Drugs were 'necessary for the cure of the various bodily ailments from which the patient may be suffering', and to 'produce necessary sleep, the commonly used being bromide, paraldehyde, chloral and bromidia'.[22] Medication was not yet used to treat specific symptoms, but to sedate disturbed and over-active patients, and those with insomnia. There was little difference in the length of hospitalisation for those with depression and mania in the 1880s through to the end of the twentieth century, most being discharged between a month and fifteen months after admission. Studies of Victorian asylums showed that about a third of admissions were discharged within a year, and a smaller proportion during the second year.[23]

In 1922, the Inspector of Stores complained about damaged clothing and bedding, mainly on G1 and G2 male wards. Five patients were very destructive and, although Dr Elgee had 'adopted every known method to try and correct them of the habit but with very little result, and they were being kept on a sedative as far as was consistent with medical treatment'.[24]

In 1923, Faith Harmsworth, a noisy, restless patient who slept in a single room off the gallery in K2 ward, was found on the staircase at 5.20 a.m. by a night nurse. She was thought safe but had apparently opened the door by continually banging on it. She went into the ward kitchen and found a bottle of chloral draught left out for another patient, and drank four draughts. 'Suitable remedies' were applied at once.[25]

From World War One through to the Second World War, there was little difference in the number and types of prescription dispensed each day. For example, in one week in April 1918, between two to eleven patients were prescribed medicine each day for physical conditions and for sedation, and one to three staff with physical conditions.[26] Even so, in 1925, the commissioners thought there should be greater discrimination in prescribing 'aperients'.[27]

On any day, generally no more than one to two patients were prescribed paraldehyde, and chloral was used less often while sulphonal, seen as safer than chloral, was used after 1918 and used in paranoia, mania, hallucinatory delusions caused by alcoholism, and in fevers, inflammatory diseases and other physical conditions. Glass syringes were dispensed to take blood from patients, to test for syphilis. In 1934, about ten to fifteen prescriptions for medication were dispensed daily.

In 1916, the government ordered that regular prescriptions should not longer be issued to staff during the war, which would become permanent, but one to two a day continued to have isolated prescriptions such as Miss Harling who had haemoglobin tablets in 1917 and Miss Collins lime juice in 1918.[28] In the 1930s, sick staff and patients were prescribed Ovaltine.[29]

Chapter 17: From Asylum to Hospital

The war ended, but restricted conditions continued in October 1919, when a new timetable was introduced to save fuel and light. A shorter working week having been introduced, day ward staff would work a six day week, doing 47 hours and 50 minutes in Week A and 48 hours and 10 minutes in Week B, including one long 12 hour day on duty from 7.00 a.m. to 8 p.m. In Week A, a morning shift began at 7.00 a.m. and, in Week B, an afternoon shift from early afternoon to 8.00 a.m. Night staff worked 95 hours and 50 minutes per fortnight, with two nights off a week.

For day staff, breakfast was at 6.30 a.m., the first dinner sitting at 12.30 p.m. and the second at 1.10 p.m. At tea, the first sitting was at 5.00 p.m. and the second at 5.30 p.m., with supper at 8.00 p.m. Night staff had breakfast at 7.30 a.m. and dinner at 8.00 p.m. For patients, breakfast was at 7.45 a.m., dinner at noon and tea at 5.00 p.m.

The revised timetable was intended to prevent a waste of man power in the middle of the day, and provide a small additional number of staff later in the day to enable 'sitting-up parties' in suitable wards: opportunities for patients to stay up later which the medical superintendent saw would help patients to be tired when they went to bed, and would sleep better without medication. Gas consumption fell, and it was decided to continue this shift pattern. In 1924, the chairman of the London Mental Health Committee requested coffee and cake be issued every night to patients who sit-up late, the cost not exceeding £2. 10s a week per one hundred patients, and charged to the 'Fetes and Entertainments Account'.[1]

Aware of difficulties in recruiting, and concerned that female staff would have too much free time, the new shifts were seen to be more ideal for enabling staff dances, staff entertainments, rehearsals, whist drives, etc., which had been impossible as only half the staff could attend. Fire drills could take place on Friday lunchtimes when double the staff would be on the wards but, one day a week, a ward would be left without its Chief Charge Nurse or Charge Nurse. The ward telephone was only to be used in connection with patients, the gate porters being instructed to ask why a call from one ward to another was being made. The hospital's outside telephone number was 'Purley 5'.[2]

The war and post-war economy led to increased annual costs and charges. In 1917, the weekly charge for patients belonging to London Unions was 12s 3d, the total annual expenditure at Cane Hill being £79,264 plus £1,173 for pensions, gratuities etc. When the commissioners visited, there were 1,058 male and 1,359 females, a total of 2,408 patients including 21 male and 34 female private patients.[3] 1n 1921, it had reduced to 2,176 patients, comprising 761 pauper males, 1,278 pauper females, 124 male private patients, mainly Service Patients, and 13 female private patients while the weekly cost for pauper patients had increased to £1.15s 10½d. Cane Hill was, in 1918, one of only seven mental hospitals allowed additions, alterations or improvements, namely £28 for serving lobbies in the main kitchen.[4]

In 1919 there were enough staff on the male side, where an eight hour working day had been introduced, but there were vacancies for trained female staff. The female side was overcrowded with over two hundred extra patients, and there was still typhoid.[5] In September 1920, the LCAC's Comptroller reported on the high rate of salaries and wages at Cane Hill, which was 16s 1½d per patient, which Dr Elgee considered was probably the result of rapidly taking on extra staff for the three shift system. The average number of patients at Cane Hill was 2,060, while the average for the other six was 2,373, which reduced the cost per patient of those hospitals.

When he arrived at Cane Hill, there were few vacancies for female staff but, on the male side, there was enough staff for 900 patients, but only 780 in residence. There were now 900 male patients, but the male nursing establishment had been reduced by 26 men, saving about 10s 7d per patient per week, and he had reverted to the previous duty rota. He hoped to reduce the staff by another seven or eight men, once the holiday season was over.

The cost of food for staff at Cane Hill was £839 more than the average of five other hospitals. Meanwhile, junior female staff complained about various issues included the quality and quantity of food, and having to pay for meals, which they did not eat, when they remained in the building at mealtimes on leave days. His observations were accepted by the sub-committee.

In December, the Comptroller reported again on the high cost of provisions: staff received more meals than at other hospitals while pork was given to patients, which cost more than beef and mutton, and they had a full meat dinner once a week, while the farm made a loss of £1,211 or 10d per head per week. Dr Elgee reported numerous economies, and no longer issued pork. With more patients in residence, there was a reduction in the cost per head.[6]

In 1923 following further economies, the maintenance cost for each patient fell from £1.8s 7d to £1.2s 9d.[7] It compared favourably with other hospitals, although furniture, property and clothing were higher because of equipping Portnalls, while Dr Elgee had insisted that stocks of towels, bedding and clothing be increased on wards. Later in the year, new dietary costs were presented. The cost of feeding one hundred male patients had risen from £17.1s 10d to £20.19s 7d and, for women, from £17.9s 8d to £20.18s 4d. After 'experimentation', it was decided some small reductions could be made. All male patients should have an average of 3,200 calories a day, and females 3,000 calories. At Cane Hill, the daily average would be 3,178 calories a day for male non-workers and 2,720 calories for female non-workers, male workers having an average of 3,580 calories a day, and females 3,182 calories.

In 1925, the sub-committee noted with satisfaction that the cost of maintenance at Cane Hill was 9d below the average.[8] The charge to London Unions for maintenance increased further to £1.8s 0d, but fell to £1.6s 10d in 1929, when, at Cane Hill, the actual cost was £1.2s 10¼d for each 'pauper patient'.[9]

Having dismissed probationer nurses in 1920 to save money, in 1924 applications fell and there were 33 vacancies for probationer nurses. The sub-committee sought permission to employ temporary nurses, not eligible to be on the permanent staff.[10] Advertisements for probationary and temporary nurses were placed in the *Nursing Mirror*, two national papers, *The Scotsman* and the *Western Daily Press*, and other advertisements for laundry and hospital maids. Two women applying to be female nurses came from Wales, arranged through the Ministry of Labour's Employment Exchange, but had 'dirty heads' when examined and were not appointed. In March 1924, 64 staff were off sick, mainly with influenza, so thirty-seven nurses had to work on their day off, being paid for overtime worked in excess of 96 hours a fortnight.

That same month, seven farm workers petitioned that they found it difficult to live, and that it seemed particularly hard that, after working all day with patients, after paying rates and rent, they were left with just over £1 to support a wife and family. The National Asylum Workers' Union applied on behalf of one farm worker, Ernest G. Richard, to increase his wages by 10s a week as he dealt with swill, dust and refuse. The sub-committee, thinking he had adequate grounds, referred all the requests to the General Purposes Sub-Committee.

In April, male nurse Thomas Wheeler appeared at the Surrey Quarter Sessions accused of stealing meat, apples and suet from the hospital, having been stopped by police when leaving the estate. He claimed he bought them on the way to work, but was found guilty. Because of his previous good character, he was bound over for twelve months in the sum of £20. Although the National Asylum Workers' Union appealed on his behalf as he had a wife and four young children, Wheeler was dismissed but, as an act of clemency, was paid up to the day he was found guilty. The butcher could not see how Wheeler obtained meat, the two patients in the butcher's shop being quite trustworthy, but an additional lock was put on the shop, one key was kept by the Steward and the other by the store's clerk.[11]

The farm workers' situation had not improved and even long-standing employees were forced to leave. In 1920, one of the carters, W. Coomber, was driving a horse and cart along the road by the piggeries when the horse bolted, frightened by a barrel organ being delivered for the fete. The cart overturned on a bend, but Coomber had already jumped off. The wheel ran over his chest, but he was able to walk to the farmhouse where a medical officer examined him and found he had one or two broken ribs and severe bruising. He was still off sick on full pay in late August. A few months later, the first tractors was ordered, which in time would replace horses. Carters could be paid 5s a week less because, without horses, they were not required to work overtime.[12] In November 1924 he resigned because of inadequate wages, although the sub-committee assured him he was welcome to reapply.[13]

The Nurse's Life

Following the disruptions of war, the Board of Control's view was that, while patients had suffered through constant changes of staff looking after them, 'neither, in our opinion, do the long hours off duty when they (nursing staff) are also bound to be spending money tend to the contentment of the female staff, especially when they are far away from their own homes. The work and wages of nursing staff needed to be carefully considered'.[14] Nurses' physical fitness should be increased, which would directly benefit patients, while they believed that training needed to improve; nothing was gained by lowering educational standards in order to recruit.

As a general rule in mental hospitals, one nurse slept in a room adjoining each dormitory, and other resident nursing staff slept in the main building but, in 1928, the Commissioners wrote that, as mental nursing was an 'arduous and exacting occupation', nurses homes were needed to provide off-duty hours which were 'quiet and uninterrupted'.[15] In 1929, the Commissioners empathised that it was 'idle to expect educated women to sleep in bedrooms of the dreariest description opening directing into the ward'. At Cane Hill, many female nurses had for some years slept in a former ward block, with the needleroom on the top floor.[16]

As well as supervising and working with patients, there were manual duties. In 1924, the London Mental Hospitals Committee instructed that 'the cleaning of the inside of windows is properly a part of the routine work of male and female nurses . . . nurses are not required to clean the outside of windows above ground floor level' in future, this would be undertaken by the fireman or by staff in the engineer's department.[17]

Living conditions meant resident staff had to keep sharp objects, such as razors, scissors, hatpins and medication, locked in a drawer in their room. Nurses' private scissors were only to be used in their own rooms. No patient was to have hatpins or private scissors. Staff could not take food or other items from the mess-room without permission.

Without specific permission from the medical superintendent, resident 'sub-ordinate officers and servants' could not have visitors, nor could resident staff could spend a night out of the hospital without leave. In June 1920, Dr Elgee instructed that, when off duty, staff must leave the building by the main entrance and drive. Any resident staff remaining in the building on a leave day would be charged for meals, whether or not they ate them.[18] Male and female staff were only allowed to 'associate' in the hospital and grounds 'under circumstances permitted by the medical superintendent'. Pre-war regulations were resumed: any female staff intending to marry had to inform the hospital authorities, as the London County Mental Hospitals Department no longer employed married women, except as temporary staff for short periods if vacancies could not be filled.[19]

Caring for Staff

Staff were dismissed if physically unfit to do the work, although sometimes after treatment had been arranged or prolonged sick leave. New staff were rapidly dismissed if found to have physical problems.

Operations were arranged for staff at hospitals in central London. Some, with intermittent sickness, were supported for many years. Dr Elgee arranged for one senior nurse to attend the Royal Bath Hospital in Harrogate for 'immediate treatment' on several occasions. In an age before antibiotics, infection could be serious and life threatening. Nurse Louisa Hibling died of septic pneumonia having scratched her finger on a patient's shoe buckle. Her mother claimed £300 compensation and, eventually, £150 was paid.[20]

When Staff Nurse John Glencross, an attendant for twenty-seven years, died in Croydon's workhouse infirmary in 1920, he was a widower with four sons aged from four to thirteen years of age. The Roman Catholic chaplain at Cane Hill became their guardian, Glencross having entrusted him with his insurance policy, his post office saving book containing £25.4s 1d and two War Certificates of 15s 6d each for his eldest son, and arranged his burial in the hospital cemetery at no cost to the sub-committee. They had lived at 226 Chipstead Valley Road, but the only alternative was a Roman Catholic orphanage. The chaplain applied to Croydon Union, the Guardians suggesting the LCC should contribute to their maintenance. Cane Hill's sub-committee paid Glencross's wages up to his death, and asked the chaplain to remind the Guardians that the 'Council pays a very large contribution by way of rates to the exchequer of their Union'. The four boys were admitted to St. Joseph's Orphanage in Orpington, their father's saving going towards their maintenance.[21]

Ordinary staff had twelve days leave a year, and nursing and indoor staff fourteen days in 1924. In 1931, it increased to twenty-four days for first assistants and nurses, and eighteen days for second assistants and nurses, rising to twenty-four days after twelve years service, while Matron had thirty days leave.

Nurses' dresses changed from pink to blue stripes in 1923, with head female nurses wearing a plain blue in a different shade. Blue overcoats were provided for outdoor wear and, although shawls could still be worn, they would no longer be issued. All nurses had four instead of three aprons, and white linen belts, but black stockings were not provided. Female laundry and domestic staff wore Peter pan collars and spotted muslin mob caps.[22] In 1925, a room was equipped with a gas-ring, sink and ironing board for staff use.

Representatives of grades of 'sub-ordinate staff' together with the kitchen maids, presented a petition in 1928 to be able to wear should wraps in the corridors because of the cold experienced when leaving warm wards. When nurses stopped wearing shawls, the remaining stock was placed in wards for communal use, but nurses disliked this arrangement. As sub-committees remained strictly responsible to the LCC, an application was sent to the General Purposes Sub-Committee for permission to issue woollen coats to laundry and kitchen maids, and were informed by the Acting Chief Officer that, at other hospitals, nurses wore their uniform coats in the hospital during cold weather, only one medical superintendent having objected.[23]

In 1929, female nursing staff could send weekly to the laundry, 1 dress, 1 cap (with strings for Chief Charges), 2 collars, 3 pairs of cuffs, 1 chemise or combinations, 1 drawers, 1 nightdress, 4 aprons, 2 pairs of stockings, 6 handkerchiefs, 1 sheet, 1 pillowcase, 2 towels, 1 slip bodice, 1 petticoat (occasionally), 1 belt, 1 blanket or quilt, curtains or toilet covers. From 1928, if permitted by their medical superintendent, qualified nurses were allowed to wear the brooch issued by the Royal Medico-Psychological Association, provided the design was modified 'so as to allow the point of the pin to be shielded efficiently'.[24]

The branch secretary of the National Asylum Workers' Union, met with the deputy medical superintendent in 1926 regarding complaints by staff about the food. Meat was hard and vegetables dirty and inedible; the amount of bread issued had been reduced as had the cheese issued after lunch while fish was sometimes soft and unpalatable. Dr Pearn responded that meat was bought for the whole hospital, but care was taken in selecting suitable joints for the staff, and admitted to isolated incidents when insects or grubs were left in vegetables. The amount of cheese was reduced from 2 oz to 1 oz because, some time ago, the cost of the food issued for staff dinners exceeded the amount staff paid for the meals, but the mess man could give out more bread.

The sub-committee agreed to increase bread and cheese as soon as the price of food permitted and, if staff wanted more food, there was no objection if they paid the increased cost. The kitchen staff were inexperienced, so that meals were not so good as they had been. The residential staff asked not to have to have their meals in the hospital, but Dr Pearn thought it inadvisable 'having more particularly in my mind the possibility that a great many of the younger nurses on the female side would not have a proper dinner and also that it was inadvisable for them to work from 7.00 a.m. to 2.40 p.m. without a break for meals. Resident staff had their meals during the time they were on duty. If the privilege was given to male staff, it would have to be extended to female nurses'.[25]

A detached nurses home was considered at Cane Hill in 1926, after suggestions from the Commissioners, to release space for patients because of overcrowding.[26] In 1925, ninety-eight staff had accommodation in dormitories and in single rooms intended for patients in E and L wards, while a day room was used as a recreational room for 105 nurses. Fourteen male and twenty-two female patients were suitable for discharge, and the Mental Aftercare Association would be asked to enquire into their home conditions, and to consider taking some recommended by the medical superintendent. If needed, the allowance of 15s a week while on trial leave could be increased.[27]

In 1926, the London Mental Hospitals Committee produced advice on patients' care when on leave, which instructed friends and relatives to be caring and supportive, and stressed the importance of returning to employment:

1 Kindness and a little forbearance by relatives and friends would do much to preventing another mental breakdown. All hurry, worry, annoyance and needless talk would certainly endanger full recovery.

2 No gossiping or joking should be allowed respecting a patient's recent illness.

3 Patients should be encouraged to employ themselves whilst out on trial in order to be quite ready to resume their ordinary work when finally discharged. In many cases patients are able to resume their ordinary work whilst on trial, and this should be encouraged where possible.

4 They should keep regular hours, have plenty of rest and sleep and, as a rule, go to bed early and rise early.

5 They should take plain food at regular times.

6 They should totally avoid intoxicating liquors which could cause a relapse or even permanent treatment in a mental hospital.

7 Care should be taken that the bowels act daily.

8 If there was any physical illness, sleeplessness or restlessness at night or abnormal mental symptoms, the patients should go to a family doctor. If the symptoms were 'urgent', the medical superintendent was to be notified at once, and the patient would be collected and returned to the hospital. On trial, a patient could be brought back to the hospital at any time without any formality and, if necessary, detained for treatment.[28]

In 1928, there were plans for a nurses home for eighty staff.[29] It was early 1935 before it opened, releasing fifty-four rooms on the female side.[30]

Security Measures

The LCC published a greatly enlarged manual of duties in 1927 defining the regulations, and the responsibilities of each grade of staff, including gate keepers whose first duty was to 'exercise a general observation' to prevent patients escaping and communicating improperly with persons outside, and to prevent the removal of hospital property. They kept a book in which all visitors, apart from patients' visitors and those visiting private residences on the estate, entered their names and addresses, and issued passes to patients' visitors.

No nurse, servant or workman could leave the hospital except 'under the normal regulations', without permission from the medical superintendent, or take any parcel, bag, basket, etc. out without it being examined unless the bearer had a pass issued by the house steward, matron or inspector. Gate keepers could search any employee or conveyance entering or leaving but, in the case of a female, had to contact the medical superintendent who would arrange for a 'head female officer' to perform the search. All employees were to ensure ladders, steps or anything that might enable patients to escape, were carefully guarded and removed from the patients' reach as soon as the job was finished.

The back gate keeper saw that vehicles containing items which were on a list provided by the house steward were weighed, the weigh bridge being on the road approaching the stores from the lodge in Portnalls Road, and the weights recorded in a book.[31]

Having served in World War One, Jim Packham worked at Cane Hill from 1919 until 1962, beginning as an attendant, polishing floors and looking after the 'inmates', and rising to the rank of night superintendent. When he began, most wards were locked, and there were only 'attendants and inmates', the latter men wearing red ties and black corduroy, while staff were issued with keys, chains, belts and whistles. Belts and chains were abolished about 1923. The patients' main entertainments were church services, dances and supervised football and cricket matches.[32]

Chapter 18: The Board of Control

With post-war austerity, the Board of Control's Commissioners published their first full report in 1923, observing that Cane Hill continued to be 'well maintained and administered', despite considerably overcrowding with an excess of 104 males and 66 females.

The Commissioners' suggestions regarding wards and dormitories were adopted, and there were now radiators in the general bathrooms. The old medical superintendent's house was now used by medical and clerical staff, with rooms for assistant medical officers, and sleeping accommodation for female nursing staff.

Always concerned about the food, the improved diet appeared 'physiologically adequate', the patients looking healthy and well-nourished. Dinner was fried or boiled fish of good quality and sufficient, potatoes, bread and milk pudding but they regretted that the kitchen's present equipment prevented all having fried fish, which was 'more appetising and attractive than the boiled variety', and 'the fish was practically cold when it arrived in the wards', staff having neglected to fill the containers with hot water.

Whereas all patients had previously worn hospital clothing, their own being returned to the Unions, some female patients wore their own 'out garments', while 'institution dresses' were now of a more modern style and cut.

Twenty men and six females were 'under special treatment for mental reasons', the rest being mainly 'either debilitated, senile, general paralytics or suffering from temporary illness'. Fourteen men and twelve women with tuberculosis were mainly treated on verandas or the isolation hospital. The numbers of nursing staff were:

Staff	Male	Female	Total
Charge	30	41	71
Ordinary	111	128	239
Night	17	23	40

Sixty-five male and fifty-three female staff had the nursing certificate of the Medico-Psychological Association, while forty men and thirty-nine women had passed the preliminary exam.[1] Much had changed since the early years of the century and, in 1927, nursing staff were directed that no assistants, who were unqualified, were to be left in charge of wards at any time, as patients needed the direct care and observation of trained mental nurses. The following year, one third of night nursing staff 'shall consist of staff nurses of long experience, tried loyalty and irreproachable character', who could be appointed as acting night charge nurses for a term of three years which might be extended.[2]

In October 1924, the Commissioners were more satisfied, the patients 'being well cared for'. Food was very good and well-served, clothing had improved with some patients wearing garments supplied by relatives, and hospital clothing in varied colours with care and attention paid to the style and trimming of dresses. Wards were suitably supplied with 'objects of interest' including caged birds. Overcrowding had reduced, with 56 extra males and 53 extra females, 229 being discharged the previous year, of which 122 had recovered. Seven were on leave, 118 having, in the previous year, had trial leave prior to discharge.

Three verandahs were to be built. The mortuary was being improved in a 'reverential character', to enable relatives to view the bodies of deceased patients, but sanitary areas needed modernisation, including shelves and a better means of keeping toothbrushes.[3] Research at Birmingham University had suggested a link between focal sepsis and insanity, leading some to believe that bacterial poisoning caused by rotting teeth could lead to mental illness.[4]

Visiting in July 1925, buildings were well maintained, with plans to replace out-of-date toilets. An electricity cable had been laid in the grounds, initially to supply the laundry, kitchen, bakehouse and treatment area, and later to light all the buildings. All but one ward were well supplied with plants and flowers but, in one or two female bathrooms, it 'would materially add to the comfort of the patients if the baths were separated by wooden partitions or even curtains', while the Commissioners hoped the sub-committee would not entirely abandon the idea of a cinema in the recreation hall. Overcrowding continued in some small dormitories. Twenty-seven patients with tuberculosis were treated in the Cottage Hospital, while enteric fever suspects had been segregated.

Regular winter entertainments with refreshments recommenced after the war, and the fete in the summer. In 1923, there was the first mention of an outing, probably by the most able patients. In September and October 1924, two group of male patients, and two groups of females, each about 15 in number, went to the British Empire Exhibition while, in December, the sub-committee accepted the proprietor of the local cinema's invitation to provide an entertainment for a limited number of patients.[5] Char-a-banc outings began in the summer in the late 1920s, men and women going on separate outings, men being given tobacco when they went.[6] In January 1929, Colney Hatch Mental Hospital's staff concert party presented an entertainment for patients.[7]

Patients generally presented 'a happy and contented appearance', with staff and patients playing cricket while, twice a week, all fit patients went to the cricket ground where the band, with about twenty-four musicians, performed for about two hours. Patients were generally tidy and 'nicely dressed', a few wearing their own clothes which the commissioners hoped would increase, and that facilities would be provided in the laundry to patients wanting to wear their own underclothes.[8] Dr Elgee thought it impractical because of problems in distributing them on their return from the laundry.

Patients were not always content. Occasional complaints were voiced to senior staff about ill treatment by nurses, but the Commissioners would report that there were no complaints, although patients would request their discharge. A 'patient revolt' occured in 1925, male epileptic patients being 'very much upset' by a shortage of vegetables at lunchtime. Given cheese instead, patients who usually worked in the grounds refused to work that afternoon and, as tobacco given to working patients was issued by the nurse in charge of the ward at the gate when the patients went out to work, they received none that day.

The next day, they again refused to go out to work and some became excited. About 10.15 a.m., seventeen panes of glass were broken in windows on the ward, three lampshades, glass on two pictures and three chairs in the dayroom. Four patients were involved, three being moved to other wards and kept in bed for two to three days.[9]

At the Commissioners' visit in November 1926, one male patient had dysentery, one female had enteric fever, probably typhoid fever, and 27 patients with tuberculosis were mainly treated in the cottage hospital or the male and female infirmaries. Two male and one female sick patient were treated on verandahs, with the approval of the Commissioners: 'provided sufficient clothing and hot bottles are supplied, verandahs should be in continual use day and night to the great benefit of patients'. There was considerable overcrowding, particularly on female wards H and K, but it was hoped that, when alterations were completed at another LCC hospital, patients could be moved there.

As ever, each year no mechanical use was recorded but, in 1926, 4 males and 27 females had short periods of seclusion, while there were two suicides.[10] More were secluded, as nursing staff had understood the traditional interpretation that it was only recorded during the daytime, but the authorities expected seclusion at any time to be recorded. Patients were kept in single and padded rooms when disturbed.

In 1924, three female staff were accused of hitting patients. As usual, allegations were investigated, and staff and patients questioned. It was reported that E.E., a female patient, was extremely violent at times and Dr Elgee ordered that no staff be alone with her. She was kept in a single room with the window partially shuttered to prevent her damaging the window: 'it was necessary in her violent moments that some amount of force should be used to control her'. The chairman and two members of the sub-committee visited the ward and talked with her, and decided the allegations were unfounded. Another patient involved told them that 'nurses were very kind and forbearing'.[11]

Renovations continued: the kitchen had been painted and its ventilation improved, the modernisation of toilets had begun and admission wards had new sanitary annexes. They praised the new cinematograph in the recreation hall, connected to the mains electricity, although films had not yet been shown to the patients. There were curtains between baths in the female general bathroom and in female wards A and B.

With three new washing machines installed, it was perhaps female members of the sub-committee who instructed in 1926 that, as women's boots went to be condemned, they should be replaced by shoes. As for stockings, the Chief Officer of Stores at the LCC suggested that the Mental Health Committee should approve whatever shade of stocking the sub-committee might select, so that the shade would be available for all hospitals, as the quantity ordered by one hospital would be too small to make up a dyeing order. The sub-committee decided that the female patients' dress be modernised, suggesting its female members should look into the matter and make suggestions. Samples of women's clothing were shown to the lady members for their approval, the sub-committee deciding to seek the approval of the Mental Health Committee for 'experiments to be made in the use of non-standard garments for certain approved types of female patients'.[12] Gradually, some female patients would be able to express some individuality.

The Commissioners recommended steam presses for the men's clothing, which had to be washed.[13] In 1925, the London County Mental Hospitals allowed the employment of male patients in officer's houses and gardens.[14] It is not known how long patients had carried money but a shop was opened in 1924 to sell tobacco and cigarettes to male patients.[15] Later, sweets were introduced, with plans to introduce a greater variety of goods in the near future.[16]

More treatment, more infection

The Board of Control was more pro-active than its predecessor in its demands for treatment, having seen the Royal Commission on Lunacy and Mental Disorder set up in 1924 whose report was published two years later. The Board and the Royal Commission agreed 'insanity in all its stages should be divorced from the Poor Law' which led to many patients being dealt with in Poor Law Institutions for long periods before reaching mental hospitals, it seeming 'indefensible to pauperise individuals merely because they became mentally ill'. There was no evidence of mental illness increasing but further accommodation, particularly admission hospitals, and laboratories were necessary because of the increased population.[17]

The Commissioners no longer recorded patients' activities in the same detail but, in 1924, noted with approval that patient labour was used in building works, while 145 now had parole within the estate and 5 full parole beyond.[18] From 1925 onwards, their reports show only male patients had parole, until 1928 when 9 men had full parole while 117 males and 10 females had parole within the estate.

In 1927, two male and four female wards were described as limited open-door wards, the Garden House for female patients, and Portnalls House for males, having full open doors. In 1928 and 1929, two wards and a villa had open doors. In five female 'turbulent wards' and two infirmaries, there was considerable overcrowding, but vacancies in one ward for 'better class and quiet patients', resulting in three male vacancies, an excess of nine female patients, and a shortage of twenty-five female nurses.

The Commissioners regretted that, particularly on the female side, few patients were allowed to undress by their beds at night, little risk having been found elsewhere. New male admissions were mixing in the overcrowded male airing courts, which were overcrowded, but it should improve with an additional verandah. They encouraged greater use of the verandahs, by day and night, 'though the patients may at first be inclined to dislike this form of treatment'. There was not yet x-ray and 'light treatment rooms', which would be 'valuable additions to medical treatment', but there were wirelesses at Portnalls, and at the Cottage Hospital where one female patient was isolated as a possible enteric fever carrier.[19]

The sub-committee had listened for the Commissioners reported in 1928 that a steam clothes press and new dough mixer were being considered, electricity was installed in the recreation hall and powered violet ray apparatus. Verandahs had home-made roller blinds instead of coloured paint or distemper. Many patients were allowed to undress by their beds.

It was 'very nice to see so many birds in the wards, of all ages, besides birds actually sitting'! Patients were clean and very contented but more books were needed in every ward, particularly picture books for patients to turn the pages, having noted staff had told them that 'the patients in this ward don't do much reading'. Portnalls could be improved and made more homely with pictures, having only one oil painting while, in some wards, all the toothbrushes were in one glass.

The women's gardens were well kept in marked contrast with the men's B, C and D male block garden which was worn and dusty and looked overcrowded, turf having been lost during the war. One ward and garden, intended for men, was used for females.

Facilities gradually improved, electricity being slowly installed, but the Commissioners consistently regretted the limited take-up of new treatments, with limited use of continuous baths, perhaps because of difficulties in recruiting medical officers, one to two houses being needed for married medical officers, but they applauded the introduction of occupational therapy and the appointment of an 'occupation officer'.[20]

Medical officers at Cane Hill appear to have performed limited surgery but, in the early 1920s, a contract was drawn up for six physicians and surgeons at the Middlesex Hospital to attend patients at Cane Hill. Using the operating theatre, several female patients had mastectomies. In a typical session in 1926, Mr Tanner performed two operations: an appendix was removed and another patient had a left iliac colostomy.[21] Throughout the 1920s, Dr Elgee and the sub-committee agreed to requests from families to transfer patients to other London asylums nearer to them. In 1922, when a male patient asked to do brush making and the equipment was at Long Grove Hospital, he was transferred there.[22] Patients still escaped from time to time but, now, staff were generally not blamed.

The Board's campaign

The Commissioners expressed their frustration in 1928 that some hospital committees were 'still too conservative in adopting new methods or installing new appliances until their utility has been demonstrated beyond any reasonable doubt'. They believed this 'ultra-cautious policy' a mistake; results 'may be disappointing but, psychologically, it is worth much to inspire the patient and his relatives that everything possible is being done to ensure his recovery'.

They believed the public and relatives 'would never regard mental hospitals as hospitals in the true sense until they are satisfied that vigorous effort directed to the individual patient is being made to effect a cure . . . it is of the upmost importance to convince the patient that everything possible is being done for him, and it is difficult to over-estimate the importance of inspiring the hope which is so important an element in recovery'. They recommended out-patient treatment centres as

> too often patients discharged from mental hospitals broke down because of the transition from the ordered and sheltered life of the hospital to the stress and competition of the work-a-day world is too sudden and too severe for the convalescent. The difficulty is aggravated by the tendency to regard the discharged patient with a certain suspicion.[23]

In December 1929, there were plans for an anaesthetic room, a massage and electrical treatment room and a dental room, all close to the operating theatre. Nurses were trained by an assistant matron who acted as sister tutor and by medical officers; in 1930, Dr Napier Pearn, the deputy medical superintendent, published *Mental Nursing Simplified*.

Statistics were important: the recovery rate at Cane Hill in 1929 was 23.3 per cent, compared with the highest rate of 32.9 per cent at Claybury, and the lowest rate of 21.8 per cent at Long Grove.[24] With 870 male and 1,250 female patients, a total of 2,120, the hospital was 'practically full' after years of overcrowding, with eighty more beds once the nurses home was built, but vacancies for seventeen female nurses. Cane Hill was 'well maintained and able administered by Dr Elgee.

Twenty-nine patients had active tuberculosis, with a small outbreak of dysentery, brought in by a patient from a poor law institution, which had been stamped out by 'energetic treatment and segregation'. For many years, great care was taken to control enteric fever, having identified eighteen known carriers now segregated from other patients but, in the Spring, 148 patients and 23 staff had influenza.[25] Outbreaks of typhoid continued: in 1929, two probationer nurses contracted the infection while working on the typhoid ward, probably where known carriers lived.[26]

Lt. Col. Elgee

As medical superintendent, he promoted the hospital's modernisation, following difficulties in funding following the war, and introduced new treatments, which the Commissioners often saw as delayed or not used to their full potential.

In the early years, he was often absent when the commissioners visited. In November 1926, his health was greatly improved but he was still unfit for work and was going away for three months sick leave. Dr Pearn had been in charge for the previous nine months, with nine permanent medical officers, one now recently seconded to the Maudsley Hospital, and two locum tenens.[27] It may have been Dr Pearn who suggested developments in his absence.

In June 1931, Dr Elgee retired because of ill health, to the regret of the commissioners, to be succeeded by Dr George Austen Lilly, deputy medical superintendent at Banstead Hospital for over five years who previously worked at Cane Hill, Hanwell, Bexley and Chartham Hospitals.

Chapter 19: The estate

In December 1924, the LCC's inspectors reported on the farm, 146 acres in size including 34 acres of permanent pasture and 75 acres of market garden crops. Lying on thin chalk soil, they thought it unsuitable milk and vegetables, and difficult to farm because of poor soil and hilly land. To meet demand, and with a small acreage of pasture, there was successive cropping, with dry cows and young stock grazed elsewhere. All concentrated feed and hay was bought, and the arable land only supplemented grassland and provided roots and cabbage for the winter. Fertility was mainly maintained by heavy dressings of farm manure. Mr Fish, the farm bailiff disagreed: the vegetable forage and root crops, including mangolds, produced 900 to 1,000 tons annually.

They thought it uneconomical to pay for grazing locally, but Mr Fish replied that the cattle did exceptionally well and conditions were exceptionally good. When they commented that the herd of black and white Holsteins yield was low, and the herd could be improved, Mr Fish thought the milk yield satisfactory. He had been offered £500 for seventeen cattle, and used pedigree bulls for breeding. Pigs were kept outdoors, using woodland, one hundred fat pigs having been sold after their visit, while there were over 2,000 poultry.

The inspectors were impressed by the efficient patient labour but thought Mr Fish more of a stockman who did not make sufficient allowance for the production of fruit and vegetables for the hospital and 'the employment of patients from the therapeutic point of view'. They recommended reducing the marker garden to forty acres as the existing size required an enormous amount of labour. The sub-committee supported Mr Fish but the inspectors' report proposed that mental hospital farms would, in future, be under a special farm sub-committee which, when in action, meant the farm bailiff would report to that sub-committee in future, although the hospital's subcommittee remained responsible for negotiating with local farmers.

In 1925, Mr Fish had 25 staff whereas he had 27 in 1912, with 66 cattle in 1912 and 124 now, as well as additional pigs and poultry. The London County Mental Hospitals decided not to provide knee boots to farm labourers when cutting vegetables, while the sub-committee informed the newly formed Special (Farming Operations) Sub-committee that local arrangements at Cane Hill to graze cattle were the best that could be made 'under the circumstances'.

Mr A.E. Cresswell, already renting grazing land to Cane Hill, offered to sell Selsdon Park Farm in Selsdon, a 376 acre farm with a farmhouse, buildings and seven cottages to the LCC at £7 an acre.[1] The sub-committee, very keen to purchase, contacted the Valuer but, following his report, decided not to purchase. It continued renting land from Mr Moule at Tollers Farm, Mr Cresswell, and Lord Marshall in Chipstead.[2]

Between the wars, farming slumped and owners looked to sell. Six acres of grazing land was rented at Southern Farm in Chipstead from Mr C.H. Cearn of Bradmore Lodge, Coulsdon who, in 1928, offered to lease or sell 165 acres of grassland with buildings at Southern Farm or at Gatwick Farm in Chipstead. They rented the 165 acres, Mr Fish receiving a special financial allowance for the extra work involved. Grazing land was still rented from Mr Cresswell.

In late 1930, grazing was renewed at Southern farm, but the sub-committee refused an offer to lease or buy Court Lodge Estate in Chipstead. They congratulated Mr. Fish on excellent results, despite the Special (Farm-Operations) Sub-Committee's report of low yielding cows in the herd. They recommended the head cowman Albert Kent have staff accommodation when a senior nurse retired and, in May 1931, he moved into East Lodge, with James Arthur Mead as the new non-resident gate keeper.[3]

Other developments

Early on, Dr Elgee encouraged the sub-committee to reorganise accommodation in the asylum. An early proposal was that his deputy, Dr Oscar Pearn and his family live in Postern House in Portnalls Road, near to the main building, then occupied by fourteen female patients. The house, with five bedrooms, was smaller than others and in a 'comparatively inferior position with rooms much darkened by overhanging trees'. Work was advanced to accommodate ninety nurses living in cubicles, with single bedrooms vacated by nurses now available for patients.[4]

Patients and staff would live in Glencairn, where the former chaplain lived, but in 1922, the Board of Control agreed to Dr Elgee and his family moving there.[5] The former medical superintendent's house, in the front of the main building, was converted into rooms for the medical officers and clerk on the ground floor, matron's quarters on the first floor and, on the second floor, bedrooms for domestic and nursing staff.[6]

There was a shortage of suitable houses for thirty-five staff to rent locally, including thirty-one who lived some distance away. Others rented rooms locally. When the couple at the farm house retired, its patients returned to the main building and the farm bailiff moved in. Coulsdon and Purley Urban District Council (C&PUDC) requested two to three attendants be housed in Portnalls, who were 'now residing in cottages in the neighbourhood so that such cottages could be placed at the disposal of people now living in gravely overcrowded conditions'. The sub-committee had no money to adapt the still empty Portnalls and was trying to evict two former employees from asylum cottages through the Courts.

The London County Mental Hospitals (LCMH) permitted female staff to live out locally from 1922 but, at Cane Hill, such accommodation was non-existent. Although female wards E and L were used for staff accommodation and E could not be restored as a ward since the dayroom was used as the nurses' mess room, the suggestion would release little accommodation, while there was no bus or train service to enable staff to be on duty at 7.00 a.m., but they could begin with workroom and laundry staff. On the estate, staff houses were at East Lodge, Back Gate Lodge, 1-28 Dunstans Cottages, the three Stoney Cottages, Well House and Postern Villa.[7]

Overcrowding continued and, in 1923, twenty-six of Cane Hill's patients moved from Brookwood to Worcester Asylum. Another thirty-one returned temporarily to Cane Hill from Brookwood, being 'not fit enough' at present, but twenty-four of them would go to Worcester when improved.[8] In 1926, female patients were transferred to Storthes Hall Hospital, near Huddersfield, by rail.[9] The Valuer reported that land north of the cemetery had been sold for building, but another fifty-two acres adjoining the cemetery was coming up for sale at about £200 an acre, but the sub-committee decided not to pursue it. It could only be used for farming, as the road could not longer be diverted.

By 1923, several former staff or their widows refused to leave their homes on the hospital estate and, with new legislation, the Rental Restriction Act of 1923, the solicitor thought they could not be evicted unless they had alternate accommodation. Mrs Russell claimed she was practically promised a tenancy in one of the first eighty houses to be built by C&PUDC, but they had not yet started building, while A.G. Paver, a former nurse, who had applied to C&PUDC and visited many agents in Norbury, Thornton Heath, Croydon and Purley, reported plenty of houses for sale but none to rent. When the C&PUDC informed Mrs Russell they could not offer accommodation to her and her two children, the Clerk at Cane Hill enquired locally to find rooms. Even when his deputy found a house with two bedrooms in Coulsdon, the solicitor doubted they could be evicted because of the children.[10]

In 1925, the Clerk of the C&PUDC wrote to the sub-committee: its housing committee was building accommodation, but a considerable number of applicants were hospital employees. The housing committee, thinking it unreasonable that the local authority should house so many staff, asked the LCC to consider providing more accommodation.[11]

In November 1923, heavy rain soaked through the walls of male F Block, damaging wallpaper on the first and second floors. The walls were treated with oil to keep the damp out, while plans began to tile the outer walls of male F and H wards in 1924-5, the corresponding walls on the female side having been successfully tiled in 1914. The sub-committee hoped to modernise bathrooms and water closets in seven female wards and the nurses' block.[12] They were only able to replace waste pipes although, on F ward, they replaced the original water closets, namely eight cast-iron pans 'the flush being operated by the seat' when the user stood up, by modern cisterns and glazed stoneware lavatory pans.[13]

A Dutch barn would be built on the farm, the kitchen and laundry modernised, and verandahs improved on two female wards and both wards at the isolation hospital. Cinematograph apparatus, costing £650, would be installed in a shed behind the stage or at the other end of the hall, and additional radiators in some female wards, but would later be delayed until electricity was installed in the wards.[14] Linoleum on male F2 ward, which was thirty-two years old, would be replaced at a cost of £85, but portions were to be used in other wards which had the same pattern.

Economies continued: 23 cwt of old account books and forms were sold for pulping. Patients were employed in officers' residences, but the medical superintendent's request to warm wards from 20 October rather than 1 November was allowed in 1925.

On the wards, a new spur of single rooms, including a padded room, would be built off the female admission ward, in connection with the LCMH's improved classification of patients. Discussions began with the C&PUDC's surveyor to connect the hospital building with the main sewer, the staff cottages, farm buildings and other properties on the estate having been connected.

In 1925, H.M. Office of Works applied to purchase a plot of ground at the junction of Hollyme Oak Road and Brighton Road to build a telephone exchange, a proposal welcomed by the sub-committee.[15]

The nurses' home

In 1929, the Board of Control commented on the new nurses home intended for 85 female nurses, with a possible extension to take 105 people, the selected site being good but remote from the female side of the hospital. There was already a home for 54 nurses on the north-west side of the main building, and they thought it should be built nearby. They wanted a dining and a recreation room in the new block, with easy access from the female side and the kitchen if it did not have its own kitchen. Regarding the existing nurses home, they suggested the needleroom on the top floor be moved and the area used for nurses' bedrooms, but the acting chief officer had already planned to convert it to a nurses' dormitory.

Later that year, the architect presented plans for the new nurses home at the north-east of the estate, with a dining room and recreation room for all ordinary female nursing staff, which would free space for 76 additional female patients. Lockers with keys were provided for all the present staff bedrooms; 40 on the male side and 165 on the female side. Electric lighting would be installed in the kitchen, but not in the dark room for the consulting opthalmic surgeon or the male staffs' billiard room.[16]

The grounds

Overhanging trees on the edge of the estate were pruned in 1920 after the London Omnibus Company complained that they were liable to injure passengers riding on the outside of their omnibuses.[17] A few months earlier, the Acting Chief Officer of the LCC's Parks Department reported that the hedge of Portugal Laurel on the main drive was badly affected with silver leaf and would eventually need to be removed. The main feature was a double row of cupressus trees: it would be desirable to sacrifice all the other trees to maintain this feature, the only exception being a row of limes.

Thujas planted between the cupressus were fine trees but should be removed. Behind the cupressus was a second line of mainly deciduous trees needing pruning, and some to be removed.[18] In June 1932, the medical superintendent was asked to remove all yew trees because of poisoning at another hospital.[19]

With the end of horse driven traffic, the gravel strip along the middle of the drive was removed in 1925, and it was arranged for the C&PUDC to tarmac it.[20] When local residents complained about 'unpleasant odours' from the hospital's sewerage farm, followed by a letter from the C&PUDC's medical officer of health, the sub-committee decided to ignore it.[21] Arrangements were made in 1931 for the local council to collect refuse daily from the Cane Hill, the hospital having always dealt with it on site, but negotiations broke down when the C&PUDC asked the LCC to contribute £331.10s a year, the sub-committee responding that it was the local largest ratepayer.

With many out of work in the country, that summer the LCMH asked if 'any works of public utility necessary at the hospital could be accelerated to relieve unemployment in the coming winter of 1931-2'. The engineer was consulted, but no projects could be identified. Even the plans which the sub-committee had would be affected by the country's economic problems.[22]

Chapter 20: From gas to electric

Dr Elgee retired in June 1931, the sub-committee thanking him for 'the zealous and efficient way' in which he 'always discharged his duties. Dr Lilly attended the sub-committee's meeting in July and immediately set out his first initiatives for the hospital.

He wanted to associate himself with psychiatric out-patients clinics at the LCC's general hospitals, which the sub-committee agreed to if his services were desired, and that the women's occupation officer's appointment be made permanent which they considered and, in October, Miss Kathleen Raistrick was appointed.

They agreed to use £8 to fund and develop the patient's shop, which could be later recovered from the Tea Fund. Finally, Dr Lilly wanted to continue the programme to light the hospital with electricity. Suggesting a store room become the staff lecture room, the electric cable could not carry a further load, and it would have to be lit by gas. He proposed an separate admission unit, and to accelerate the modernisation of sanitary annexes, particularly on female wards. In the meantime, those on three male wards would be modernised.

There were other necessary expenses: ovens in the kitchen needed to be replaced by a two-deck drawplate oven costing £1,000 while local residents complained of the sight of the new Downland Telephone Exchange being built on the edge of the estate. Lombardy poplars, fifteen feet high and ten feet apart would be planted and maintained by the Postmaster General. A few months later, it was agreed to lease land at the corner of Chipstead Valley Road and Lion Green to H.M. Office of Works to build a post office.

With the tender was due to go out to build the long intended 84 bed nurses home, Dr Lilly objected to its site because of its distance from the female wards. When he proposed the female nursing staff's dining room, intended for the new nurses home, be in the main building near to the kitchen, the sub-committee decided to informally seek the Board of Control's opinion.

In September 1931, the LCMH's General Purposes Sub-committee passed a resolution that, in view of the severe economic crisis in the country, the Council approved the action of chairmen and other authorised members during the current situation in suspending proposed expenditure. All committees were instructed to secure all possible reductions 'consistent with the maintenance of the efficiency of the . . . several services, in both capital and maintenance provision for the year 1931-2'.

Cane Hill's sub-committee resolved to continue with planned cleaning and decorating, but to postpone the nurses home and ask the architect to modify the plans. Two weeks later, they decided it was essential but to reduce the bedrooms from 100 square feet to 84 square feet, and site the dining room next to the general bathroom on the female side of the main building. With the number of bathrooms reduced, and washbasins in bedrooms, it would cost £24,671, a saving of £455. Sick nurses were nursed in side rooms in the infirmary, but the sub-committee accepted Dr Lilly's suggestion that they use Matron's quarters while she moved to rooms in the front block, known as the Central House, occupied by nurses. Firegrates in dayrooms where fires were still lit, would be modernised to economise the consumption of coal.

In September 1931, Mr Sherwell offered to transfer his lease on Leyfields Farm, adjacent to the hospital estate, to the LCC, which the sub-committee thought could be substituted for the land at Southerns Farm three and a half miles from the hospital. The Valuer reported that it could be rented for 18s an acre for five years, with only patients working there whom the medical superintendent considered 'quiet and inoffensive'. The LCC would undertake to prevent any nuisance or annoyance caused by the patients as it should save £1,200, £600 compensation being paid to the outgoing tenant. In the end, it was decided not to lease Leyfields Farm because of the outgoing tenant's terms, and grazing continued at Southerns and Tollers Farms.[1] In 1933, milking machines were not installed as it was a breeding herd, and might affect 'breeding capabilities'. New cattle were still purchased from Norfolk and Suffolk.[2]

The Special (Farming Operation) Sub-Committee (SFOS) commented on the comparatively high labour costs incurred in keeping poultry. Ten cockerels were bought for breeding while 160 surplus fowls provided meals for working and infirm patients instead of the usual meat. One hundred gooseberry bushes and twelve apple trees were purchased, and 30,000 replacement cabbage plants after slug damage. Earlier, in 1930, 11 cwt of cauliflowers were sold to Tooting Bec Mental Hospital and 2½ cwt to Fountains Hospital.

In January 1933, it was decided to lease 284 acres comprising Southerns Farm with 163 acres, Noke and Shabden Farms for six years at £25 a year, and 40 acres at Reeves Farm on a yearly tenancy, all from Lord Marshall of Chipstead, and about 85 acres adjoining Noke and Shabden Farms from Mr Bowering for six years at £85, and no longer rent at Tollers Farm.[3] A 30 cwt second hand motor lorry was purchased to replace the horse and cart for transporting milk and farm produce, and to collect waste food from Tooting Bec Hospital for pigs, which had meant three journeys a week with a horse and cart. A second lorry was purchased in 1934. Potatoes and vegetables were sold to Tooting Bec. Swine fever struck in 1934, with some pigs slaughtered and the remaining 120 kept at Noke Farm until they were sold, and more purchased.[4] Nursing staff were informed that 'hog wash from the wards was not being kept sufficiently free from harmful elements for the pigs, tea leaves, ashes and dressings having been found in the food.' They were instructed to keep waste food free of other ward waste.[5]

In March 1935, there was foot and mouth on the hospital farm, starting with the pigs. The fine herd of 84 Fresians and up to 300 pigs were slaughtered, with £2,834.5s 10d paid in compensation by the Ministry of Health. Now, all milk was supplied by contract.[6]

In 1935, the sub-committee agreed to negotiate to lease land fronting Lion Green Road to C&PUDC as a site for a public library.[7] Local facilities were being built close to the estate, to the benefit of its staff and local residents.

The new nurses home

In June 1932, Dr Lilly suggested building the nurses home 'at the top of the drive below and to the south of the administrative centre', which was provisionally accepted, remodelling it on one at Horton Hospital. With a steep slope on his suggested site, it required an additional £1,000 and it was decided to revert to the original site east of the administrative centre, between the main building and the isolation ward. His suggestion was accepted for a proposed 30 bed female ward when the present dining rooms were released.[8] The Council had approved £29,050 for the new nurses home but, in January 1934, the cost was reduced to £13,898.

Several staff were permitted to install a 'wireless receiving apparatus' in their rooms and, in 1933, an 'all-mains receiving set with a gramophone pick-up' was purchased and, at a later date, extension leads to the wards. An eight-roller calendar, costing £1,700, was purchased for the laundry. Cupboards were bought for occupational therapy in sixteen wards, an order repeated for other wards, and three hard tennis courts laid down for staff.

In 1936, other improvements included water flushing urinals in airing courts, a power-driven sausage machine and a chapel for Roman Catholic patients. The majority of cottage tenants voted to have electricity in their cottages, although it meant an increase in rents. Electricity would be installed to the whole hospital in stages, beginning in 1936-7, the first part costing £4,000. The refrigerator was replaced in the main kitchen, small refrigerators were purchased for each of the ten villas and a chlorinating plant installed. Radiators would be installed in 54 rooms in the old nurses home, as the heating was inadequate. £256,920 was approved for additional accommodation for 500 additional female patients at Portnalls.[9] In early 1937, it was decided not to go ahead with the scheme.

That year, they agreed to lease land on Lion Green Road to the C&PUDC as a car park. It meant losing two allotments belonging to the cottages, but the SFOS identified alternative plots close to the cottages.[10]

Football

Dr Lilly pursued another campaign in December 1936, complaining that the football field had little grass and was extremely muddy after recent heavy rain. The SFOS would be asked if part of Long Meadow, grazing land, could be used. The following February, with the field still very muddy and unfit to use because of continuing heavy rain and increased use by patients, he asked about a plot on the northeast side close to the potato shed and the male side.

The SFOS replied that about two acres would be seriously detrimental to farming operations, and would restrict opportunities available for patients to work on the land. They suggested extending the cricket field into adjoining pasture.

Dr Lilly and the sub-committee still felt their suggested field more convenient but, as an alternative, suggested a site between Portnalls Villa, Portnalls Stables, used as a garage, and the public road. The Superintending Bailiff for the Portnalls estate agreed and offered to spend £1,000 removing a belt of conifers improving the badly drained field, which would take about two years' work.

In response, Dr Lilly objected to the suggested field and to two others on the south-west side, being too distant from the male side to permit 'a considerable number of crippled and infirm patients watching football'. The field he had earlier suggested on the north-east side was the best, and the SFOS would be asked again about this site.

In May, the SFOS agreed to his suggestion, and to use part of the kitchen garden, provided telephone lines were moved and the field fenced, but the sub-committee decided not to hand over the present field to the SFOS for farming. The SFOS stated in July that the new football field would be sufficient and the hospital should not retain the old one, but the sub-committee responded that if the SFOS only used it for grazing, it could be used for football probably no more than once in three to four years when the new field was unfit for play.

Dr Lilly changed his mind again in January 1937, and now suggested the previously proposed land close to Portnalls Villa and Portnalls Stables. An estimate was received that it would cost £27.10s to remove the conifers.

At least two staff were dissatisfied with their homes. In 1938, Mr F. Arkle, the engineer complained of 'disagreeable sights and sounds arising from using Postern Wood and an adjoining field close to his house for pig breeding'. The SFOS agreed to convert the corner of the field next to his house into a shrubbery. At the same time, the hospital fireman asked to live out of the hospital because his house was near to a coal dump, a urinal and the mortuary, and was a 'serious menace' to his wife's health. The sub-committee agreed to improve the conditions or find alternative accommodation.

Upgrading

In 1937, funding was agreed for major upgrading. £3,150 was granted in addition to £17,000 already authorised in 1935-6, 1936-7 and 1937-8 to complete installing electric lighting, renew fire alarms, telephones, and other smaller works, and to provide electric lighting in 28 staff cottages in Chipstead Valley Road. Another £500 was needed to electrify Portnalls, the Cottage Hospital, farm buildings and piggeries.

In April 1938, there was no provision to install electricity in staff cottages, and the County of London Electric Supply Company agreed to install electric lighting and two points in 28 cottages at a cost of £425. Gas fittings would be removed and the cottages 'made good' at a cost of £55. The tenants agreed, although it meant a rent increase of 7d a week.

Furnishings in the wards were improved with cushions for settees in the day rooms while forty large dining tables were converted to make eighty smaller ones. Forms would be replaced by 145 dining chairs.

Many staff appointed before World War One now reached retirement, including Charge Nurse Richard James Yandle. Most early nursing staff were born far away, but settled in Coulsdon, and their children now worked at Cane Hill. In 1936, the first two of the female chief charge nurses were appointed as 'sisters' including Miss Dowling. Dr F. Morres, an important member of the cricket team, retired as first assistant medical officer in 1937, Dr Alexander Walk, being appointed to his position. Dr Walk left in 1938 to be deputy medical superintendant at Horton Hospital, but would return as medical superintendent. Dr Pearn remained as deputy medical superintendent.

There were other new and different faces. In 1934, Dr Sudhindranath Banerji having previously worked at Cane Hill, did six months as an unpaid clinical assistant.[11] Dr Pauline Stirling, the first female doctor at Cane Hill, was appointed and promoted soon after as second medical officer in October 1938. A year later, she was joined by Dr Winifred Porter.[12]

The first intimation of war came in 1937 when the Board of Control reported they were getting enquiries about air raid precautions, as hospitals might be mistaken for military establishments.[13] The sub-committee's minutes in October 1938 report that Mr. Hampshire, an assistant clerk, was unable to take all his leave because he was an anti-gas instructor.[14]

From May 1939, the sub-committee met four weekly instead of every two weeks, 'to enable officers to be devoted to the preparation of measures of civil defence'.[15]

Chapter 21: Freedom for some

Resident staff had more freedom. In July 1931, two female probationer nurses complained of being assaulted as they walked up the hospital drive at 12.30 a.m. The police were informed and the Chief engineer was asked to report on the practicability and cost of making the hospital grounds inaccessible to unauthorised members of the public.

There were a number of entrances to the hospital estate. A nurse was placed on duty at each of two gates on the hospital boundary from 8.00 p.m. to 10.00 p.m. to prevent unauthorised people entering. It was proposed to close the gate to Coulsdon South Station at 8.00 p.m. and to keep a nurse on duty at the main gate. Gates 4, 5 and 7 would have locks, gates 3 and 8 would be replaced by unclimbable gates and gates 6, 9 and 11 kept locked. Gate 10 would be locked at 10.00 p.m., gate 8 locked when not in use and gate 12 locked at night.

In October Ethel B., a female patient was found to be pregnant. She was interviewed by the hospital's solicitor, as were the two workmen whom she accused. They denied it and, as the patient was vague about dates, with no corroboration of her story, it was thought no jury would convict. Both men were transferred to other institutions, preferably for male patients only, while Dr Elgee was instructed to tighten up arrangements for supervising patients so that, as far as was possible, it would not happening.

The following month, Mrs A. Peer of Coniston Road wrote twice complaining that her dog was shot by someone on the hospital estate, and wanting reimbursement for veterinary treatment. The farm bailiff reported that no one used a gun that day, but eight pure bred pullets were killed by a stray dog on a previous occasion. Because of the danger to livestock, the sub-committee asked the solicitor for advice about warning notices. They considered a gate at the entrance to the deputy medical superintendent's house while the chief engineer, at Postern Villa, complained of having to keep opening his gate for visitors to his house.

Staff still stayed out late. In February 1932, a temporary maid was found 'in a state of collapse' at 12.35 a.m. on the drive, by two male nurses. She alleged that she was struck by a strange man, but had no bruises or injury and no strangers were seen by other staff walking up the drive at the same time. However, it was decided to again place a gate porter at the main entrance, East Lodge, from 6.00 p.m. to 12.30 a.m., and to charge the tenant a suitable rent to make up for the necessary accommodation. James Arthur Mead was employed as a non-resident gate keeper from June, at 12s a week.[1]

In 1932, staff asking for late leave or a pass for a night out, were instructed to ascertain that it had been granted. Staff returning late after leave and claiming the train was late, or that they missed it, 'must bring with them a note from the Station Master or other official confirming statement'.[2]

A lack of freedom

While the life of resident staff became less restricted, in the 1920s there was a steady decrease in the number of patients, especially females, allowed parole both in the grounds and beyond the estate. In 1929 118 men and 6 women had 'the privilege of being in the grounds and just 6 men could go beyond the estate.[3] Two years later, the Board of Control noted that no female patients were allowed parole. Two men could go beyond the estate and 101 in the grounds. Two wards and one villa on each side had open door access to the ward gardens, but not beyond. They noted similar figures for parole until 1936, the last year details were recorded, the Commissioners considering it 'remarkable' no females had parole, particularly because of the small size of many airing courts.

Perhaps it was a reaction to Ethel B's pregnancy and Cane Hill's proximity to an increasingly busy main road, despite the Board of Control having, in 1933, stressed that

> parole is valuable not only for the effects on the patients who are given this measure, but also because it gives other patients something to look forward to and is an inducement to good behaviour ... The freest measure of which the circumstances of the hospital will permit should be encouraged.

Radically, the Board commented that 'safety-first' is not the best motto for mental hospitals.[4] They noted in 1931 that only two of the four ward gardens on the male side were in use, the number of patients in the gardens being too large while draining water from the gardens should be a priority.[5] In the years before World War Two, residents in Chipstead saw patients, in their distinctive hospital clothing, being walked locally in crocodile file.[6] However in 1930, patients had become more restricted in the main building. Instructions were issued that

1 Working patients, during their slack intervals, should not be allowed to wander about the corridors.

2 Patients are not to be sent on messages to the stores or kitchen unaccompanied.

3 When patients ask to be allowed to go into the garden, they are to be sent back to their own wards, so that they can take exercise in the garden belonging to the ward, and are not allowed to exercise in the garden opposite the messroom.

4 When the staff ask the patients to do out their rooms for them, though there is no objection to this, it must be done under supervision.

5 The parole granted to patients to go backwards and forwards to the needleroom and workshops has been cancelled and they must now be escorted to and from work.

That same year, staff uniforms were updated. Head and male nurses had two serge suits a year, one for the winter and one for the summer, a cloth cap, a straw hat for day duty and an overcoat, as required. Ordinary nurses still had a belt chain, a belt and hook and a whistle. Inspectors wore a frock suit as well as one jacket suit for the winter and another for the summer. Staff working in the potting sheds, or tractor work or required to attend funerals, had a black rubberproof coat.

Nurses had three galatea dresses, one cloth overcoat, six collars, six pairs of cuffs, four caps, twelve aprons, a storm cap, three belts and a cord, belt, hook and whistle. All night nurses had one pair of 'silent shoes'.

Assistant matrons had two grey alpaca dresses a year, with six collars in embroidered muslin and six matching pairs of cuffs and six Sister Dora caps. Matron no longer wore a uniform, her dress being left to her discretion and the sub-committee's approval.[7]

1930 Mental Treatment Act

The 1930 Mental Treatment Act created three classes of patient: certified patients, temporary patients admitted without certification for six months on the recommendation of two medical practitioners, a medical report having to be produced within seven days of admission, with power to extend for a further six months if two independent medical practitioners thought a further period of treatment was desirable, without the involvement of a magistrate and, for the first time, voluntary patients. Temporary and voluntary treatment was intended to 'obviate recourse to certification'.[8]

The Act highlighted the need for out-patient treatment, convalescent homes and aftercare and, in its progress through Parliament, the Board of Control repeatedly suggested that voluntary and temporary patients be treated in admission units wholly separate from the main buildings.[9]

In 1931, four hospitals had less than 5 per cent of its patients who were voluntary, while Cane Hill was among nineteen where only 5 to 9 per cent of its patients were voluntary; Portsmouth had 67 per cent and Swansea the most with 68 per cent.[10] When the Board visited Cane Hill that year, there were thirteen male and five female voluntary patients, with seven males and seven females on trial leave. Told that only one temporary patient had been admitted, they expressed their disappointment since certificates could have been avoided in 10 per cent of admissions. There was a shortage of suitable accommodation to which patients could be discharged.[11]

In 1935, 10 to 14 per cent of Cane Hill's admissions were voluntary, but less than 4 per cent were temporary.[12] The following year, the Commissioners were disappointed to learn of only eight temporary admissions, all female, in 1935. When they visited in 1936, seeing 26 male and 14 female voluntary and two temporary patients, they commented that it 'appears to indicate the provisions of the Mental Treatment Act 1930 are not understood or appreciated by most of the medical practitioners and relieving officers in the area which the hospital serves'.[13]

While the opportunity to go outside the estate or even the main building, unless working on the farm or estate, was now limited to a few patients, organised outings began. In 1929, six parties each of 25 working patients went to Box Hill by char-a-banc in August.[14] Char-a-banc outings were mentioned in 1931 and, two years later, Mr A.W. Cozens of Canterbury requested to take a party of patients out for an afternoon, having already done so satisfactorily at Banstead, and so the sub-committee agreed to it.[15] The number of patients on trial leave gradually increased and, in January 1937, there were twenty-five: eleven had no allowance while nine had the maximum of £2.3s 4d.[16]

In 1931, films were popular at Cane Hill, and the sub-committee now considered a 'talking-film apparatus'.[17] The Board of Control commented that

> Probably nothing has done more in recent years to add to the happiness and contentment of the patients than the installation of the cinema. The weekly or fortnightly entertainments not only afford great pleasure in themselves but, by giving patients something to look forward to, they help to deaden the monotony of institutional life.[18]

Local awareness of the hospital's patients may have increased for, in 1937, Messrs F.W. Woolworths gave £5.5s 0d worth of Easter eggs as presents for the patients.[19]

Caring for patients

There were fewer complaints by patients of ill treatment, although it is not known if incidents actually reduced. As in previous years, most of those were reported because they were observed by senior staff. How much did other staff see and condone?

In 1930, a patient, Henry Thomas Frost was sent by a stores porter to tell patients working in the butcher's shop that their tobacco ration was ready. Frost reported that the butcher, Mr Wickens, used bad language to him, hustled him out of the shop and kicked him on the back of the leg, resulting in a fairly large bruise. Wickens denied it, stating that he was working at high pressure and might have closed the door sharply on the patient, while the porter saw the door shut as if the butcher was irritated, but did not see him kick the patient.

The kicking could not be proved but Wickens was interviewed by the chairman and informed that pressure of work was not a valid excuse for irritability or short temper, and he must exercise the greatest possible restraint in his relationships with patients.

Staff nurse Joseph E Rice, reprimanded in 1932 for quarreling and using abusive language to a probationer nurse when working with a party of patients on the farm, was warned that a repetition would 'lead to the determination of his appointment'.

The previous year, night charge nurse Catherine Davies had two severe prolonged struggles with a patient in November and December, after which she developed neurasthenia and, in 1931 was considered permanently unfit for mental health work and given retirement and, eventually, £150 in compensation in 1933, with the suggestion that, after a short stay at the seaside, she should 'be fit for some light employment, preferably of a home character'.

In January 1933, an assistant matron saw a nurse shake and slap a patient on the head. She admitted losing her temper and was suspended, but the sub-committee decided against criminal proceedings. The following month, the deputy medical superintendent saw a female staff nurse shaking a patient by the head. She admitted holding the patient by the hair, but said she caught the patient by the arm and head to prevent her breaking a window. With insufficient evidence, the nurse was given a warning.[20] As in earlier years, it was a senior member of staff saw an incident and reported it. However in July 1933, three nurses reported seeing Charge Nurse Lilian Ryall pull a patient's hair at 5.00 p.m., and hit the same patient with a papier maché chamber pot at 7.00 p.m. As the patient confirmed the charges, Ryall was dismissed. Although liable to criminal charges, the sub-committee decided not to prosecute. When, in 1934, a patient committed suicide by hanging himself from a bracket in the ward's lavatory, the charge nurse was found guilty of neglect and dismissed.[21]

In 1929, a female patient Mildred G. had very fixed amorous ideas about the deputy medical superintendent. Dr Elgee, fearing 'these ideas would militate against her recovery' arranged her transfer to West Park Hospital where her brother was a patient.[22] A male patient, who thought he was persecuted by medical staff, was transferred to Banstead or Epsom Hospitals, his relatives living in Epsom.[23]

Patients could keep money and, in 1933, a showcase was set up in the shop where patients could see the goods they wanted to buy. A chief charge nurse reported that £2.7s 8d, handed to him by patients for safe keeping overnight, was taken from the knife box where he hid it. He was informed not to let patients retain more than 2s each, that the box should have been locked in the store room, and was required to refund £1, the remainder being repaid from the Tea Fund.[24]

Conditions

Many improvements were undertaken in the 1920s but, in 1931, the Board of Control commented that much remained to be improved, acknowledging that it would be some time before there was a change from gas to electric lights.[25]

In 1932, nurses were requested to have baths before 7.00 p.m. as the heating did not allow hot water for evening baths. Two years later, staff were requested to be as sparing as possible in using hot and cold water as, due to the previous summer's drought, water levels at the hospital's pumping station were low.[26]

Wards were neat and tidy, many having recently had wirelesses, but were overdue for redecoration. They congratulated Dr Lilly on his appointment and looked forward to 'great expansion'. However, bed-linen continued 'to be a bad colour', still having to be 'rough dried', as the laundry awaited modernisation. Out-door coats had been introduced for some better patients, but the majority still had shawls. Underwear was very old fashioned and 'perhaps allowed to last longer than their condition warrants', but they were glad to find Matron was anxious to improve the women's clothing. As ever, patients were generally quiet and well-behaved. There had been two suicides: one by hanging and the other by a patient away on trial leave.

Ignoring the country's economic situation, the Board noted the 'great economy of space' in the size of bedrooms in the planned nurses' home, brought about by financial cuts, and regretted the lack of clinical rooms and store rooms in the hospital. Malarial and light treatment continued, and frequent x-ray examinations with the necessary apparatus brought to the hospital. The hospital was free of dysentery and other infections.[27]

In 1935, the Board noted endeavours to improve the hospital under Dr Lilly's 'able administration'. Wards remained tidy but a great deal of redecoration was needed. Two male wards were completed, but wiring the wards for electric lighting had been postponed. A new eight-roll calendar in the laundry improved the finish to bed linen and women's clothing. More modern women's clothes were being introduced.[28] The following year, they generally commented that 'A woman, particularly a young one, cannot and ought not to feel normal in shapeless clothes and with limp and bedraggled hair. A little vanity . . . is a hopeful sign in any mental patient'. As for men, 'steam presses are well worth what they cost, not only because a decent Sunday suit lessens the sense of being institutionalised, but also because patients take more care of clothes in which they can feel some pride'.[29]

The nurses home had opened, releasing fifty-four bedrooms on the female side while rooms were adapted as libraries for the patients, and nurses needed a new lecture room and desks. They thought it inappropriate that fifty-four Roman Catholic patients attended Mass in the medical officers' billiard room, and noted the number of patients attending Church of England services and entertainments was below that of all the mental hospitals.

There were 863 male and 1,312 female patients, a total of 2,175, with an excess of 6 men and 22 females. Registers of female patients survive to 1935 and show groups of patients being transferred to Cane Hill, presumably having been boarded elsewhere. In 1933, seventeen women aged 57 and over came from Leicester City Mental Hospital, twelve mainly elderly patients from Horton Hospital and, in 1934, twenty more from Leicester, the youngest aged 48. Between 1931 and 1934, twenty-eight women came from Netherne Hospital.[30]

The nursing staff's establishment was complete, with 74 charge nurses, 272 ordinary nurses and 42 night nurses. 247 nurses held a nursing certificate, and 70 had passed the preliminary examination. All patients were inoculated against enteric fever which included typhoid and re-inoculated as necessary, and the hospital free of typhoid for years. Eighteen patients had TB, six of whom were active, and were treated in open verandahs 'under ideal conditions'.

Some improvements

In 1936, the Board of Control noted numerous alterations and structural improvements at Cane Hill: a few dayrooms on the male side were redecorated and had electric lighting. They congratulated Dr Lilly on the 'most pleasing appearance' and 'the success of his colour schemes, but many dayrooms were dark and dilapidated with a lack of flowers and very few plants. They specifically noted that no female staff were employed on wards.

More able patients lived in better conditions: Portnalls was 'a most pleasant building' and the Garden House, for convalescent females, was attractive, and due to be redecorated. Meals were cooked in the villas and the isolation hospital. There was a 'talking picture apparatus' in the recreation hall and all wards had wireless sets. The weekly charge for maintenance had risen from £1.2s 9d in 1931 to £1.5s 8d.

The patients were 'generally quiet and orderly . . . [they] seemed content and comfortable' and they thought the diet, on a four weekly rota, was well varied with fresh fruit or salad daily, and green vegetables three times a week, and there was a new fish frier. Eighty women patients made dresses and other garments in the needleroom: the women's clothing was 'very pleasing . . . [with] a good variety of patterns and colours' but garments were still marked with an ink stamp which looked very unsightly and rotted the garments. They suggested marked tapes.

Physical exercise was important in the 1930s. Male staff and patients played football and cricket, and female staff hockey. Male staff played tennis and golf, and many staff cycled. In 1936, a physical training class began for twenty female patients.[31] Staff taking the 'patients' drill classes' were issued with a navy blue gym tunic, navy blue knickers and mottled plimsolls.[32]

When they visited, there were three cases of dysentery but patients had been inoculated on affected wards. Twenty-three patients had TB and it was a hot day: temperatures of 102F on B1 female verandah and 92F on G2 male verandah. They suggested patients be moved inside, and electric fans used in future.[33]

The sub-committee responded: they would try to increase the number of men and women on parole, regarding fifteen female patients in the Garden House as on parole. Flowers and plants would be redistributed to all wards where patients could be trusted with flowers. There was no need for electric fans, as patients were moved from verandahs to dormitories in very hot weather. They would try to start a physical training class for male patients.

In late 1936, the London County Mental Health Committee decided that each year up to one hundred working patients, in hospital for over a year, at each large London mental hospital would have two weeks holiday at the Mental Aftercare Association's seaside homes.[34] From 1937, separate groups of male and female patients went from Cane Hill at separate times.

No more visits from the Commissioners were reported until 1940, when very different conditions prevailed.

Chapter 22: Occupational therapy

In 1928, the Commissioners praised the 'gratifying results' obtained in some mental hospitals by the development of occupational therapy and wanted to see more occupations officers employed. They observed that, in the past, staff had concentrated on patients 'whose readiness to work was spontaneous or needed only the urge of some reward, and upon work which is of some economic benefit to the institution' but, it was

> increasingly recognised that many apparently unemployable patients, in the hands of staff trained in teaching handicrafts, can be occupied with great benefit to themselves if sufficient care is taken to select, often by repeated experiment, the particular kind of occupation best suited to the patient's mental condition. Recent experience in some Dutch hospitals, in which occupational therapy has been highly organized, emphasises afresh that there are many patients, not excluding violent types, who benefit by occupation and who can be far more easily handled if they are kept suitably employed. Carefully organized occupation has a definite therapeutic value ...

Dr Elgee and the sub-committee recognised its value and employed a 'temporary occupational officer'.

In 1929, the Commissioners were enthusiastic about its development at Cane Hill, having seen one 'occupational officer' working on the women's side of the hospital, a temporary appointment not yet on the establishment, probably working with shorter stay patients expected to recover. Twelve female patients attended in the morning and eighteen in the afternoon doing excellent raffia work, with 'much activity in making Christmas presents'.

There were no plans to introduce 'occupation centres' on the wards and, on the male side, no occupation officer, and little attempt to introduce activity other than in the workshops. Men still worked in the gardens and farm, and as ward workers. The Commissioners considered that, at Cane Hill:

> The value of teaching patients to employ themselves in unaccustomed ways, such as weaving, basket work, book binding, as a means of treatment, would more than justify the trouble and expense involved . . . [However] An obstacle arises in an unexpected way from the use of the words 'mental hospital'. We were told that many patients, when invited to do raffia work, replied that they were in a hospital and not expected to work.[1]

In 1931, the Commissioners continued their support of occupational therapy (OT) and found it

> distressing to go around many hospitals and find scores of patients left to deteriorate in wearisome idleness. It is bad for them and bad for staff, for idle hands find as much opportunity for mischief in a mental hospital as outside. The idle patient has far too much time to brood over his real or imaginary troubles.

Regarding working patients, they disregarded the statistics given by hospitals as they made no distinction between remedial occupation and employment designed to reduce maintenance costs, and not to benefit the patient. In many cases, they thought it better to give a patient work to which they were not accustomed as 'the concentration required may be far more beneficial as a distraction than the most or less automatic performance of familiar work which requires little attention and leaves the patient free to mope or brood'. Gardening was very popular, and allotting small gardens to patients willing to cultivate them often had beneficial results. They stressed the need of a specialised trained worker for the effective organisation of OT in large hospitals.[2]

In 1933, the Commissioners felt sure it led to 'the amelioration of conditions which hitherto have not been successfully dealt with in any other way' and to 'maintaining interest in life and happiness'. They stressed its importance in 'milder forms of mental disorder' as patients became 'happier and more ready to accept the need for hospital treatment. Few of these cases can be treated effectively in their own homes' and it helped them to bear the separation from their families.

They stressed that OT should be used with those who became 'chronic or continuing cases': it 'should never be stopped as the effect is progressive and therefore demands close continuity. The mind must either find activity in the ordinary things of life or it must pass into a condition of lethargy and social uselessness'.[3]

The first occupational therapy training school having opened in Bristol in 1930, the Commissioners declared in 1934 that it was not enough to train nurses do simple crafts: 'to attain any real measure of success there must be under medical direction an occupation[al] therapist in general charge who has made a special study of the methods of approach to the unemployables and who has acquired some knowledge of the working of the disordered mind. The occupation[al] therapist needs to be constantly on the look-out for the patient who can be transferred to some more interesting task'. Knotting cloth cloths was suggested as a basic simple task.[4]

Soon after Dr Lilly arrived in 1931, he asked the sub-committee that the women's occupation officer's appointment be made permanent and, in October, Miss Kathleen Raistrick was appointed. Little is known of her work. Cupboards were ordered for OT on sixteen female wards and more ordered throughout the 1930s, and she may have directed nurses to do activities. £7 from the Tea Fund defrayed expenses in connection with the exhibition of patients' work at the Public Health Congress in November 1934.[5]

The LCC Mental Health Committee agreed to appoint male occupations officers and handicraft instructors from April 1935. All mental hospitals were to report in January 1936 on the development of occupation officers and the results achieved. At Cane Hill, a report was requested in November 1935 on occupational therapy. Unfortunately, it has not survived.[6]

When the Commissioners visited in June 1935, they noted handicraft work being developed with a good number of patients on male wards C2 and G1 and female ward D1, and an OT room on the female side.[7] The following year, they noted great progress in OT, which was almost entirely on the wards, and a great credit to nursing staff. An 'occupational mistress' trained patients in the Arts and Crafts department on the female side, but she had only trained one nurse: it would be more productive if she trained more. On the male side, excellent work was produced in dayrooms, but the commissioners thought they attend a central 'occupations unit'.[8]

In June 1936, in response to the Board of Control's comments, the sub-committee would later in the year consider sending staff to train in occupational therapy, and to change the wards in which occupational therapy took place, although they were not convinced that concentrating on the male side was in the patients' best interest. They would try to begin physical training classes for male patients.[9]

Chapter 23: World War Two and its aftermath

The sub-committee appears to have met four to six times a year during the war, its minutes becoming shorter and shorter, perhaps because of a paper shortage. However, the Board of Control Commissioners visited annually and reported fully.

In the late summer of 1940, in the Battle of Britain, Cane Hill lay some two miles west of RAF Kenley, a fighter station, and three miles south of Croydon Airport. The Commissioners visited on 6 August, days before Croydon Airport was bombed on 15 August. 180 bombs fell on RAF Kenley on 18 August, although the station was back in operation twenty-four hours later. A month before the Battle of Britain began overhead, they found the patients quiet and orderly and, on the whole, contented, largely due to the staff's sympathetic and tactful attitude. They were impressed by their intimate knowledge of patients' idiosyncrasies, particularly on the female side, while medical care was very thorough.

The wards were in good decorative repair, apart from four female wards, but windows were protected from blast by fixing hessian to the glass and varnishing it, making wards very dark and depressing. As it excluded more light than methods used in other London hospitals, the Commissioners felt the health and cheerfulness of staff and patients might suffer in winter.

Hot water was not available at night, as staff could not keep the furnaces stoked because of the possibility of air raids 'and the need of hot water in quantity for casualties'. As water was boiled in kettles, they suggested gas or electric water heaters in wards.

The hospital was overcrowded. An emergency hospital, set up in the main building, meant 6,000 to 8,000 extra items weekly for the laundry, resulting in many heaps of soiled linen awaiting sorting, on which flies were settling. 344 patients, including 322 women from Horton Hospital, had been transferred to Cane Hill in late 1939. There were now 792 male and 1,613 female patients, a total of 2,405 patients and, at night an excess of 126 men and 323 women patients in dormitories. On 20 August, forty patients, accompanied by staff, arrived from Gibraltar's mental hospital.

The mortuary had been 'thoroughly unsatisfactory' for years, while male airing courts remained in a dangerous condition and needed relaying which they thought could be done with patient labour, but there was an excellent new cafeteria for nursing staff.

One patient had dysentery, another scarlet fever, and twenty-six TB, but all patients received a T.A.B. vaccine on admission. Dr Lilly had kept the hospital free from epidemics for many years by inoculating all patients with a 'polyvalent vaccine' in any wards where diarrhoea occurred on several consecutive days.

Worsening conditions

When the Commissioners visited in August 1941, there were fewer nurses, despite the Council having, in March, decided that female nurses could remain on the permanent staff after marriage.[1] 'Good spirits' prevailed with Dr Lilly well supported by his staff, including Miss Littlejohn who remained Matron. There were 2,399 patients, and 23 on leave, including 59 service or ex-service patients and 40 private patients (35 females and 5 males).

With patients from Horton and Gibraltar, and air-raid precaution arrangements, at night the hospital was overcrowded by 19 per cent on the male side and 25 per cent on the female side but, through careful placing of beds, was not too obvious. There was considerable strain on staff, due to vacancies caused by war work, but staff co-operated well, and married women returned as temporary staff.

The Emergency Hospital, was run by Mr. O.S. Tubbs F.R.C.S., with two female house-surgeons and visiting specialists available from Horton Hospital. With 268 beds, it was formed out of B1, B2, C1 and C2 wards on the male side, and included the operating theatre, while a plaster room had been built.[2] Dr Lilly was responsible for it, being asked to report on its organisation and work from the outbreak from the outbreak of war to 31 December 1942.[3]

The Commissioners, impressed by the neatness and good quality of patients' clothing 'free from monotony of pattern', praised the sewing room for ensuring dresses were bright and pleased their wearers, wishing to see it extended to all patients.

Great care was taken with the diet, which accorded with restrictions laid down for the public, rationing have been introduced in January 1940 which, in 1941, included butter, bacon, sugar, tea, margarine, cooking fats and cheese, dairy herds having been slaughtered to provide arable land. For some months, a highly experienced chef had taught kitchen staff to make the 'best and such appetising meals' possible with available ingredients, which would become a full-time post. Irish rabbit would be purchased.

The Board of Control had never recorded seclusion but, in August 1941, they noted 173 women and 7 men secluded in the previous twelve months. It is not known if this was a gradual increase, or sudden because of the pressures of overcrowding and reduced staffing. In October 1940, 204 women had dysentery and in November 69 men. Since their last visit, two men and six women had died from dysentery, with three women and eight men still under treatment. Two men and ten women had enteric fever, probably typhoid fever, one having died, while thirteen man and seven women had died of TB. There were 40 men and 183 women being treated in bed, the former lower and the latter higher than usually seen in mental hospitals. The Commissioners thought the use of x-ray at Cane Hill remarkable in diagnosing injuries, mainly among elderly female patients, which might otherwise have been missed.

Despite wartime conditions, they complained that there was no admission ward for men and, while some road and paths had been repaired, three male wards badly needed redecoration. They suggested changing pictures around and introducing plants, flowers, books, magazines and other 'objects of interest'. Portnalls, now occupied by 55 male working patients, still lacked a bathroom and patients continued using the general bathroom in the main building.

Their main concern related to the patients' activity. A small number of male patients worked in utility departments, 11 per cent in the farm and gardens, and others did ward cleaning. Less than eighty women (5 per cent) worked in the laundry. They thought the number employed small, but were pleased that only about a quarter worked on the wards, whereas other hospitals often had as many as half.

They were pleased to see senior nurses 'encouraging patients of the chronic type to occupy themselves usefully', particularly noting vegetable plots cultivated by patients in several ward gardens, and suggested that, in present war time conditions, more men and women should work in the farm and gardens, wearing suitable outdoor clothes, as a 'healthy and valuable experience'.

Many patients were in the ward gardens, 'where the terraced formation adds the attractiveness of their appearance', resulting from builder's rubble left there sixty years before, but they just walked. They suggested more organised work in utility departments and occupational therapy, to be 'dealt with in a vigorous and comprehensive manner', but stressed that this was not exclusive to Cane Hill.

Few patients went to church services or entertainments. The Anglican chaplain remained shared with St. Bernard's Hospital, and so responsible for nearly 5,000 patients and 600 staff, while a Roman Catholic priest and a free church minister still visited. While the cinema was popular, the authority which granted licences for performances restricted viewings.

Increasing difficulties

In September 1942, only one commissioner, Isabel G.H. Wilson, visited. She noted that 'Difficulties must often have been great and the very way in which they have been faced shows a commendable spirit of perseverance'. Resources had been found for medical treatment and consultation, with the first mention of electrical treatment, probably ECT, and she observed 'thoughtful and steady work' by staff. 'The contribution to the national effort has not been made without affecting the staff and patients . . . and any further changes which may be contemplated should be considered in the light of actual conditions on the wards'. They remained overcrowded, and redecoration had stopped: some wards were attractive but others were deteriorating. Blackout protection meant wards remained dark in the day, although light curtains were taken down when they needed washing, and not returned.

Having increased in price, fewer books and less tobacco could be purchased while physical training classes had stopped. Staff attendance at air raid precaution lectures and fire prevention prevented outings in some wards, even to ward gardens, and there were no social workers. At some time during the war, men from the Canadian Army, based on the estate, would visit and liven up the Social Club.

The number of patients reduced to 2,316 in the hospital with nearly 30 on trial, so that there were vacancies for 95 male and 77 female patients. While 27 patients died of TB, 27 were still being treated. Dysentery continued: out of 32 men and 59 females, four had died. It was scattered through the hospital with 17 out of 20 wards affected and 9 out of 11 villas, but had reduced with treatment including sulphoguanidine. The Commissioner suggested Dr Lilly revise his procedures, but he replied that he worked with many inexperienced staff. Dr Pearn, deputy medical superintendent for over twenty years, had retired. The hot water supply to patients' wash basins had to be discontinued, and hand towels removed.

Meat, sugar, teas, jam and marmalade were at the full civilian ration, while bacon was 20 per cent of the civilian ration, and cheese was only for working patients. Many men worked on the farm, and a 'contented group' of seven women. The female OT department provided activities for thirty patients at a time, while men did handicrafts including carpentry, with activities on the wards, but difficulties in getting materials.

Old clothing was still worn, with new items only issued if necessary. The sewing room remade old frocks and jumpers to produce new garments: 'not only economy of material but a quite unusual beauty and attractiveness of styles and colour schemes. This work is so good that it has turned the necessity of using scraps into a real satisfaction and benefit for the patients concerned'.

Endurance

The Commissioners, in June 1943, visited 'this important hospital', and were 'satisfied that the high standards of administration and care of patients for which this hospital is well known are well maintained in this fourth year of war'.

Wards, especially on the female side, needed redecoration, compared with those decorated 'with such good taste before the war'. They were overcrowded with 2,313 patients and 32 on leave, care still being taken to minimise the effects of overcrowding, every use being made of available space. The Commissioners were pleased that as many as 30 out of 77 patients given leave in 1943 received money allowances. There were now 77 voluntary patients in the hospital, admissions having dropped to only 125 in 1942, with 31 voluntary admissions and 94 certified admissions. Even so, there was now an excess of 83 male and 264 females beds, while the weekly maintenance charge for rate-aided patients was £2.1s 5d.

As in pre-war years, few females had parole, the commissioners commenting that Cane Hill's authorities were more generous to men, with 81 having parole beyond the estate, and 26 in the grounds.[4] Despite rationing, the sub-committee provided light refreshments for visiting and hospital cricket, tennis and football teams.[5]

Patients continued to look neat and well-cared for, the women wearing 'new and very attractive' garments: 'the patients in the sewing room took an obvious pride in the transformation they were assisting to make'. They considered the main meal very satisfactory, and noted arrangements made to protect bulk food supplied from gas attack.

Most patients now worked in utility departments, the Commissioners suggesting some patients doing handicrafts might rather be in workshops as well, with acute staff shortages and tasks essential to the running of the hospital. Patients' allotments in ward gardens continued to be successful 'and aroused much interest among patients', while the charge nurse on female ward E had started rug making and basketry.

Despite a shortage of medical staff, 'special electrical treatment' was in use, and they were considering leucotomies. There were 132 male and 284 female nurses, with 11 male and 24 female night nurses, of which 109 male and 159 female were qualified, with no female staff nursing male patients. Infections had reduced, with no typhoid, although 36 died of TB in the previous year, which was higher than average, although the mortality rate was 6.3 per cent in 1942, compared with 8 per cent for all mental hospitals.[6] In September, the commissioners were informed no action would be taken to install running water in wash basins on dormitories where infections were treated until after the war but, in early 1944, female dysentery carriers stopped working in the laundry.[7]

In June 1944, at the time of the Second Blitz of London, 63 male and 95 female patients, with accompanying staff, were transferred from St. Bernard's Mental Hospital in Southall until February 1945. Four men died while at Cane Hill, but the remainder returned to St. Bernard's.[8] Soon after D Day, heavy bombing of Croydon had recommenced, with V2 rockets.

The number of patients in Cane Hill had increased to 2,423 when the Commissioners visited in November 1944, declaring patients 'enjoy kindly care and treatment upon the most progressive lines'. Admissions in 1943 rose slightly to 142, but still well below pre-war levels, while 31 patients were out on trial, of which 18 had money allowances. Just 96, a small proportion, were voluntary patients, but there were now 62 service or ex-service patients, and 37 male and 49 female private patients who paid up to £2.6s a week, while the weekly maintenance charge for rate-aided patients was £2.0s 10d.

The interior decoration still looked deteriorated but wards were generally comfortable and homely. Lavatory doors and seats were being renewed and missing washbasin plugs replaced, the commissioners having discussed ward hygiene with Dr Lilly who assured them any defects would be remedied.

Eighty female patients still made and renovated clothing, displaying 'great ingenuity and taste' while parties of women patients worked on the land, and patients' allotments were maintained. Despite shortages of materials, occupational therapy continued in wards and centres. The diet was good and varied, and there was no dysentery or typhoid, but a large number of dysentery carriers were scattered through the hospital, including a few of the sixty men in the laundry. 54 patients and 3 staff had TB, including 22 men from Banstead Hospital, some treated on a leaking verandah.

The use of ECT was observed to be very successful in treatment, seven leucotomies had been performed, the results being disappointing although one patient had greatly improved.[9]

The War ends

The first mention of food donations came in March 1945, with the gift of 500 lbs of full cream dried milk and 240 lbs of milk chocolate powder received from the American Red Cross.

A report, which has not survived, was made in July 1946 regarding the continued use of ornamental grounds, playing fields, etc. for food production. In November, food arrived from Adelaide and Melbourne in Australia, as well as the South Australian and Tasmanian governments. 3,402 lbs of jam came from the New South Wales government who, in April 1947, sent 63 cases of jam and two cases of tinned rabbit. 29 cases of All Bran and 15 cases of macaroni came in late 1947 from the Canadian Red Cross.

In March 1945, it was hoped to have the first fête after the war in the summer of 1946. Three staff nurses who returned from military service in October 1945, were seen by the sub-committee and thanked for their service in H.M. Forces. In March 1946, sixteen nurses and nine of the engineer's staff had returned. Six staff left, included two married female nurses, their services not longer required. Chief Male Nurse Henry Samuel and three other staff retired. In September, a bronze plaque was proposed, costing no more than £75 from the Tea Fund, to commemorate those who had died serving their country: Dr Winifred Porter in 1941, Alexander Sheriff in 1943 and Kathleen Bond 1944.[10]

Post-war difficulties

In October 1945, the number of patients had reduced to 2,248, with 127 male and 252 female staff although, in 1944, admissions rose to 274 including 78 voluntary patients. There was now a social worker, and a male occupation officer who took a physical training class for about twenty patients.

'Blast-walls' were swiftly removed, and the absence of curtains and shutters greatly improved lighting and ventilation in wards, although there was difficulty replacing large number of windows damaged in the war.[11] The deep shelter on the hospital estate was securely sealed, the Ministry of Works had checked and it and carried out constructional work. In 1950, there were negotiations with a company to use it temporarily to 'grind and polish mirrors for optical purposes.[12]

Wards looked well-kept and comfortable despite the lack of renovation and decoration, while food was good and had returned to a four-weekly diet. Supper consisted of soup or cocoa, with bread and cheese, or tea and bread with marmalade, and clothing was good although the effects of wear and tear was now evident, including 'attractive and cleverly designed dresses and other garments' made from black-out material.

Recreational activities included the cinema and dances for patients twice a week, at least four nursing staff having music qualifications. Occupational therapy continued, including activities with disturbed patients and with great ingenuity shown in overcoming the shortage of materials. The library was re-organised and was looked after by a visiting chaplain and his assistants.

Earlier in the year, just two women had dysentery, and two men enteric fever the previous year, of which one died, but TB was now an important issue: 21 had died of it in 1944, while 30 males and 16 females were treated, over half of the men having come from Banstead Mental Hospital. Four nurses were treated, with up to fifty suspected cases, and Dr Campbell, the T.B. Officer visited monthly. Even so, the mortality rate was 6.1 per cent compared with 6.9 per cent in all mental hospitals.

The Commissioners met medical staff, deciding that they gave much careful thought to patients' mental and physical care. Older methods of treatment, not identified, were used together with electrical and insulin treatment, the latter being used for some time with males and more recently with females. Leucotomies were used with selected patients, with varying results. They paid tribute to the way in which staff had carried out their duties, and maintained the standard of care 'over a period of years of anxiety and danger'.

The number of patients remained much the same when the Commissioners visited in October 1946. The closing days of the war saw a greater proportion of female admissions: 49 men and 212 women, only 23 coming from their own homes. The majority were voluntary admissions, only 128 being under the Mental Health Act.

Medical and nursing care was seen as excellent but there was a marked lack of 'remedial occupation', with overcrowding, a shortage of materials, and a shortage of female nursing staff, and no likelihood of an immediate improvement.

The diet was very good, as was the women's clothing, but the men's was less satisfactory.[13] The commissioners were informed that men's working clothes looked well worn because of limited supplies, but each had a Sunday suit. They had unsuccessfully advertised ten times for an assistant work mistress responsible for cutting out.[14] The hard-pressed needleroom planned to appoint two dressmakers, rather than seamstresses.

Wards were well kept, with at least one domestic on each female ward, and very clean, and curtains put up again, but several female wards were 'so dilapidated and depressing as to call for immediate attention'. In November, Dr Lilly reported inadequate facilities to wash and dry horsehair to remake mattresses.[15] He suggested a lean-to shed near the upholster's shop.[16]

They criticised the library facilities, as being exceptionally poor. There were about 2,000 books but male patients could not choose, and the inadequate stock on wards was only changed monthly, with a maximum of twenty-four books on male wards.[17] The sub-committee replied that it was impossible to get library books in the war, but they were arranging for 3,000 books from the Red Cross, while public libraries hoped to send unwanted books and they wanted, in time, to get new Penguin books. The males' library was closed during the war, but men could use the females' library. A central library was being considered.[18] Staff had a good lecture room, but no library with technical books for nurses.[19] Priorities were bed linen, and painting the main kitchen as materials became available.[20]

The Emergency Hospital had left, releasing wards, and it was intended to open one as a 'treatment unit': Insulin treatment on the male side took place in an open infirmary ward. There had been no recent dysentery epidemic, but two women had typhoid earlier in the year, while they planned to treat several paratyphoid carriers. 44 patients had TB, with 22 deaths in 1945, while the laundry's sterilizer was inefficient. Later that year, there was one case of dysentery, one of paratyphoid and a patient contracted poliomyelitis.[21]

Shortages

Married staff were unable to get local housing, their families living considerable distances away such as Staff nurse F.W.N. whose wife and children were in North Wales. The local authority did not seem prepared to give resident staff at the hospital the same order of priority for housing as was given to other residents in the district. Dr Lilly would write to the local medical officer of health asking him to contact the C&PUDC to give equal priority.[22]

There were 2,247 patients when the Commissioners visited in October 1947, including 57 male and 136 female patients. Nine female patients who were typhoid carriers were segregated at the end on K1 ward, together with seven who had dysentery in the past, although sulphur drugs had greatly reduced the spread of the latter in recent years. 74 males and 198 females were treated in bed. Insulin treatment and ECT were regularly used, and a number of patients of both sexes had undergone pre-frontal leucotomies. In 1948, a list of 48 potential patients was made in the female register.

As elsewhere, there was a serious shortage of female nurses whom, the Commissioners noted, were hard pressed and working in poor conditions which could not be altered at present: overcrowding, large wards, a lack of hot water in basins, a shortage of lavatories and lockers for patients' possessions. Outside painting of the buildings had begun, but they thought the state of some wards so bad as to need attention if they were to be used by patients. In particular, two small dormitories each containing three patients with 'defective habits' were 'dark, stuffy with dirty walls and poor floors', which Dr Lilly rightly considered unfit to be used.

They still criticised library facilities, and an acute shortage of bed linen and material for patients' clothing which resulted in 'a reversion to the old fashioned type of institutional clothing'. Dinner was excellent, with a varied menu, and the Commissioners paid 'high tribute to the work of the nurses', the general attitude of patients to nurses and medical staff seeming 'to be a very happy one'.[23] Sport was important, and £604.4s, plus £150 from the Tea Fund, was approved to construct two hard tennis courts.[24]

They stressed the need to introduce occupational therapy 'as a means of improving habits and making life happier for deteriorating patients as well as for those who are improving'. It would make the nurses' work easier but the Commissioners reported that it was rare in any mental hospital to find such low numbers of patients employed as at Cane Hill, being 50 per cent of males and 30 per cent of females, reflected in the unusually large number of patients sitting inactive or wandering restlessly outside.

By occupational therapy, they included not only work in the two Centres but the introduction under medical direction of physical training and recreations including patients' social clubs where they organised their own activities, as well as more outside activities for men and women, increased numbers in workshops, a greater range of occupations for patients, and habit training on the wards. The Commissioners saw these would lighten the nurses' work by producing 'a more co-operative attitude amongst the patients' and taking more patients off wards during the day.[25]

The sub-committee advertised for Cane Hill's first qualified occupational therapist. Miss Alice Sharpe, the only candidate, was appointed in January 1948 with a salary of £475 a year. They were satisfied that about one hundred patients were employed in the farm and gardens.[26]

Miss Edith Dignum Littlejohn, matron since July 1935, retired in June 1947, to be replaced by Miss Webber.[27] [1] Dr Lilly remained,

---

[1] Miss Littlejohn died in 1956.

being given the title of physical superintendent in October 1947, with Dr Alexander Walk who succeeded Dr Pearn as deputy, and Dr Fahy in charge on the male side

Mrs M.M. Dollar, a member since 1931, became chairman of the sub-committee in 1939, with Mrs Girling as vice-chairman and two other women on the sub-committee. She retired as chairman in 1940 but resumed in 1944. The LCC would hand over control to the new National Health Service, and the sub-committee resigned. Cane Hill's new hospital management committee (HMC) would be responsible to the Ministry of Health, through the South East Metropolitan Regional Hospital Board (RHB).

Chapter 24: The National Health Service 1948-1962

When the Board of Control's Commissioners visited on 9 April 1948, there were 2,281 patients in the hospital, and 35 on leave. 180 patients were due to return to Horton, but 22 male and 20 females from Gibraltar remained in Cane Hill in 1949, some having died there.

There were 79 vacant beds on the male side, but 312 excess female patients and it was thought female admissions would increase. The female side remained overcrowded and, in 1955 more male beds were needed, and the male nurses block needed to be enlarged to accommodate more staff. 45 patients returned to Horton in September, but 112 remained in 1950.

Well into the 1950s, six members of the HMC, including the chairman, met monthly for the discharge of patients, two being present when it was discussed with the patient, and interviewed all newly admitted patients.

Redecoration of the wards began, and cleaning and washing of walls, but there were difficulties in obtaining bed linen and female underwear, a shortage of library books and no central library, or reading room and library on the male side. In 1952, lockers and easy chairs began to be placed in female wards, and electric shavers issued to male wards as an experiment. A subscription was made to the National Gallery to obtain prints, and to borrow twenty pictures a year from the Red Cross Society.

Staff shortages continued, not only among nursing staff, with difficulties in recruiting. Despite the shortages, there were good indoor games and recreation but few outdoor activities for women. Patients were particularly quiet and contented, 'considering few were occupied' but they praised the new system of rewards for patients, which was much appreciated. Patients working on the farm in the evening received 1d, but the HMC considered it inadequate and it was raised to 3d and then to 6d.

Meals were well presented, a catering officer having been appointed but with problems in always serving good meals because of staff shortages. In 1949, with continuing food rationing, a gift of honey came from the Australian Department of Agriculture and cooking fat from New Zealand's National Patriotic Fund. The Fat for Britain Fund, in Melbourne, Australia sent toilet soap. However, in 1950, the shop could sell sweets, crisps, cakes, cigarettes, tobacco, cosmetics, haberdashery and other items to staff and patients. Menus altered, as more ready-made items were purchased. Food ordered in 1952 included steak pies, ice cream, Energen bread, buns, luncheon sausage meat, beef sausages, fish paste and biscuits. In 1954, with a reduction in funding, the HMC considered it impossible to raise the standard of the diet to that recommended by the RHB. Staff ate in the cafeteria where, in 1956, breakfast cost 1s 9d, lunch 2s 3d, tea 9d and dinner 2s 6d.

Opportunities for parole increased considerably. 73 men and 89 women went beyond the estate in 1948, while 95 men and 91 women had parole within the estate, the commissioners regretting there were 'no enclosed grounds which can encourage parole, as they are open to the surrounding country and to the town of Coulsdon', but a considerable number of patients had restricted liberty within the hospital buildings, even though 49 per cent of admissions were now voluntary.

There were occupation centres on both sides, the female department run by Miss Sharpe, a qualified occupational therapist with a sister and three student nurses, with plans to recommence work on the wards where large numbers of patients sat around unoccupied, and a male department with a male occupation officer and two assistants.

A medical officer ran group therapy sessions for patients having ECT, where 'daily efforts were made to help patients to understand and respond to their situation'. Continuous narcosis and insulin treatment were used, with leucotomies for selected patients. Two female social workers visited patients in hospital, and their homes, and there was talk of a boarding-out scheme.

The hospital ran as a single unit with its own management committee of thirteen members meeting monthly, while members made fortnightly visits. Mrs M.M. Dollar was chairman, and local authorities and welfare bodies in South London, from where patients came, were invited to nominate a representative. Dr Lilly retired in 1949, to return frequently as a commissioner, and was succeeded by his deputy, Dr Walk, with Dr Charlton as the new deputy. In 1951, he had no deputy, but Dr Mitchell covered for him when he was absent. Known for his pioneering work in music therapy, and 'popular and deeply appreciated', Dr Mitchell died suddenly in January 1952. Dr Walk continued living in Postern House, and Glencairn was converted into two flats. Miss V.H. Webber, matron since 1947, retired in 1956 and was succeeded by Miss Dowling.

Medical officers were seen by the Commissioners to take a great interest in their work. There were insulin units on both sides, with deep coma treatment used in some cases. ECT was established, some eighty patients had pre-frontal leucotomies and psychotherapy would be extended when a new medical officer arrived. A physiotherapist was appointed and, in 1951, a part-time psychologist. There were out-patient clinics at St Giles Hospital in Camberwell and St Olaves Hospital in Rotherhithe and later at Beckenham Hospital but, at Cane Hill, with the country's ongoing financial problems, there was little improvement in the buildings – and still no hot water in washbasins. The commissioners were impressed by the nurses' very good care and efforts to make the patients comfortable, with patients expressing appreciation of their kindness and thoughtfulness. Many wards had open fires as well as central heating, and female patients were provided with warm decorative woolly bed jackets.

The female side remained overcrowded: seven had dysentery, one having died while six contracted typhoid, with one death. None of those with typhoid had been on those wards where fourteen typhoid carriers lived, being kept apart from others as much as possible. Over forty patients had TB, most kept on verandahs, with some men in the Cottage Hospital.

Outings, the fête and summer holidays to MACA's seaside homes recommenced. In 1949, the new patients' social club was a new success, with Dr Mitchell's active support. Its activities included discussions on current affairs, play reading, music appreciation and an art class. Coaches took patients to play cricket, football, billiards and darts at other hospitals, as part of the patients' inter-hospital league. Staff took in part in similar hospital leagues, and played local teams at football, cricket, tennis, hockey, golf and cross-country running.

There was a well organised library organised by the Red Cross and funded by the HMC, with a librarian. In 1950, a television was hired to use in the Cottage Hospital, after which the King Edward's Hospital Fund provided new cinematograph equipment and more television sets. The HMC bought records for patients' dances, wireless sets and a grand piano for concerts. From 1954, films were shown on wards to patients unable to get to the recreational hall. Fancy dresses dances had long been a part of the patients' life, and £130 worth of outfits were replaced. Patients had more freedom with 87 males and 259 females able to go out beyond the estate. At the same time, the general issue of pass keys to individual staff members was stopped: heads of department would issue keys as required.

A special tea was held for patients to celebrate the Coronation in 1953. The RHB held a ballot to allocate seats to members of HMCs to observe the coronation procession, Cane Hill's two seats being won by Mrs Hailstone and Miss Larkin. A dinner in the autumn attended by representatives of all grades of staff, celebrated the seventieth anniversary of the hospital's opening.

Civil Defence

In 1950, with fear of the Cold War, the government decided mental health nurses were exempt from recall to the Forces. Cane Hill, being less than four miles from Croydon, was designated as a 'Cushion Hospital' which would receive casualties from the scene of attack. It would not be evacuated.

The RHB requested information as to where beds and bed linen could be stored, as well the number and type of vehicles on the estate, and were informed by the hospital secretary, Mr Chapman, that there was insufficient space for normal needs. In an emergency, 3,000 staff and patients at Cane Hill would require feeding, and 72 patients from Tooting Bec Hospital, 235 from St. James Hospital and 175 from St. Mary's Hospital, both in Portsmouth, would be transferred to Cane Hill.

Using a drawing sent by Mr Chapman, the RHB decided that four sites of about twenty acres near to the junction of Portnalls Road and Hollymeoak Road could be used for a tented hospital providing about nine hundred beds. Into the 1960s, training courses were provided for staff and, in 1966, there were ten Civil Defence volunteers at Cane Hill.

Working patients

Fewer patients were willing to work in the laundry, so its staff had to be increased from fifteen to nineteen. In 1949, the practice of employing patients to do painting work had stopped long ago. Dr Walk had no objection to it, but there was now 'no surplus of patient labour regularly available'. He suggested that they could paint and stain furniture. The foreman builder discussed the matter with the trade union representatives who agreed to patients being employed, provided he did not have to provide staff to take charge of them but, in March 1950, it was decided to discontinue patients doing painters' work. In 1953, washing painted walls was again approved as a suitable occupation for patients.

In 1951, the HMC informed the Coulsdon Area Farm that transporting patients doing farm work in uncovered lorries was open to criticism, and to ensure they went in covered lorries in bad weather, and to ask what action was being taken to prevent patients riding on the sides of lorries. Patients had more freedom: a patient escaped in December 1950 taking a portable typewriter belonging to the hospital, and pawned it. The pawnbroker offered to return it, on payment of £5, which was accepted. Patients were already employed outside the hospital and, in 1950, arrangements were made to recover part of their wages to cover the cost of keeping them in hospital.

Probably because of difficulties in recruiting staff, a letter was received in 1951 from the South West Metropolitan Branch Association of Hospital Management Committees asking for the HMC's observations on diverting patient labour from OT departments to utility departments. Its reply was that work in the latter should be stimulated, but work in OT departments was desirable, and suggested spending time in both.

When the Grouped Farms Sub-Committee wrote regarding the needed employment of patients on the farms, Dr Walk informed the HMC that he proposed a 'propaganda campaign' with patients, to stimulate their interest in the work of the hospital, with a view to stimulating their interest in 'occupational work' with a booklet for new patients, describing the hospital and why 'occupation is expected'. There would be articles in the *Cane Hill Chronicle*, lantern shows and announcements at patients' entertainments and a female nursing assistant employed to supervise women patients employed in gardening.

The Estate and the community

Dr Lilly announced that no animals could enter or be kept in the hospital buildings without permission. It was 1959 before the League of Friends hoped to provide two aquaria for female wards, and a caged bird for one male and one female ward. However, in 1953, a local resident complained that trees in an enclosure at Dr Walk's garden were being damaged by the doctor's horses. Dr Walk's application to rent and enclose a grass strip behind the cricket pitch for them, was turned down. He was informed that the appearance of the frontage of Postern House, and the condition of the land left much to be desired, and allowed to pay for a hospital gardener for a half day a week. A wattle screen was erected opposite to the gate of K block garden to screen patients from being seen from Portnalls Road.

Asking advice about trespass by local people in 1950, the hospital secretary wrote to the solicitor that the hospital estate had never been completely fenced in. a number of people cut across the estate to reach the railway station and bus stop, while dogs were exercised on the farm land and children played on the estate, especially in the woods. Where most people entered, there was a fence reinforced by barbed wire, and substantial fencing in places, but neither had the slightest effect in keeping people out. Children and older boys had damaged hospital property, often throwing stones, climbing the walls of the ward gardens, etc. Patients on parole in the grounds complained of being followed and jeered at by boys and girls. When caught, they complained of having nowhere else to play, the nearby recreation ground being insufficient. Kenley Police advised that they could do nothing about trespass, and only intervene if there was damage.

The HMC formally objected to the C&PUDC's plan to build a housing estate adjacent to the hospital, as local residents already complained about noise from two blocks containing 'noisy turbulent patients', and suggested turning the ground into a recreation field. It agreed to sell land to C&PUDC for a community centre and to extend the car park, and to lease land to Coulsdon Post and Sorting Office.

In August 1953, the *Coulsdon & Purley Advertiser* expressed concern that two small girls were approached by a parole patient. One incident was not serious and, in the other case, when she asked him to tell her the time, he seized her by the shoulder and stroked her hair. In October, the Secretary of the Chipstead Residents Association petitioned the Minister of Education for bus transport for local children, to ensure their safety. The following summer, two male patients left the grounds without permission. One followed people while the other was said to have 'attacked' a woman but it was noted there were only four complaints in three years. With a lack of space for exercise by parole patients, Dr Walk considered it was a temptation to leave the estate. When wards were locked, it was not because patients were potentially dangerous 'but in order to ease the task of oversight of the patients by the depleted ward staff'.

Notices were erected to warn against trespassing. In 1954, the Chipstead Residents Association again complained of the danger to children from patients given parole outside the estate, but Dr Walk assured them that a patient's history was carefully checked before being given parole, and it would be reviewed if anything happened.

In June 1955, a local resident complained that a male patient was 'acting in a frightening manner' in Portnalls Road. The chairman of the HMC, Mr Geere, asked to meet with the RHB's Complaints Sub-Committee, agreed with precautionary measures taken by Dr Lilly regarding this patient, being against undue restriction for patients fit to have parole outside the hospital because of lapses of behaviour on the part of individual patients.

In 1956, there were several examples of trespass, with the fear of introducing disease to the livestock. Dogs were found in the fields, strangers fed uncooked food to the pigs, horses were grazed in fields by strangers, and even found in the airing courts. Dr Walk's horses were found galloping in a pasture field while outsiders continually cut and broke wire to enter the estate.

In 1952, the HMC agreed to the Railway Executive's proposal to remove the roof of the railway line through the estate, subject to a bridge being built to carry the existing footpath, wide enough to carry a farm tractor, with unclimbable fencing on both sides. The Railway Executive agreed to replace the trees along the footpath with trees or shrubs recommended by the HMC.

Again in 1954 and 1955, and later in the decade, the RHB refused the C&PUDC's application to set aside land on the estate to build council houses, because of the need to retain land around the building. In 1950, it was decided that funerals would be at Streatham Park Cemetery, unless a request was made for burial in the hospital cemetery.

Links increased with the outside community. From 1950, books came from C&PUDC's library. The public were invited to dances where alcohol was sold, and in 1951, the HMC agreed to the Sports and Social Club inviting the public to a four week trial of Old Time Dancing. In March 1951, a public meeting was held in South London to publicise the work of the hospital.

Discontent

In January 1951, sixty-two female nurses petitioned the Ministry of Health that, in the past four years, members of staff at Cane Hill had 'undergone humiliations and unpleasantness, causing extreme dissatisfaction and bad feeling'. The HMC tried to investigate, but only three ward sisters and a staff nurse gave evidence, and it concluded the grievances were unsubstantiated, and it had been 'unwise and irregular' not to bring it to their attention first. Matron Webber had their full confidence and they were determined to uphold her authority.

However, in May 1951, the Chief Male Nurse stated a lack of interest by Dr Walk in the male side of the hospital, reflected in the work of other departments, including delays in providing wireless sets and renewing lavatory pans. He was concerned that part of male F1 ward would become part of the OT centre, resulting in hardship to the patients on the ward, and that casualties among male nurses were increasing as they were apprehensive about being criticised about their manner of dealing with fractious patients: the failure to recruit male students nurses partly stemmed from the male staffs' unwillingness to recommend friends to work there.

Perhaps to boost morale, a hospital badge was introduced incorporating the crest of the London County Council, the Southwark Cross, devices representing medicine and a Saxon ornament commemorating archaeological finds in the estate before World War One, which male nurses agreed to wear. All wards were given names rather than the existing initials.

Renovation and new developments

Redecoration began slowly in 1949, despite dampness due to leaking roofs and gutters, with damp patches on walls. They awaited the Treasury's permission to replace the boiler house. In January 1952, the Commissioners described Cane Hill as 'an old Hospital, and it suffers from years of past neglect ... many corridors, staircases and dormitories have not been decorated for twenty years or more, many bedsteads need replacement and much new furniture is required'. Some worn stone staircases on the male side were dangerous. The HMC responded that they felt they had acted correctly in giving priority to redecorating the outside of the building, and those parts inside which were most used or most in need. The planned programme had not been realised because of cuts imposed on the HMC's estimates.

'Comparatively few wards have any hot water in the ablution rooms, and except in a few of the departments, the electric lighting is quite inadequate'. The HMC replied that, when the Commissioners visited, lighting was not used during the day because of economies and to meet the Electricity Board's request for care in using electricity during peak periods. Electricity blackouts were still common, especially at mealtimes. Consumption rose from 166,115 units in 1948 to 228,630 units as more electrical appliances were used, while fluorescent lighting was being introduced.

Wards were clean and tidy, but lacked plants and flowers. The Commissioners' opinion was that Cane Hill was allotted less than the share it should have had of money available in the Region, which may partly have been due to a failure by Cane Hill to indicate its minimum needs.

There were new developments: a new verandah for female TB patients, a small shop and café, a training school with lecture and demonstration rooms in part of the former general bathroom, an excellent pathological department, a dental room now ensuite with the operating theatre, and bathrooms would be installed in staff cottages.

The Commissioners thought the OT centres excellent, and other departments concerned with the patients 'rehabilitation and resocialisation' were exceptionally good. Dr Walk had accepted their suggestion of more ward activities. A small 'habit training class' had begun on a male ward for patients 'degraded in habits' where great improvements were shown. In 1950, a physical training instructor was employed for two sessions a week.

Overcrowding continued on several wards, particularly on the female side, but the main problem was the difficulty in nursing groups of similar patients together, because of the number of very large wards especially on the female side. A start was made with L block being divided into two wards, and Queens and Olave wards were used for admission patients. The commissioners congratulated the nurses in overcoming various difficulties, considering the patients 'tolerant of the conditions under which a large number of them had to live'. There was no hairdressing service, and they recommended a hairdressing saloon with a professional hairdresser when funds allowed, eventually agreed to by the RHB in 1958 and opened in 1959 for female patients, while men still had to wait.

Clothing became available for patients. In 1950, orders included two gross of men's vests, four gross of men's underpants, three gross of women's vests, three gross of women's knickers, five gross of women's stockings, three gross of men's ties, and seven dozen trilby hats. This was followed by all kinds of clothing, including material for 'strong dresses', and material to make bed linen, sheets, and pillowcases, pillows, and mattresses as well as hessian, coloured leathercloth, sail cloth canvas and drill khaki. Strong dresses were still won in 1955.

All but two wards on the female side had been redecorated in 1951, but had made little impression in the 'great mass of arrears' in redecoration. In 1954, Dr Lilly was one of the Commissioners who congratulated Dr Walk and the HMC for improvements in the previous year, despite so little money being available. Even with a new boiler house, opened by the Minister of Health in 1953, not all wash rooms had hot water and some top floor dormitories had no heating.

In 1954, at least 35 per cent of beds were still 'of the old fashioned wooden type', alongside 'obsolete' iron bedsteads. Dr Walk took up their suggestion of making spring mattresses in the upholstery department. Many wards now had curtains. Portnalls still had no bathroom and no water closet on the dormitory floor for use at night. Cane Hill, in common with all mental hospitals, had many elderly patients: nursing was of a high standard, with every effort to keep as many sitting up as possible to prevent them becoming bedridden. However, patients did not yet have their own individual underwear.

In the dayrooms, there were a 'depressing' number of long wooden benches with wooden backs and seats, some with a long cushion. Patients sat on them five abreast, or on hard wooden dining chairs, unless fortunate enough to secure one of the ten upholstered armchairs introduced on each ward.

In March 1955, Dr Lilly reported to the HMC about an article in the *Evening Standard* in which he was quoted as describing the hospital as a 'slum', but he said he was misquoted. Mr Geere thought Dr Lilly's use of the word was unfortunate. During the discussion, the RHB's representatives suggested that, in the early years since 1949, there was consistent underspending by the HMC, and that unspent money should have been used to buy more furniture and decorate wards, while certain items of work, not identified in the minutes, were criticised. The Chairman was 'quite satisfied' that, apart from 1951-2 when £5,000 was not used in a year when they 'had been urged to effect every possible economy', the HMC spent all the money available for building and for furniture. At the same meeting, they decided to apply for £5,000 to modernise and extend the Cottage Hospital as a neurosis unit although a few years later, after renovation, it housed old incontinent men, and for £2,350 for a new physiotherapy building and an extension to the treatment units.

Dr Lilly visited again in 1955, noting the important modernisation of this 'large and progressively managed hospital', money having been made available and well used. More wards had bright curtains, cushions and modern pictures, but the majority had a 'bleak' appearance and remained poorly furnished. More money had been spent on furniture with a grant from King Edward's Hospital Fund to refurbish admission wards, a source of funding much used in subsequent years.

The commissioners thought occupation and recreation particularly well organised, with a very full entertainment programme. Almost every evening, the hall was used for the cinema, concerts, old time dancing classes and dances. There were frequent coach outings, and patients' football matches at home and away, patients going by coach to see away matches. In 1954, the Staff Sports and Social Club requested a bowling green lawn for staff and patients in front of Queen's ward. It was 1961 before King Edward's Hospital Fund visited and agreed to a grant of £6,000, now apparently just for staff.

The League of Friends, formed in 1953 by people already visiting patients, raised money, visited lonely patients, organised special tea parties on wards using hospital provisions, provided presents for patients without friends or relatives, outings to pantomimes and the circus in coaches paid for by the amenity fund. Since 1951, the HMC had purchased televisions for the wards, long before most people had them in their own homes. From 1955, the League of Friend's offer to provide them as well was accepted. Two female patients were allowed to bring their own televisions to be used in their wards. By 1960, sets were in nearly every ward. In 1955, a member of the League of Friends suggested setting up clubs for discharged patients and those on trial leave, and Camberwell Borough Council agreed to provide premises. The club opened in September 1956, initially for three months and funded by the LCC, but continued successfully and, from 1957, a coach took selected patients there from the hospital.

Patients' clothing, worn by long stay patients, was neat but drab, particularly men's suits. Some better male patients had tweed jackets and flannel trousers, but all were spoilt by being sent to the laundry. In 1956, it was intended to introduce personal underwear and to create a small room on each side, close to the laundry, where patients could do their personal washing, but this did not happen until 1959.[1]

Chapter 25: Activity and rehabilitation

In 1952, the Commissioners discussed with Dr Walk and the hospital secretary, Mr Chapman, pocket money and incentives for patients doing work which would otherwise have to be done by paid staff. A few patients received comforts to the maximum amount allowed of 4s, but some old people, formerly good workers, received nothing. The following year, working men had 'fairly satisfactory rewards' but few women received them: in the laundry, with a shortage of female labour, rewards might be 'an inducement to many more to co-operate for the general welfare of the hospital'.

The HMC replied that about 690 patients received awards in tobacco or cash at £8,000 a year. Although an extra £1,000 had been allocated, the total cost would be £9,000 which would mean diverting other monies, which would only be 'to the disadvantage of the patients in general'.

In 1956, indigent patients, who had no other available funds, received a maximum of 5s in cash or an ounce of tobacco. There still appeared to be less given to women, with no free issue of sweets or cigarettes. Male working patients, 'doing something useful' received up to 7s 6d a week, and women up to 6s. The Commissioners believed patients doing work, which would otherwise be done by paid staff, should receive more. Pocket money in cash or kind for indigent patients was increased by the Ministry of Health to 10s in 1958.

Up to fifty male patients attended the male OT dept in 1953, making rugs which were sold back to the hospital, stools, chairs, painted wooden articles, and had a lathe, while those in the female OT mainly did embroidery. The RHB agreed to a new x-ray department, partly funded by £3,500 from the King Edward's Hospital Fund. The next year, the Ministry of Health agreed to extend central heating throughout the hospital.

Ward gardens remained, separated from the estate by walls and, in 1955, the fence between Dickens and Ellis wards was altered to allow patients in Ellis to use a high mound to be able to see the recreation field. In 1957, walls of gardens belonging to Guy, Faraday and Ellis ward would be lowered to two feet high, and the curved length of wall bounding part of No. 3 male wall garden demolished, its path within the former wall becoming a footpath besides the road.

The HMC was eager to employ more qualified OTs and, in 1954, two were appointed provided they passed the final examinations of the Association of Occupational Therapists, which they did in January 1955. That summer, the RHB approved posts for another male and female OT, and a part-time clinical psychologist. A radiographer, shared with Warlingham Park Hospital, came for a half day a week. The King Edward's Hospital Fund visited to discuss applications for funding to refurbish wards and an OT department mainly for the admission wards. They also contributed towards modernising the main kitchen and ward kitchens.

From December 1955, individual patients were treated with Largactil, a new major tranquilliser, in order to see how many would benefit from its regular use. This and other new medications would soon have a great effect on patients and life in the hospital.

The new male OT dept opened in May 1956 and, in 1957, a new female occupational department, mainly funded by the King Edward's Hospital Fund. In 1958, old wash basins were replaced and the Commissioners hoped that, before long, all the 'half-size water closet doors', with their lack of privacy, would be replaced. Ten of the fifteen men's wards and nineteen of the twenty-three women's wards had open doors. Over 1,000 patients went freely within the grounds, and 585 were allowed beyond. Fishing trips were arranged for male patients.

On nearly every female ward, there was a craft class, with a rehabilitation programme in the female OT department including dressmaking, cookery, and art, despite ongoing difficulties in filling posts. With a limited establishment of four qualified occupational therapists, even these few posts were not filled. 146 female patients attended the OT department, and 512 were treated on overcrowded female wards. A physiotherapist did physical training and dance classes, and a new physiotherapy department was being built.

In 1958, the Ministry of Health recommended that hours for nursing staff be reduced to 88 hours a fortnight, but the HMC informed the RHB that nurses needed to continue working at least 96 hours because of the acute nursing shortage. In 1959, the nursing staff's union agreed to initially introducing 88 hours for male staff only. With ongoing difficulties in recruitment, in the early 1950s male and female nursing assistants were recruited from Austria. In 1959, matron reported that foreign female nursing students had been limited to one quarter of the total employed, and that only coloured student nurses recommended by the Colonial Office were engaged. To encourage nursing staff, an annual nurses' prize day ceremony was introduced in 1961.

Miss Sharpe, the head OT, resigned in 1958, the HMC again drawing the RHB's attention to the urgent need 'to strengthen the staff of OTs', and its desire to provide recreational standards at Cane Hill of a standard found at other mental hospitals. Despite shortages, the OT departments took part in the Coulsdon Residents Association's arts and crafts exhibition. In 1959, the RHB agreed to an additional OT. In 1960, it was proposed to ask the RHB for permission to extend the female OT department to include rooms for dressmaking, cookery and housewifery classes, and to ask the King Edward's Hospital Fund for a grant.

Daily life changed rapidly. In 1959, with 2,229 patients in the hospital, 1,588 went freely in the grounds, and 738 beyond the estate. Despite having no separate admission unit, admissions rose from 1,115 in 1957 to 1,272 in 1958 and discharges from 974 to 1,002. With 207 excess patients on the female side, some slept in beds in day rooms. Staff shortages continued, especially on the female side. Many elderly people with senile dementia were admitted, spending their last days at Cane Hill.

In March 1960, the Board of Control made its final visit, commenting that 'In a hospital of such high standing, it is not surprising that many recent improvements are evident'. Wards were 'bright, cheerful and very suitably comfortable' and they noted 'a cheerful and harmonious atmosphere'. There was much new furniture including beds with interior sprung or dunlopillo mattresses, replacing old wooden ones. All ward bathrooms were modernised and floors renovated, with new linoleum laid in fourteen wards. There were still open fires on wards, and several chimney fires. Gardens were well kept, with the help of patients, and 'beginning to look very beautiful'. With a lack of accommodation for female nurses and married male nurses, two staff hostels were planned next to the nurses home.

The Cane Hill Chronicle

The patients' magazine began in 1950, under the aegis of the patients' social club, the '48' Club, initially all female patients, put together by the patients with the chaplain as Advisory Editor. A medical officer helped to collate the pages. It gives the clearest view of how life had changed for patients for, in its first edition, one wrote of the 'pulling down [of] many unnecessary restrictions . . . making a fairer prospect for the Patients . . . a great deal of freedom and many social and cultural entertainments.

There was something every evening, often with doctors and senior staff involved. In March 1951, Mr Williamson, a charge nurse, gave a talk about being a regular soldier until selected to serve with the Chindits in Burma, and the patients put together an 'Impromptu Concert, with a pianist and soloists, tap dancing and a compere. There was a party day for deaf and dumb patients.

In April, in the Gramophone Club, Dr Walk played classical records, Dr Gibb presented 'The Feast of Belshezzar' by Walton, while Dr Mitchell talked about Haydn and Mozart. Having come recently, he started the patients' orchestra which gave their first performance with triangles, castanets, tambourines, cymbals, drums, bells, one-note trumpets, rattles, cuckoos and nightingales. Any patient could join, provided their doctor gave permission.

A coach party went to 'Merrie England' at Lewisham Town hall, accompanied by Matron and Mrs Dollar, the chairman. Miss Anna Pollack and Mr Howard Allport from the Sadlers Wells Operatic Company gave a concert as did a professional celloist. Local combined choirs sang Stainer's 'Crucifixion' in the hospital church, and the Countess of Munster and Dr Mitchell's wife gave a concert together.

That same month, Dr Stalker gave a talk about his recent trip to the USA, Father Hickey a slide show on his holiday to Denmark, Dr Walk a lecture called 'Bussing to Bath, or a week in Wiltshire' and Mr Mallet, from Coulsdon Toc H, a talk about fishing.

Already in 1950, there were outings such as trips to Whipsnade and to Brighton, with lunch on the beach, the afternoon watching boating and swimming, tea and then a shopping expedition. In June, the Ramblers Club, with thirteen patients, ended up in Banstead at 5.00 p.m. and found an inexpensive tea shop. A male patient on B1 reported:

Banstead seemed altogether too fashionable for us. One of our party eventually had the courage to enter a tea shop and to our surprise beckoned us inside . . . There were one or two old ladies who eyed us with disfavour. We literally swamped the place . . . I had a feeling of horror that someone was going to produce a packet of sandwiches or a bottle and place it on the table. What they must have thought of us I cannot say . . . we luckily had enough money to pay for our tea so all was well. We raced home, arriving back at 7.00 p.m.

On another occasion, they walked to Reigate, returning on the 404 and 414 buses at 8.15 p.m., having taken a camera with them.

The radio group listened to the Proms while the play reading group met in the Club Room every Thursday at 5.30 p.m. One month, they read *Pygmalion* by Bernard Shaw, *Cuckoo in the Nest* by Ben Travers, and *The Linden Tree* by J.B. Priestley. Patients went to the two cinemas in Purley and, when the new cinematograph equipment came, 'the equal of any outside cinema', the chairman and members of the committee, Dr Walk, Matron and the chaplain came to the showing.

In June 1950, the patients' cricket club played at Botley's Park, Darenth, Springfield and Warlingham Park Hospitals, as well as two evening matches against the clerks and the men in the stores. That same month, a former female patient returned and recalled

the Red Kitchen' in the hospital as a Mecca for many female patients. When the dormitories were opened at 7.00 a.m., a number of patients went down and made an early cup of tea, a few owning their own kettles while the rest used an ordinary clean tin . . . you had to learn to cope with a lidless, handless object filled with boiling water . . . All you require is a piece of rag to twist firmly round the top . . . tea made and poured out, maybe you want to send a cup of tea to an elderly friend who is still in the dormitory.

Over several editions, Dr Fahey and Mr Trenowden, the dispenser, wrote about the trees, shrub, flowers and wild life, describing the whole estate. Tway blade orchids pushed up their twin leaves on the front lawn while wrens were 'trilling sweetly' in Posterns Wood.

In 1951, it described 'The Paint Unit', patients who painted all kinds of items: furniture, fire extinguishers, railings, beds, seats and screens. They had eight-five beds to paint, and eighty-five seats in the women's court yards, having painted those in the men's court yards.

One exchange of correspondence reflected Dr Walk's relationship with his patients, when he wrote to the Editor requesting that if a male patient, 'Reformer', ate his soup instead of drinking it, the Superintendent, sometimes called the 'Supper Attendant' would come and eat it with him. 'Reformer' replied that he wondered why the 'Supper-intendant' wished to eat rather than drink soup – perhaps he drinks his meat instead. Soup having greatly improved since his first letter, he would let the matter rest. At the Commeration Staff Dinner in October 1953, celebrating the hospital's opening seventy years earlier, patients served the staff before their own dinner in the patients' canteen and then returned to hear the speeches – 'a novel idea'.

A patient wrote of being 'the recipient of much kindness and friendliness' during her stay but, in 1956, another complained of having to stand while the nurse in charge said Grace at the end of meals. In 1958, a patient wrote of the 'growth of friendliness . . . a much brighter happier place . . . It's a change from a prison to a hotel . . . More freedom to move about and the angel of kindness everywhere, a Christmas spirit for all the year round'. With the new 1959 Mental Health Act, some were concerned that those who had been patients for a long time would be unable to find employment, or a home for themselves.

Patients obtained employment. One wrote that, after years of illness, she enjoyed working in a doctor's house and had her own room: 'Let the people know what excellent work the Hospital is doing'. A man who left aged 64, after thirty-one years at Cane Hill, and was very happy in full-time employment, wrote that the local council offered employment to former patients in various departments.

However, in December 1961, Dr Walk retired and the Rev, D.V. Davies, chaplain and editor since 1950. Both must have been active supporters, medical staff were no longer involved in supporting the patients' social club and the next edition did not appear until June 1962, as not enough material was submitted. The new chaplain's editorial became a mini-sermon, with the magazine full of his religious and 'uplifting essays' and it ceased in 1965.[1]

Medical treatments

The Commissioners saw rehabilitation and 'habit training' as important but, although there was a very high standard of medical and nursing care, there was an inadequate number of medical staff: the Regional Board agreed to increase it from twelve to sixteen. Medical staff did ten sessions a week in out-patient clinics in general hospitals in South London, and many domiciliary visits at the request of GPs and the duty social worker, while a day hospital had opened at St. Olave's Hospital. Unilateral ECT was used while selected patients, who failed to respond to other treatments, received intensive psychotherapy, with 'encouraging results'. A full-time clinical psychologist was appointed in 1957. Five leucotomies were performed in 1958 and three in 1959. Patients' physical conditions were now treated at Redhill Hospital, and surgery at Dulwich Hospital.

In 1958, four female patients who excreted typhoid organisms, and four other women who no longer excreted organisms but were treated as carriers, were still kept separate to prevent a spread of infection. It is not known how long they remained in Cane Hill. In 1960, one patient had dysentery and fourteen patients TB, mass radiography having been undertaken in December 1959. With the end of the Board of Control's reports in 1960, few records survive of infectious diseases but there was an outbreak of dysentery on the male side in 1963.

Following a trial with Largactil in late 1959, and its introduction as a regularly used treatment, other extensive therapeutic trials took place. Stelazine was provided free by its manufacturers for a considerable time before a charge was made, while Tofranil was successfully used to treat depression. In September 1959, the Group Secretary reported on overspending on medication as, that summer, a further trial of Stelazine took place which, if successful, would continue to be used.

Dr Hutchison reported that it was only at large hospitals, such as Cane Hill, that controlled trials could be carried out, and that many patients benefited and were able to be discharged more quickly, a factor justifying increased expenditure. They were asked to maintain a careful control on expenditure, to report back on their effectiveness and show how much the average length of stay in hospital had reduced.

With new medication, the total number of patients dropped rapidly to 1,686 in 1960. The number of beds having reduced, there remained an extra 182 female patients but 77 vacancies on the male side. In 1959, out of 1,062 admissions, 883 were voluntary, while 661 were admitted from home. Despite this, when a charge nurse was reduced in rank to staff nurse, having been on duty when goods were stolen from Wren Ward, he did not feel he was negligent as, due to an acute shortage of staff, there were seventy-six patients on the ward during the day, and one hundred at night, the goods disappearing in the evening.

In 1957, the RHB revised Cane Hill's catchment area to include Bromley Borough. Two years later, with the 1959 Mental Act, the commissioners envisaged 'a period of much interest and value will be opening at Cane Hill, where so much good work has been done in the past'. The HMC were concerned that treatment of acute mental illness in general hospitals would mean only ill old people would be referred to mental hospitals. Cane Hill served a larger catchment area than any other hospital in the Region. Dr Walk retired in December 1961, the HMC choosing to fill the vacancy by a consultant psychiatrist with clinical duties only, agreed with the RHB.[2]

Chapter 26: Planned Reduction

The Ministry of Health's document, *A Hospital Plan for England and Wales* published in 1962, described Cane Hill as a most efficiently run hospital, but old with large wards, and lacking such facilities as admission units. It must be closed, when alternative accommodation became available for the population which it served, and suggested Cane Hill would amalgamate with Springfield Hospital before its eventual closure in the mid or late 1980s, its responsibilities being taken over by Springfield. Mr Geere saw hints that the closure would be by 1975.

The hospital in 1962 had just under 2,000 patients, with about 700 staff and 300 acres of land.[1] Meeting with the RHB, with Cane Hill's catchment population of 665,000, it was decided there was a future need for 1,000 beds. The RHB concurred that it would be 1977 before a start was to close the hospital.

When it was suggested to dispose of surplus land, the HMC replied that the whole estate including the farm should be retained to give patients reasonable seclusion and necessary facilities for recreation and exercise, apart from the possibility of some land on the periphery for housing. Tranquillisers were the highest expenditure: too much was prescribed and junior doctors should be encouraged not to over prescribe. With continuing staff shortages, the matron and chief male nurse visited areas of severe unemployment to recruit staff: Liverpool, Glasgow, Sunderland, Middlesborough, Belfast and Cardiff.

Life continued: Princess Marina, having made an informal visit in 1961 was invited to the nurses' annual prize giving in October 1963 and open the new female OT centre. If she could not make it, they would ask the actors Brian Rix or Jack Warner or the musician Mr. Semprini, who performed several times at Cane Hill. However, she agreed. In the meantime, the matron and the chief male nurse suggested that visitors continue seeing patients on the wards, rather than return to using the recreation hall on visiting days. Visiting hours were extended to 2.00 to 4.00 p.m. every day, and 6.00 p.m. to 7.30 p.m. on Mondays to Saturdays.[2]

Why?

From 1960 onwards, with the end of the Board of Control, only minutes of the teams managing Cane Hill survive, with some additional reports. The Board of Control had provided a view from the outside, being determined to promote the highest standards and new ideas, but often appearing oblivious to the economic problems of hospitals reliant on central funding, most recently the RHB and, ultimately, the Ministry of Health. The Board was succeeded by the Hospital Advisory Service, who performed a similar function but their reports do not appear to have survived. There can only be supposition as to why the RHB decided to close Cane Hill before Oakwood, in Maidstone, and Bexley Hospitals.

The three mental hospitals admitted patients from south and south-east London, but Cane Hill was situated on land within the South-West Metropolitan Regional Hospital Board (SWMRHB) and seen as being away from its catchment area. It had supported and been involved in bringing services nearer to where its population lived, which reduced the medical presence at Cane Hill identified in the 1950s as having an inadequate number of medical officers.

In that decade, there were many developments in the hospital but much of the funding came from the King Edward's Hospital Fund rather than the RHB. Regular reference was made to Cane Hill receiving lower funding than other mental hospitals. Once the SWMRHB had decided to close Cane Hill, it would appear that only enough funding was given to keep it going at what they appeared to see as an acceptable level, while the management at Cane Hill endeavoured to maintain the building and to introduce new services not only to maintain and improve conditions for the patients but also for its employees, in order to recruit and keep staff and, perhaps hopefully to keep the hospital open in the long term.

A regional drug unit was set up on Salter Ward but, with only seven patients, was considered uneconomical and was closed. A larger improved nurses training school was needed in 1965, but the Chairman thought it a remote chance that it would be funded.

Meanwhile

In 1963, the Ministry of Health announced its intention to sell or lease hospital farms and, by 1967, the farm was leased out, the tenant farmer barring access to two paths and depriving patients of recreational walks. An opening would be made in the fence beyond the cricket pavilion and, perhaps, a footpath to Lion Green Road.

Much ready made food was bought in for both staff and patients, such as fish fingers and cakes, veal and ham pies, sausage rolls, steak and kidney puddings, saveloys, cake, dried carrots, frozen peas and strawberries, as well as tins of broad beans, blackcurrants, peaches, plums, rhubarb, fruit salad, 221 cases of baked beans, sardines and 3,600 tins of tomatoes. Christmas meant two tons of cooking fat and 1,000 tons of turkey. A patient's daily diet should include 5 oz of boneless meat, 2 oz of bacon, one egg and 6 oz of potatoes. The needleroom still made articles including dresses, female nursing uniforms, aprons, sheets and repaired clothing.

In 1965, there had been no burials in the cemetery for many years. It was tidy but headstones and surrounds were badly damaged and strewn about because of vandalism. The head gardener made a site plan and moved the headstones to safe storage within the cemetery, it being suggested that the local council might take it over and convert it into an open space.

With fewer patients, the old and the new farm houses were adapted for staff accommodation. In 1968, when the Greater London Council requested to buy the land between the hospital houses in Chipstead Valley Road, the HMC refused as it was ear-marked for much needed hospital housing. The HMC suggested a swimming pool next to the social club and bowling green in 1966, which was built and available for patients and staff, at separate times, while the staff social club was enlarged in 1966. Up to 160 patients went on holiday to MACA's seaside homes.

Elderly patients were now discharged within four to six weeks of being ready to local authority accommodation in Southwark and Lewisham. It took longer for Bromley and Camberwell, as less accommodation was available. Bermondsey and South Southwark were removed from the catchment area in 1965 but, from July 1965, patients who previously went to Tooting Bec Hospital were accepted. Out patient sessions began at Stepping Stones in Bromley.[3]

In 1966, the King Edward's Hospital Fund was approached for a grant towards a patient's social centre in the laundry yard. Nursing Officers wanted a small hall, tea bar, library, reading room, shop and office estimated at £45,000 for 200 patients and visitors, but the HMC thought a smaller hall adequate. Amenity funds were used for a nine-hole golf pitch and putting course adjoining the swimming pool, and a putting green adjacent to the staff social club's car park, for the use of staff and patients. A recreations officer was appointed to 'organise and further develop patients' leisure and recreational activities and to co-ordinate hospital voluntary activities.

Occupational and industrial therapy

Prior to the 1959 Mental Health Act, industrial therapy was carried out separately in the male and female OT departments. Subsequently, the male OT department became responsible for all industrial therapy for male and female patients while the female OT department, run by qualified occupational therapists, provided assessment and rehabilitation in the other aspects of a person's life, and ran OT sessions on the wards.

The female OT centre was run by a head occupational therapist with a very small number of qualified staff and a growing number of unqualified staff. Unlike neighbouring Warlingham Park and Netherne with large OT departments of a high reputation, Cane Hill's establishment was small and it had difficulty recruiting qualified OTs. In 1969, permission was sought from the Department of Health to employ six OT assistants to assist in keeping elderly patients mobile and to extend OT in the wards.

A census was taken in October 1972 to show how patients were 'occupied' in the hospital:

Women	Total	Under 1 yr in Hospital	Long stay
OT dept	84	35	49
IT	79	2	77
OT & IT on wards	210	33	177
Utility depts	80	3	77
Ward workers	124	8	116
Gardens & grounds	9	1	8

Working outside hospital	23	3	20
Hall group	45		45
Mitchell orchestra	5		5
Total	659	85	574
Pts unoccupied on wards	257	62	195
Pts receiving rewards	280	39	241

Men	Total	Under 1 yr in Hospital	Long stay
OT dept	17	11	6
IT	64	11	53
OT & IT on wards	13		13
Utility depts	45	10	35
Gardens & grounds	55		55
Working outside hospital	21	10	11
Hall group	61	1	60
Total	248	22	226
Pts unoccupied on wards	137	60	77
Pts receiving rewards	248	22	226

In the OT department, women did physical training classes, housewifery, dressmaking, art, cooking, musical appreciation and worked in the typing pool. Women worked in the laundry, needleroom, kitchen, stores, cafeteria and the sewing group.

In OT, men attended physical training classes, art, the typing pool and musical appreciation. They worked in the laundry, kitchen, stores, tailor's shop, upholsterer's shop and tinsmith's shop.

Staff shortages

Despite the reduction in beds, overcrowding continued, the intention being to have 34 beds in each ward. Miss Dowling retired in 1969, and Mr. Philand, acting chief male nurse, recruited in Northern Ireland, hoping twenty-five people would join. In 1970, he became Head of Nursing Services, eventually replacing the matron and chief male nurse.

In 1969, the *Regional Hospital Plan* stated that the Bethlem Royal and Maudsley Hospitals would provide a district service in

Camberwell for short and medium stay patients, long stay patients still being admitted to Cane Hill. The following year area health authorities were set up, Cane Hill becoming the responsibility of Bromley Area Health Authority.

In 1970, the majority of patients were aged over sixty-five, some of whom could live in the community, with about 40 per cent of Cane Hill's patients classified as psycho-geriatric, having dementia. Many of the latter could go to appropriate homes, but approaches to local authorities were unsuccessful as many patients could not conform to their standards, including hygiene, without help and supervision. Dr Thrower, disturbed to see a large number of unoccupied long stay patients, wondered if some could live in hostel-type accommodation.[4]

Unable to recruit nursing staff in the UK, from the 1950s, people were recruited from abroad, mainly from Commonwealth countries. £400 a year was paid to Croydon Borough for a lecturer to take two classes a week teaching colloquial English.

Fewer patients

In 1971, following the conversion of H and K blocks to each house three wards with thirty beds, there were 1,629 beds, 997 female and 632 male. The proposal was to eventually reduce to about 1,300 beds, with lifts installed in all three storey blocks. With increased freedom, fire damage increased on wards, largely the result of patients smoking in bed. The previous year, three 'protected rooms', formerly known as 'padded rooms' were padlocked for a six month trial, their retention to be reviewed in the light of the experience of staff having to nurse disturbed patients without the rooms being available'. It is not known how many remained or for how long.[5]

In 1971, the average bed occupancy was 1,533, leading the Group Secretary to report that the hospital 'was building up a hard-core of long stay chronic patients'. Some consultants tried to restrict the numbers of psycho-geriatrics admitted, by placing them in nursing homes, but no patient who really needed hospitalisation was denied admission.[6] Many patients had no family and, in 1971, it was decided to continue removing corneas from unclaimed bodies for use in corneal grafting.[7]

Plans began in 1973 to prepare a group of nine patients in hospital for discharge to live in a group home, but there was nowhere for them to go. Beckenham Mental Health Association, later Beckenham MIND, was interested and approached Bromley Council to see if they would make a house available, and Lambeth Mental Health Association looked at setting up a house. An out-patient clinic had already opened A day hospital had opened some years earlier at Steeping Stones in Bromley and, now, a day centre for psycho-geriatrics opened there three days a week.[8]

The final meeting of the HMC took place in March 1973, having been informed that a Hospital Management Team (HMT) would run the hospital. It consisted of four men: the finance officer, the administrator representing all the administrative and estate departments, the chairman of the Medical Staff Committee representing clinical staff, the industrial manager, the co-ordinator of voluntary services and the chaplain, and the Chief Nursing Officer representing nursing staff, the recreation officer and the pathology laboratory nurse. Six statutory visitors would visit on a rota basis to report on the state of the hospital and to interview sectioned patients.[9]

Chapter 27: The Hospital Management Team

After its first meeting in April 1973, the Finance Officer submitted to the Area Treasurer a budget of £2,052,932 for the year 1974-5. Croydon Area Health Authority would provide acute hospital facilities for an indefinite period, and supply services. Allowances paid to patients would be increased by £7,500 to £42,500. Working patients who had earned up to £2.99 a week, would now earn up to £4.50. The fête would be as usual in July, but 'tapered' down to entertainments already booked.

As a priority, the HMT looked at the development of OT and Rehabilitation Services. The OT establishment and nursing establishments would each be increased by six assistants, to expand rehabilitation. The chief male nurse, head OT and the recreations officer, Barry Vines appointed in 1972, viewed the physiotherapy department with a view to using it for OT, unable to fill the vacant physiotherapy post, while the chaplain co-ordinated fund raising for a mobile home as a rehabilitation group home.[1]

Mr G.K. Davies, occupations officer and then industrial therapy manager, retired in 1975, to be succeeded by Peter Webster. Coulsdon Rotaract created a garden for patients to look after under the supervision of the OT department, while Barry Vines arranged the first of many day trips to the continent for small groups of patients.

East Lodge, at the entrance to Cane Hill, would be converted into a rehabilitation house preparing groups of patients from the Cottage Hospital for discharge while the former needleroom was converted into seventeen single rooms for nursing staff. A tailoring department, needleroom, mending room and scheme to loan 'hostess dresses' to patients remained, run by the clothing manager. It was still not possible to achieve the objective, decided three years before, that patients visit the clothing department to chose and try on their own clothes.

The SWMRHB sold Stoney Cottages, the HMT asking the RHB for some or all of the proceeds to purchase more accommodation to help alleviate recruitment problems, most local houses remaining too expensive for the majority of staff. The following year, the operating theatre closed. The greenhouses were gradually rotting away, but would be repaired, while trees destroyed by Dutch elm disease needed to be replaced.[2]

More developments were seen in 1976: horse-box doors on ward toilets, would be gradually replaced with full length doors, but there was a backlog of carpentry work. Barry Vines formed a new patients' social club while the new head OT set up groups for admissions, 'mid-term' patients and geriatric patients, ward groups, a domestic rehabilitation group and a projective techniques group. Meanwhile, junior doctors complained that nursing often exerted clinical judgements in areas where they were not trained, and did not exert clinical judgement when they could do. Nursing officers were said to display an off-hand attitude to them.[3]

The HMT appointed the head OT, Mrs Warren as its fifth member, and set up three clinical area multi-disciplinary teams to work in three areas: South Southwark and Lewisham, Camberwell and Bromley.

In 1977, it was suggested that a purpose built secure unit be built on the tennis courts, with a new tennis court next to the swimming pool. Up to £1,000 would be spent to level ground between H and K blocks for a garden to celebrate the Queen's Jubilee, while residents of Portnalls Road were invited to hold a Jubilee Party on the recreation field, provided they accepted full responsibility for looking after them.

As the number of patients reduced, it was planned to close Salter ward, and look at re-allocating beds when wards fell below thirty beds. Nightingale would be closed, its patients transferred to Pugin and Pugin's patients 'decanted' to wards throughout the hospital, the beginning of a steady closure of wards. It was hoped Cane Hill's 'flexible bed reduction plan' might be an example for other hospitals to follow. In the meantime, groups of patients spent weekends in Brighton, with volunteers as escorts. Others went on day trips to Boulogne.

A new beauty salon was set up, run by volunteers and, in 1978, it was hoped to improve the men's clothing and find alternative ways of marking clothing. As volunteers ran an evening social club from 8.00 p.m. to 10.00 p.m., the evening meal was moved to 6.00

p.m. to fit in with patients' social activities. A group was set up by Miss McCoughlin and Barry Vines for patients who frequented the hospital shop area and did nothing else, which would in time move to the former Nightingale Ward.

The head OT produced the *Long Stay Working Party Report*, accepted by the HMT who expressed their support for her recommendations. The rehabilitation programme was running well in the Cottage Hospital and East Lodge, the OT department had produced a detailed assessment showing what each patient could do when discharged, and Bromley Council would be asked for another house in Bromley.

The number of short stay patients at Cane Hill would decrease, and the number of long stay patients increase. According to the *Area Strategic Plan*, there would be no need in ten years time for Cane Hill as it was now: 'resources should be within the community'.

To save money, many traditions ended. In 1978, some patients asked for the fête's reintroduction, but most wanted the money spent on river boat trips and other outings. Each ward would have just one newspaper, and other magazines were reviewed: a saving of £4,000 a year. There was no objection to selling razor blades in the hospital shop. The staff approved the use of the Garden House for patients working out of the hospital, Unions being consulted for their views. Five patients would live in three single rooms and two would share.

Croydon Borough must have refused to buy the cemetery, for the HMT anticipated getting £16,000 from its sale by the RHB. The sale of Cane Hill's farmland was brought forward and the HMT asked to be able to keep the money from the sale. OT and physiotherapy services were reduced because of staff shortages. Unable to recruit newly qualified OT staff, social workers, OTs and physiotherapists proposed a multi-disciplinary day assessment area.[4]

Further economies

Into the 1980s, throughout the country, with overspending in acute units, there was not yet ring-fencing for mental health facilities, so that funding was taken from the latter, vacant posts were frozen and there was less money for building and maintenance.

In 1979, with a serious shortage of nursing staff, and unable to retain staff because of a shortage of housing for married staff, it was announced that Bromley Health Authority was short of £500,000 for the current year, with a need to prioritise redecoration. The reopening of the male residential block for single men was planned, as it was thought men could be recruited from the North of England. 'It would soon become very difficult to provide adequate nursing cover'.

East Lambeth would have only sixty-two beds, consistent with long term plans to concentrate services on Bromley Borough. Asked to make 3 per cent energy savings, heating was reduced in places such as corridors and the chapel. The swimming pool only opened from June to August, a saving of six weeks' energy and labour. However, it was decided to hold a fête in June 1980, to raise money for the amenity fund and to get 'positive publicity', which raised £2,000 for physiotherapy equipment, garden seats, a mobile disco and a record player. In December, the social club's sequence dancing section raised £500 to replace the film projector. The interim medium secure unit opened in the main building in September 1980.

No patients lived in Portnalls which was now dilapidated, and they were trying to close it, but two married couples still lived there in flats. As wards closed, remaining wards were upgraded, as much as capital funding allowed, curtaining for cubicles being a priority. The billiard table in Faraday Ward was sold to pay for improvements in that ward.

Unlike neighbouring mental hospitals, there remained a separate dining room for medical staff: junior doctors complained of its withdrawal, with its waitress service, as they said problems would arise if 'bleeped' while queuing in the cafeteria. One consultant wrote that 'he felt Cane Hill was being denuded of money by the savings which had to be made'. On the other hand, probably assuming that Cane Hill would remain open although reduced in size, and to recruit and retain staff, a post-graduate multi-professional training centre was opened on the top floor of F Block.[5] The hours which nursing staff worked would reduce to a 37½ hour week by April 1981, and a five day week was being negotiated. In March, patients stopped working in the main stores.

The South East Thames Regional Health Authority having sold the cemetery for housing, the developers were to arrange the removal of the thousands of bodies to Mitcham Road Cemetery, Bromley Area Health Authority accepting their offer to create a small memorial garden in the hospital grounds, with Sir James Moody's headstone and a plaque. Great distress was expressed in local newspapers as reports came out about the methods used, including bundling bones into black plastic bags.

The statutory managers visited three wards in 1981, reporting that, in Vanbrugh, 'lavatories were deplorable, there was no privacy in the washroom and poor curtaining in the bathroom and the dormitory carpet was heavily impregnated while its court was full of litter', the result of a demarcation dispute. There was damp in Webb Ward and water penetration in Dickens Ward, while the staff canteen's kitchen appeared a health hazard.

In August, it was decided to sell land to fund projects, particularly to reinstate the Cottage rehabilitation unit, and suggested that laundry be taken in from other hospitals to help Cane Hill's income. The cafeteria's kitchen was cleaned and repaired but, to fund the patient's boutique, the patients social centre, and half the cost of improving the cafeteria, it was suggested approaching The Kings Fund. In September, the RHB authorised land between 81 and 97 Chipstead Valley Road, a children's playground for many years, to be sold to build seven houses, income from the sale to be first used at Cane Hill, the HMT agreeing to the sale in November. When the Area Planning Group questioned if retention of the Cottage was necessary, the HMT responded that, if it closed, rehabilitation would cease as there was nowhere else suitable.

In the ongoing effort to reduce nursing shortages, a new nurses training school opened in 1982. Many ward doors were locked during the day because of staff shortages. The Head of Nursing recommended just twenty-five beds in psychogeriatric wards because of staff shortages and dangers resulting from low staffing levels. Smoking at night by patients could not be solved because of low staffing levels. Three wards were no longer used for nurse training as there were insufficient trained staff. The nursing budget remained underfunded for 1982-3, the HMT sending a letter of concern to Bromley Health Authority (BHA), particularly because of staffing levels on Vanbrugh, Zachary and Wesley wards.

In 1982, the rehabilitation unit was resited in the Garden house and the Cottage closed. The bell on the clock tower needed repairs to bring it back into action costing £1,300, but was not undertaken in the present economic situation.[6] That year, a request was submitted to demolish York and Zachary Block, and an ESMI (elderly senile mentally ill) ward was transferred to Farnborough Hospital.

When an article appeared in the local press about the closure of four wards, it was news to the HMT. The district administrator wrote to ask when an ESMI ward, in addition to four wards, would close. From October, no vacant posts would be filled because of a need to make savings in Bromley Health Authority. Hill Ward needed redecoration, but there were 'many other areas in just as poor or worse conditions'. The HMT was able to increase therapeutic earnings for patients working in IT from £4 to £8.

The South East Thames Regional Health Authority still saw a use for part of the site, for building began in December of a Special Assessment and supervision Service, known as a SASS or, informally, a secure unit, for completion in February 1984.

Poor conditions continued. In November 1982, the statutory visitors 'visited Queens, Olave, Blake and Chaucer. The impression these, some of the worst maintained wards, gave was that the surroundings were having an adverse affect on the quality of life of the patients and staff morale . . . the condition of Blake as an admission ward was deplorable . . we feel very strongly that more attention should be paid to . . . the home of so many patients. Not all was so bad: in January 1983, Shaftesbury and Rossetti were 'bright and cheerful' but one corridor had 'dangerous pot holes', while the boutique eventually opened in May 1983.

The HMT complained that physiotherapy and other budget holders were moving resources from Cane Hill to 'solve a problem at Farnborough Hospital' without any consultation. There was a blockage of patients in group homes on the estate because places were not available in the community. Sixty to ninety patients could go to group homes and other patients to supervised accommodation.[7]

Chapter 28: The Nurses' View - how did we do it?

It was hard, so all had to work together, but there always someone to turn to. Until the mid-1980s, there were over sixty patients in a war, and nearly one hundred in one ward which was on two floors. A ward of sixty contained thirty dependent and thirty independent patients. Lifts were gradually put in where there were blocks with a ground floor and three floors above.

How did we do it? Working with psycho-geriatrics, patients had to be feed, washed and bathed before 8.00 a.m.: it was mass production. Some dormitories had curtains around beds, but not all. We started about 7.15 a.m. and breakfast was served at 8.30, which we dished out. Patients were well fed with a choice of porridge, prunes, kippers, bread and butter, bacon, eggs and baked beans. Afterwards, patients were toileted and made comfortable in chairs: many patients were crippled with contractures, having not been helped to move regularly, a problem with a shortage of staff and time.

We then made the beds, the linen being changed about every ten days unless soiled. It came crisp and white, ironed and folded, 'as white as milk' and smelt of bleach. Dirty linen was carried to the laundry shute.

Mid-morning, the patients had tea and a biscuit: the nurses making the tea with loose tea leaves. Milk and sugar was put in the teapot, as there was no spare time. Some patients went to OT, IT, the garden gang or, until about 1974-5, the farm. Others worked in the kitchen preparing vegetables and washing up. Every working patient had his slot in the work force. Some had jobs outside the hospital, such as Ron who worked in the 'Red Lion'. Another bought newspapers in Coulsdon and sold them in the hospital. Social activities were organised by Barry Vines, the medical staff having done it until he was appointed.

For men, there was communal shaving with one lather for ten to thirty patients, staff queuing the patients up and one staff gave each a lather.

A two to three course lunch was served at 12.00 a.m.: fruit juice, meat and two veg, with pudding and custard (rhubarb, sponge, lots of fruit), lots of bread and butter and tea. The more able had their own teapot on the table.

Patients were then cleaned up, their face and hands washed and bibs removed, and returned to their chairs for a snooze with their feet up. Tea was at 4.00 p.m. with a slice of cake, and supper at 6.00 p.m. Supper was a proper two course meal with meat and two veg, and a pudding. In later years, it became sandwiches or a salad. In the last years, they were ready prepared plated meals.

Nurses spent the afternoon bathing patients, putting laundry away and getting out clean clothes for the next day. Until individual clothes were labelled in the late 1970s, patients were given whatever fitted them. Later, clothes were sorted, put into cubby holes and, later on, there were wardrobes with hangers.

The main bathroom was divided into cubicles with curtains not always fully drawn. There were so many patients and so few nurses: it took three nurses one and a half hours, there being three nurses to sixty patients, and a shortage of staff.

There were no fridges on the wards: as cold storage, there was a low cupboard built onto the north facing side wall of the ward, each with a slate shelf. Milk was delivered in one pint bottles. Later, with fridges on the ward, milk came in a big plastic container, with a 'teat', and called a 'cow', and stored in the fridge.

Unlike other mental hospitals at that time, the male and female sides remained very separate. Patients could only meet in the communal areas in the middle, not even in the corridors on either side.

The hospital was a community within itself: many a marriage started and ended in the staff social club. There were staff cottages in Chipstead Valley Road, Portnalls Road and Vincent Road, while doctors lived near Portnalls. The chief male nurse lived in East Lodge, which became a half-way house for patients, while Back Lodge was originally occupied by the chief male nurse and then his deputy.

The tailor made uniforms for the male nursing staff: a three piece suit with a waistcoat, and white coats to wear on wards. Female nurses had six frocks. Nursing assistants wore white, staff nurses light blue, enrolled nurses green and sisters dark blue, while student nurses wore striped blue, all with a belt which varied depending on the grade, black tights and shoes and a cap.

Later days

For a long time, there was talk of Cane Hill closing, but no-one really believed it. Everything was provided in the hospital for staff and patients: both could buy food and clothes there. In the staff social club, beer was half the normal price. Staff formed friendships, but were institutionalised. They supported each other: there would be a whip-round for a funeral if someone's relative died.

For patients, on the positive side, in the last years, there was dignity, independence, more privacy, more say and control in their lives. On the negative side, they had to remain because they had nowhere to go to - they got low and depressed at Christmas and the New Year. There was more entertainment but nowhere to get a job, apart from going to OT and IT.

It was an enclosed secluded environment, away from society. Patients would live, eat, socialise and die there. There were bonds of friendship with each other and with staff. One didn't have to behave or measure up because the behaviour was accepted. Living in the community, people have to work to be accepted.

Chapter 29: Planned Closure

In 1985, the South East Thames Regional Health Authority (SE-TRHA) published its *Regional Mental Health Strategy 1985-1994*, concluding that the future of Cane Hill was 'at risk'. '£3.4 million pounds needed to be spent over the next five years . . . for it to reach an operationally acceptable standard'. There was an evident lack of resources available for rehabilitation and care of the long term mentally ill, and no sign of the situation improving. The chronic low funding was reflected in low staffing ratios and the deteriorating physical condition of the hospital.[1]

The Cane Hill Site Management Group began in April 1986 and, in May, Bromley Health Authority published its *Cane Hill Hospital Reduction Control Plan*, intending to run down the hospital and create local comprehensive services within the areas covered by Bromley, Lewisham and North Southwark, and Camberwell Health Authorities. Since 1992, wards had closed by transferring patients to Farnborough, Hither Green and Dulwich Hospitals, and the revenue had moved to those health authorities, so that staffing ratios at Cane Hill were little improved. It acknowledged that the revenue funding of the hospital had been low compared to other psychiatric hospitals for many years.

The hospital now occupied about 192 acres, of which less than a quarter was occupied by hospital buildings. From 1979 the north side, originally for male patients, had gradually closed down being in a worse state than the south side, having received less maintenance for many years.

By the end of 1985, fifteen of the forty-one wards had closed, the remaining wards having a maximum of thirty beds, and with 636 patients in the hospital: 274 long stay, 102 long stay and now elderly, 200 with elderly senile mental illness (ESMI) and 60 acute patients. It was the policy in 1985 to integrate male and female together on the wards, but only ten wards were suitable.

As for staff accommodation, there were thirty houses dating back to the 1880s, ten new houses bought to assist in recruitment and, on the estate, eight for staff with families and ten units for single staff. By 1991, it was estimated that the hospital would become unviable with just 52 patients left, each costing over £19,000 a year to maintain, and the responsibility of Bromley Health Authority. It should then close.

The nursing staff

There were mixed feelings. Some welcomed the future, while many others resented the closure and an unknown future.

Throughout Cane Hill's existence, there were very good, good, indifferent and poor nurses, and every decade a few recorded cases of abuse, at its worst in the 1890s. Many patients made complaints, all of which were investigated, but supporting witnesses could not always be found. With ongoing serious staff shortages since World War Two, they worked year after year in incredibly difficult situations to keep the institution going, although, once the hospital was closed, some staff spoke of a number of staff who regularly ate patients' food, strictly against the rules, and appropriated part of patients' tobacco rations and reward money.

Joe Callanan began at Cane Hill in the late 1950s, becoming a charge nurse in 1967, and wrote in 1986 that he never saw any cruelty there but, when he began 'staff were organised with military discipline; the charge nurses were mostly ex-army. The staff had to toe the line – or else. Everything was very regimented'.[2]

Resettlement Teams

While an administrative team did all the overall planning and organised the closure of Cane Hill, three multi-disciplinary teams were created, one for each health authority, to assess patients, recommend the most appropriate type of accommodation and prepare their patients for discharge from Cane Hill. Each team decided on different types of accommodation, depending on the patients' needs, and local facilities.

Bromley's team, formed in early 1988 and later known as the Positive Futures Team, was the last to be put together as its patients were the last to leave, working with patients in Cane Hill and Oakwood Hospital, the latter transferred to Cane Hill for six months before discharge. Apart from its nursing staff, who had worked in Cane Hill, the remainder of the team were recruited from outside: a clinical psychologist, social worker, two occupational therapists and a secretary. The hospital's consultant in rehabilitation was part of the team.

Each patient had an individual worker who got to know him or her well, finding out about his or her history, skills and hopes. Staff from the resettlement team and patients went out together for the day to the house and neighbourhood where the patients would live, visiting shops and other places, shopping and cooking lunch together. Fried eggs were a great favourite as, because of fears of salmonella, they were no longer served in hospital, with fried bacon. Patients were helped to choose furniture, curtains, etc, a difficult challenge for many who had not exercised choice for many years.

A few were initially transferred to Farnborough Hospital, and ESMI patients to nursing homes, but most went to live in five bedroomed houses in Bromley Borough, purchased by Bromley Health Authority and run by Bromley Care Services, now known as Community Options.

Nursing staff from Cane Hill who were appointed to work in the new homes, where they would support residents, being trained in new concepts and likewise prepared for their new life. Now people would, with help, have their own rooms, keep house and shop, and learn to cook their own meals. Two houses, with less able patients, had cooks.

Work and Play

While a social club was opened one afternoon a week in Bromley, house staff helped people to do ordinary things in Bromley, although many missed seeing their friends daily in Cane Hill's corridors. For those wanting to work, Horizon House, a clubhouse, was set up in Bromley based on the Fountain House model, and the first to be set up within the NHS, where staff and members worked together to develop work skills.[3]

* * * * *

Although the SASS unit continued on part of the estate, Cane Hill Hospital's last patient left a few days before the end of March, 1992, nearly ninety years after the first arrived. In 1992, it was the largest mental hospital closure so far.

As the country became increasingly industrialised and people began to move into urban areas early in the nineteenth century, asylums had become warehouses for those whose behaviour was such that the family or the community could not cope with them.

Medical superintendents and hospital committees were careful to ensure that patients were discharged to a safe environment and, if there was no family, until the 1960s, there were few places where a person with ongoing mental health problems could live in the community. Workhouses were full and generally did not want them and the asylums, later mental hospitals, were left to care for them, usually until death.

Asylums were built away from communities but they were not immune from national life. Wars, economic crises and national policies had their impact on both staff and patients. Now, most of Cane Hill Hospital has gone and those who resided and worked there, in its last days, live amongst us again.

Appendix 1

In 1887, the following description of Cane Hill Asylum, prepared by A. Henry Frend, an architect in London and related to Dr Moody's wife, was sent to Dr. Thomas Morton, Chairman of Pennsylvania's State Committee on Lunacy.

Situation. – The third and most recently built asylum for the county of Surrey is situated about five miles from the town of Croydon and two and one-half miles from Caterham Junction Station, in joint use of the London, Brighton and South Coast and South-Eastern railways. It is close to the main coach route from London to Brighton, which forms south-eastern boundary of the estate and runs somewhat parallel with and near to the railway line, passing this position in a deep cutting in the valley. For the use of the asylum there is a private goods siding at Stoat's Nest, about three-fourths of a mile distant.

Estate. – The estate lies in a hilly and very open country, and is one hundred and fifty-one acres in extent. The sub-soil is flinty chalk, thinly covered by loam, there being in one corner a bed of flints, gravel and sand valuable for road and path making and building purposes. There are two approach roads with lodges, and the area is apportioned as follows:

	Acres	Roods	Poles
Main buildings, including airing courts	11	0	0
Sewerage irrigation for growing Italian rye grass	8	0	0
Pasture land, including cricket field	18	0	0
Arable land, for potatoes and other vegetables for the patients and staff and roots for the stock	42	2	0
Kitchen, garden, fruit trees and bush fruit	17	3	0
Ornamental or pleasure grounds	3	1	0
Cemetery	2	0	0
Roads, boundary and other plantations, woods and detached buildings and ground to be developed	48	2	0
Total	151	0	0

The sewerage is to be alternated every three years. With the exception of some old woods, everything in the way of laying out and bringing land under cultivation has had to be done since the erection of the asylum, and though very much has been done, the work is not quite finished.

Site of Main Building. – the main building stands upon an elevated platform 450 feet above the sea level and 180 feet above the Brighton coach road. It faces the south-east and commends extensive and beautiful views of the surrounding countryside. This, as also the detached buildings, are constructed mainly of stock bricks, with red bricks and Portland stone dressings and slate roofs, the main front being faced with second malms, but the chaplain's house and cottage hospital have tile roofs and have been faced above the ground floors with weather tiling.

Design. – As will be seen by the plans, the asylum is on the block system, with covered ways connecting everyway thereof, and by the forethought of Mr. Howell, these have been so sloped as to dispense with steps, although the levels differ as much as 26 feet, starting from the front. At the south side stands the medical superintendent's house and office. The center is occupied by the hall porter and entrance hall, and on the east side are the ground floor committee rooms and clerks and medical officers' offices. First floor, medical officers' quarters: second floor, accommodation for dispenser, assistant steward and assistant clerk, with common sitting room. Thence in succession backwards are the chapel, with retiring rooms, chaplain's room and library surgery, recreation hall, sculleries, officers' mess room, kitchen, dairy and meat store, steward's store, bake house, laundry and wash house, engine and boiler house, water tower, coal stores, work shops and mortuary. These are common to and separate the south-western or female blocks from the north-eastern or male blocks.

Administrative Offices. – The chapel has been cleverly designed by contrasting a moderate proportion of red cutters and sundry other varieties of superior bricks amongst the stocks, a small quantity of Portland and Forest of Dean stone being so judiciously introduced as to produce a singularly effective whole at the minimum cost. It contains the usual fittings, including a fine organ, and is capable of seating 840 person, as follows: Nave, 433; north aisle, 145; south aisle, 145; north transept, 33; south transept, 48; chancel, 36.

The recreation hall has a ground floor space (exclusive of stage) 94 feet 6 inches long and fifty feet in width, besides which there is at one end a gallery to seat 130 persons and at the other is a large stage, with property and dressing rooms beneath. In the recess on one side a refreshment counter has been fixed in direct communication with the culinary department. The seats are all movable, so as to admit of suitable arrangements for either dancing or theatricals, concerts and the like entertainments, and the stage is exceptionally well fitted with the most modern and approved appliances. This hall has been built with a view to its being some day used as a dining hall should it ever be considered advisable to apply it to that purpose.

The kitchen is provided with means for cooking by steam, gas or coal.

The steward's stores have a tunnel leading through the cellars to the yard, for the purpose of conveying heavy stores into the center of the building without passing through the covered ways used by the patients.

The laundry department is unusually spacious and fitted with the most convenient modern appliances both for hand and machine washing. The drying (when not in the open air) is done by drying closets heated by steam, and these are far beyond the usual allowance. Soft water from a tank, in which all the rain water is collected, is available for washing.

The water tower is 107 feet high, and its cistern is capable of holding 34,000 gallons of water, which can be thrown over the highest parts of the building.

Wards. – The wards vary greatly in form and size. The cubic space per patient varied from 788 to 613 feet in the dormitories, and 491 to 619 feet in the day rooms. The superficial area per patient is 50 feet in the dormitories and 40 feet day space. The single rooms range from 1,267 cubic feet in the infirmaries, and 876 in ward D, to 787 cubic feet in ward H, which is the least space in any ward. Ward A, specially adapted for the reception and treatment of the sick and infirm, is two stories high, and both floors have day and night accommodation, thus obviating the necessity of continually carrying helpless patients up and down stairs. B and C wards, for the epileptic and suicidal cases, are also identical in construction. They also are of two stories, with day and night accommodation on both floors. Connected with their dormitories are single rooms, planned with a view to continual night supervision, having open panels to the doors and a gas lamp throwing a light into the room. In ward D, for the treatment of general acute cases (first and second floors actually acute cases, third floor chronic cases subject to exacerbations of their disease), the proportion of single rooms is high, and two of them are padded; but the dormitories contain fewer patients.[2] E, F, G and H wards are for the chronic working cases, where a large proportion of attendants and nurses is unnecessary. Each ward is most complete in itself, containing day rooms, dormitories, single rooms, attendant's rooms, small sculleries or kitchens, store rooms, lavatories to both day rooms and dormitories and closets, and in A, B, C and D wards bath rooms on each floor. For the other wards, there are in either division two large general bath rooms, containing nine baths, with dressing rooms attached.

Though all cooking is done in the large kitchen, and the food conveyed to the ward in very large covered dishes and by means of trucks, and the dinners are *quite* hot when they get to the wards, ward sculleries have cooking ranges, and for summer use gas stoves, for keeping food hot if required, warming beef tea, cooking a chop and such like accessory work.

Ward and other fittings. – The ward fittings of every description are very complete amongst those coming into my province and especially worthy of note are: Lock lever stops to the bath valves to prevent the hot water being turned on before the cold; sashes deeply sunk to the sills, thus enabling the windows to be raised sufficiently to admit fresh air at the meeting rails, without their being open below (these also afford an additional safe guard against driving rains); and locks to the sashes so that they can be thrown open to air the wards when the patients are all out, and, when locked, can only be raised five inches high.

Throughout the buildings are anti-percussion taps (hot and cold) to prevent waste, by being set to run only a certain quantity,

---

[2] At the bottom of the page, the wards are described more fully: 'Ward D has a larger proportion of single rooms than any other ward in the building, therefore it is more suitable for acute cases. Cases are admitted in four classes: I. Infirm into A; II. Suicidal into C; III. Epileptics into B; IV. Acute mania, D. they are then drafted off into other wards according to circumstances. The class that sleep on the third floor of D are chronic cases subject to exacerbations of their disease. The actually acute cases are on the second and third floors. General paralytics are located according to the stage of their disease. The advanced cases are in the infirmaries A; those in a stationary condition in the chronic wards; a few of the more troublesome in B'.

until turned on again. The locks are to master keys. Electric bells and telephones are used, and night attendance is checked by an electric tell-tale clock, indicating in the superintendent's office.

Decoration. – All the internal woodwork has been stained and varnished, and the wards and other parts of the asylum have been most tastefully painted, papered and otherwise decorated under the superintendence and in accordance with the designs of Dr. Moody, the medical superintendent.

Lighting. – the lighting is by means of gas laid on from the town of Croydon – a gasometer, though proposed, not having been erected on the estate.

Warming and Ventilation. – The warming and ventilation have been carefully considered. The former is effected by hot water pipes, supplemented by open fires. The latter by the introduction of fresh warmed air at the floor levels and foul air flues, and at the ceiling levels, with extracting shaft to each ward.

Water Closets and Drains. – The water closets are separated as far as possible from the wards and are freely ventilated. Each apparatus is supplied by an anti-percussion valve, worked by seat lever action. The soil pipes run down the external faces of the outside walls and ventilate above the eaves of the roofs; and they have inspection plates at convenient intervals. All drainage is efficiently trapped, and the drains are carried outside the buildings. They flow into intercepting chambers, and finally discharge into tanks forming the reservoirs fore the sewerage irrigation, which is carried out by taking advantage of the natural fall of the land.

Water. – Water is obtained from an unfailing well ninety-seven feet below the level of the Brighton road and eight feet in diameter. A distinct service runs from the main cistern to an adequate number of fire hydrants, which are inclosed in cupboards having glass panels, and every other requisite: but beyond this there are many other and most careful precautions for fire extinction and life saving.

Airing Court Wells. – The airing courts (tastefully laid out and planted) have sunk walls in order not to obstruct the view or give an air of confinement. Where the level of the ground requires it, they have cuttings on both sides.

Detached Buildings. – The detached buildings will be seen by reference to the sketch plan of the estate (also vide ground plan). I may however add the following remarks:

The cottage hospital is for infectious diseases. So long as it is not required for this purpose, it is occupied by quiet women in charge of a married nurse.

The accommodation for patients (male only) in the gardener's and farm bailiff's houses is nearly similar top that of the cottage hospital.

There are two cottages at the gas or water works.

The green houses are for the raising of plants for the wards.

The cottages for married attendants are built in two blocks of eight cottages each, the end cottages of both blocks being double dwellings, viz: for distinct occupations, that on the ground floor having its entrance at the back, and the floor being entered in front.

The Lodge at the Brighton road entrance is occupied by the clerk of the works. That at the goods or back approach by the engineer.

The stables are for the visitors and medical superintendent.[3]

The farm buildings are for the accommodation of the farm horses, thirty milch cows, breeding and slaughter pigs, and such live stock as may be from time to time purchased for the consumption of the asylum.

New Buildings. – The new buildings, to accommodate about nine hundred patients, will be similar to the old; their designs, however, are as yet in course of preparation.

All the present *administrative* offices were designed in anticipation of this enlargement of the asylum.

---

3   The 'visitors' would be the visiting committees.

Bibliography

Primary sources: printed

R. Adair, J. Melling & B. Forsythe, 'Migration, Family Structure and Pauper Lunacy in Victorian England: Admissions to the Devon County Pauper Lunatic Asylum, 1845-1900', *Continuity and Change*, 12 (1997). A. Millicent Ashdown, *A Complete System of Nursing*, (London, 1917, 1924 ed.), pp. 336-51.

P. Barham, *Forgotten Lunatics of the Great War*, (New Haven & London, 2004, 2007 ed.).

P. Bartlett, *The Poor Law of Lunacy* (Leicester, 1999).

P. Bartlett and D. Wright, *Outside the Walls of the Asylum* (London, 1999).

P.J.N. Buttrey, Quiet and orderly: the administration, placement and treatment of pauper lunatics in Croydon from 1875 to 1914, 2008, pp. 39-40. Unpublished MA dissertation.

Commissioners in Lunacy, *Annual Reports*, 68 vols (London 1845-1913).

Commissioners of the Board of Control, *Annual Report*, (London, 1915).

Croydon Union, A Statement of the Union Accounts and a list of the Guardians, Officers etc of the Croydon Union for the year ending Lady Day 1889, Chairman's Annual Statement.

S. Fowler, *Workhouse* (Kew, 2007).

D. Henderson and I. Batchelor, *Henderson's and Gillespie's Textbook of Psychiatry* (1927, London, 1962 edn).

Journal of Medical Science, Review of the Forty-Seventh Report of the Commissioners in Lunacy, 7 June 1893, vol. 39.

C. B. Ker, Claude Rendle (rev.), *Ker's Manual of Fevers*, (Oxford, 1911, 1927 ed.).

N. Longmate, *The Workhouse* (1974, London, 2003 edn.).

K. S. Lynn, *Charlie Chaplin and his Times*, (London, 1997).

D. Mellett, *The Prerogative of Asylumdom: Social, Cultural and Administrative Aspects of the Institutional Treatment of the Insane in Nineteenth Century England* (London, 1982).

P. Michael, *Care and Treatment of the Mentally Ill in North Wales*

1800-2000, (Cardiff, 2003).

W.L. Parry-Jones, 'Model of the Geel Lunatic Asylum', in A. Scull (ed.), *Madhouses, Mad-Doctors and Madmen. The Social History of Psychiatry in the Victorian Era* (London, 1981).

Report of the London County Council for the year 1904-1905, (London, 1906), p. 50.

I. Scales (ed.), *A History of Coulsdon*, (Bourne Society, 2000).

A. Scull, *The Most Solitary of Afflictions. Madness and Society in Britain, 1700-1900*
(Yale, 1993).

V. Skultans, *English Madness: Ideas on Insanity, 1580-1890* (London, 1979).

L. D. Smith, *Care, Comfort and Safe Custody: public lunatic asylums in early nineteenth-century England* (Leicester, 1999).

The Croydon Advertiser and East Surrey Reporter.

The Croydon Guardian

The Croydon Guardian & Surrey Gazette.

The Croydon Times.

The London County Council Record of Service in the Great War 1914-18 by Members of the Council's Staff, (London, 1922).

The Times

D. Wright, 'Getting Out of the Asylum: Understanding the Confinement of the Insane in the Nineteenth Century', *Social History of Medicine*, 9 (1997).

D. Wright, *Mental Disability in Victorian England* (Oxford, 2001).

Secondary sources

R. Adair, B. Forsythe and J. Melling, '"A proper lunatic for two years": pauper lunatic children in Victorian and Edwardian England: child admissions to the Devon County Asylum, 1845-1914', *Journal of Social History*, 31 (1997), pp. 371-405.

R. Adair, B. Forsythe and J. Melling, 'A danger to the public? Disposing of pauper lunatics in late-Victorian and Edwardian England: Plympton St. Mary Union and the Devon County Asylum, 1867-1914', *Medical History*, 42(1998), pp. 1-25.

M.A. Crowther, *The Workhouse System 1834-1939* (1981, London, 1983 edn.).

M. Finnane, 'Asylums, Families and the State', *History Workshop Journal*, 20 (1985) pp. 134-48.

W. Ll. Parry-Jones, *The Trade in Lunacy. A study of Private Madhouses in England in the Eighteenth and Nineteenth Centuries* (London, 1972).

C. F. Patterson, 'Rationales for the Use of Occupation in 19th Century Asylums', *British Journal of Occupational Therapy*, 60 (1997) pp. 179-83.

A. T. Scull, *Museums of Madness. The Social Organisation of Insanity in Nineteenth-Century England* (1979, London, 1982 edn.).

A. Scull, C. MacKenzie and N. Hervey, *Masters of Bedlam: The Transformation of the Mad-Doctoring Trade* (Princetown, 1996).

A. Scull (ed.), *The Asylum as Utopia: W.A.F. Browne and the Mid-Nineteenth Century Consolidation of Psychiatry* (London, 1991).

E. Showalter, *The Female Malady: Women, Madness and English Culture, 1830-1980* (1985, London, 2007 edn.).

P. Wood, *Poverty and the Workhouse in Victorian Britain* (Stroud, 1991).

D. Wright and A. Digby (eds), *From Idiocy to Mental Deficiency: Historical Perspectives on People with Learning Difficulties* (London, 1996).

Abbreviations

BC   Board of Control
CA   Croydon Archives
CL   Commissioners in Lunacy
LMA   London Metropolitan Archives
T.C.A. *The Croydon Advertiser*
TNA   The National Archives

Notes

CHAPTERS
The Background
1. D. Mellett, *The Prerogative of Asylumdom: Social, Cultural and Administrative Aspects of the Institutional Treatment of the Insane in Nineteenth Century England* (London, 1982), p. 28.
2. V. Skultans, *English Madness. Ideas on Insanity, 1580-1890* (London, 1979), p. 114.
3. D. Wright, *Mental Disability in Victorian England* (Oxford, 2001), pp. 16-8.
4. P. Bartlett, *The Poor Law of Lunacy* (Leicester, 1999), p. 41.
5. A. Scull, *The Most Solitary of Afflictions. Madness and Society in Britain, 1700-1900* (Yale, 1993), pp. 315-33.
6. Mellett, *Prerogative of Asylumdom*, pp. 39-43.
7. Scull, *Most Solitary*, pp. 355-8.
8. Skultans, *English Madness*, pp. 132-3.
9. N. Longmate, *The Workhouse* (1974, London, 2003 edn.), p. 219.
10. Scull, *Most Solitary*, p. 362.
11. Bartlett, *Lunacy*, p. 48.
12. R. Adair, J. Melling and B. Forsythe, 'Migration, Family Structure and Pauper Lunacy in Victorian England: Admissions to the Devon County Pauper Lunatic Asylum, 1845-1900', *Continuity and Change*, 12 (1997), p. 394.

Planning the Asylum
1. Now called Springfield Hospital.
2. LMA, H46/SP/A/02/005.
3. *The Croydon Advertiser*, 6.2.1875.
4. *T.C.A.*, 6.2.1875.
5. CL, 35th *Report, 1881*, pp. 300-2.
6. LMA, LCC/MIN/854.
7. *T.C.A.*, 10.7.1875.
8. *T.C.A.*, 17.7.1875.
9. *T.C.A.*, 9.10.1875.
10. *T.C.A.*, 18.9.1875.
11. *T.C.A.*, 25.9.1875.
12. LMA, H46/SP/A/02/006.
13. LMA, H46/SP/B/01/001B.
14. LMA, LCC/MIN/854.
15. TNA, RG11/807/86.
16. LMA, LCC/MIN/856.
17. Ian Scales (ed.), *A History of Coulsdon*, (Bourne Society, 2000), p. 118.
18. LMA, LCC/MIN/856. Scales, *Coulsdon*, p. 101-2: the Croydon, Merstham and Godstone Iron Railway, a horse-drawn railway, which ran from Croydon Old Town, opened in 1805 but was unsuccessful and was bought by the London & Brighton Railway. Part of its embankment survives at the back of the car park, formerly part of the Cane Hill estate, in Lion Green Road
19. Scales, *Coulsdon*, p. 34.
20. LMA, LCC/MIN/857.
21. LMA, LCC/MIN/856.
22. LMA, LCC/MIN/862.
23. See Appendix 1.
24. LMA, LCC/MIN/859.

[25] LMA, LCC/MIN/857. Strong dresses were used as a means of restraint for females, the ends of the sleeves being sewn so as to enclose the hands.
[26] LMA, LCC/MIN/862.
[27] LMA, LCC/MIN/856.

Opening Cane Hill

[1] *T.C.A.*, 26.1.1884.
[2] LMA, LCC/MIN/857.
[3] LMA, LCC/MIN/862.
[4] LMA, LCC/MIN/858.
[5] LMA, LCC/MIN/862.
[6] LMA, LCC/MIN/657.
[7] LMA, LCC/MIN/858.
[8] LMA, LCC/MIN/862.
[9] LMA, LCC/MIN/863.
[10] LMA, LCC/MIN/858.
[11] LMA, LCC/MIN/859.
[12] None have survived but, at other asylums, photographs were taken on admission and discharge.
[13] CL, *41st Report*, 1887.
[14] LMA, LCC/MIN/858.
[15] LMA, LCC/MIN/859.
[16] CA, CAN/1/1.
[17] CL, *39th Report 1885*, pp. 287-9.
[18] LMA, LCC/MIN/858.
[19] CL, *40th Report*, 1886, pp. 239-42.
[20] CL, *42nd Report*, 1886, p. 240.
[21] CL, *41st Report*, pp. 261-3.
[22] CL, *41st Report*, 1887, pp. 261-3.
[23] CL, *42nd Report*, 1888, pp. 252-4.

Staff and patients 1888-1889

[1] CA, CAN/5/1/3
[2] CA, CAN/5/2/1
[3] CA, CAN/5/1/3
[4] LMA, LCC/MIN/859.
[5] LMA, LCC/MIN/863.
[6] CA, CAN/5/1/3. From 1887, patients were transferred to Gloucester Asylum.
[7] LMA, LCC/MIN/859
[8] CL, *42nd Report, 1888*, pp. 252-4.
[9] CL, *43rd Report*, 1889, pp. 273-5.
[10] These books are in the London Metropolitan Archives.
[11] CA, GUA/1/1/13, p. 62.
[12] CA, GUA/1/1/12, p. 376, p. 603.
[13] CA, GUA/1/1/12, p. 494.
[14] CA, GUA/1/1/12, Assessment Committee 13 Nov. 1885, Settlement & Removal Committee, 1 Dec. 1885.
[15] CA, GUA/1/1/13, p. 62.
[16] CA, GUA/1/1/13, pp. 146-7.
[17] CA, GUA/1/1/14 pp. 104-5.
[18] CA, GUA/1/1/11, p. 364.
[19] CA, GUA/1/1/12, p. 300, p. 323.
[20] CL, *40th Report*, 1886, p. 242.
[12] CA, GUA/1/1/11, pp. 233, 269-70.
[22] CL, *39th Report*, 1885, p. 108.
[23] CA, GUA/1/1/11, 16 September 1884.
[24] Journal of Medical Science, *Review of the Forty-Seventh Report of the Commissioners in Lunacy, 7 June 1893*, vol. 39, pp. 560-70.

[25] P.J.N. Buttrey, *Quiet and orderly: the administration, placement and treatment of pauper lunatics in Croydon from 1875 to 1914*, 2008, pp. 39-40. Unpublished MA dissertation.
[26] LMA, H46/SP/B/01/111.
[27] CA, CAN/2/1/1/1
[28] LMA, LCC/MIN/862.
[29] LMA, LCC/MIN/859.
[30] CL, *44th Report*, 1890, pp. 218-22.
[31] LMA, LCC/MIN/862.
[32] LMA, LCC/MIN/857.
[33] LMA, LCC/MIN/862-3.
[34] CA, GUA/1/1/12, p. 300; GUA/1/1/13, p. 100.
[35] CL, *42nd Report*, 1888, p. 240.
[36] CL, *39th Report*, 1885, p. 96.
[37] CL, *41st Report*, 1887, p. 81.
[38] CL, *44th Report*, 1890, p. 83.
[39] CL, *43rd Report*, 1889, p. 94.
[40] L. D. Smith, *Care, Comfort and Safe Custody: public lunatic asylums in early nineteenth-century England* (Leicester, 1999), pp. 201-2: Sir Alexander Monson of the Surrey Asylum considered blistering the nape of the neck was 'beneficial' to patients by producing 'counter-irritant effects'. It was commonly used to treat those with mania, melancholia, epilepsy and general paralysis. Cold shower baths were believed to help calm patients with mania, while warm baths helped to lift depression.
[41] A. Scull, *The Most Solitary of Afflictions. Madness and Society in Britain, 1700-1900* (Yale, 1993), p. 322.
[42] CL, *44th Report*, 1890, pp. 218-22.
[43] CL, *44th Report*, 1890, p. 86.
[44] LMA, LCC/MIN/863.
[45] LMA, LCC/MIN/858.
[46] LMA, LCC/MIN/859.
[47] LMA, LCC/MIN/864.

Overcrowding

[1] LMA, LCC/MIN/857.
[2] LMA, LCC/MIN/862.
[3] LMA, LCC/MIN/863.
[4] CA, GUA/1/1/12, p. 563.
[5] LMA, LCC/MIN/859.
[6] CL, *42nd Report*, pp. 252-4.
[7] LMA, LCC/MIN/859.
[8] Ian Scales (ed.), *A History of Coulsdon*, (Bourne Society, 2000), p. 103. It was renamed as Coulsdon South Station in 1923, and the goods yard closed in 1931.
[9] LMA, LCC/MIN/859.
[10] CL, *44th Report*, 1890, pp. 218-22.
[11] LMA, LCC/MIN/859.
[12] CA, GUA/1/1/14, pp. 162, 176, 187, 203, 220, 248.
[13] C.A., Croydon Borough Lunacy Visiting Committee, vol. 1.
[14] CL, *45th Report*, 1891, pp. 167-9.
[15] CL, *46th Report*, 1892, pp. 183-5.
[16] CL, *47th Report*, 1893, pp. 182-4.
[17] CL, *49th Report*, 1895, pp. 233-5.
[18] CL, *49th Report*, 1895, p. 367.
[19] CA, GUA/1/1/16, pp. 186, 416, 447-8, 460, 478.

[20] CA, GUA/1/1/18, pp. 2, 56-7, 140.
[2] CA, Croydon Union, *A Statement of the Union Accounts and a list of the Guardians, Officers etc of the Croydon Union for the year ending Lady Day 1889*, Chairman's Annual Statement, p. 3. 1889.
[22] CA, GUA/1/1/18.
[23] W.L. Parry-Jones, *Model of the Geel Lunatic Asylum*, in *Madhouses, Mad-Doctors and Madmen. The Social History of Psychiatry in the Vistorian Era*, ed. Andrew Scull, London 1981, p.212.
[24] P.J.N. Buttrey, *Quiet and orderly: the administration, placement and treatment of pauper lunatics in Croydon from 1875 to 1914*, 2008, pp. 11-6. Unpublished M.A. dissertation. On 1 January 1914, 92.9 per cent were in asylums, 6.7 per cent in the workhouse, nearly all being imbeciles, and 0.4 per cent (two people) had out-relief.
[25] CA, GUA/1/1/18.

A time of change 1889-1899
[1] CA, CAN/1/8.
[2] V. Skultans, *English Madness. Ideas on Insanity, 1580-1890*, (London, 1979), p. 122.
[3] Cane Hill Asylum was not alone in not having enough beds. In 1893, the Commissioners reported that 'asylums are almost everywhere overcrowded and that accommodation for the insane is in so many places so inadequate as to amount to a crying disgrace . . . 33 of the 67 existing asylums are overcrowded [and only 3] have prospects of relief in the near future'. Journal of Medical Science, *Review of the Forty-Seventh Report of the Commissioners in Lunacy*, 7 June 1893, vol. 39, pp. 560-70.
[4] CL, 44th *Report*, 1890, pp. 218-22.
[5] CL, 46th *Report*, 1892 pp. 211-2.
[6] CL, 46th *Report*, 1892, pp. 48-9.
[7] LMA, LCC/MIN/864.
[8] LMA, LCC/MIN/867.
[9] LMA, LCC/MIN/864.
[10] LMA, LCC/MIN/867.
[11] LMA, LCC/MIN/873.
[12] LMA, LCC/MIN/870.
[13] LMA, LCC/MIN/871.
[14] Journal of Mental Science, *Asylum Reports*, 1891-2, vol. 39, p. 276
[15] LMA, LCC/MIN/866.
[16] LMA, LCC/MIN/870.
[17] CL, 47th *Report*, p. 2.
[18] LMA, LCC/MIN/871.
[19] CL, 50th *Report*, 1896, p. 291.
[20] CL, 52nd *Report*, 1898, p. 305.
[21] LMA, LCC/MIN/868.
[22] LMA, LCC/MIN/870.
[23] LMA, LCC/MIN/871.
[24] LMA, LCC/MIN/872.
[25] LMA, LCC/MIN/871.
[26] LMA, LCC/MIN/873.

Staff and patients 1890-1900
[1] CL, 45th *Report*, 1891 pp. 193-4.
[2] CL, 46th *Report*,,1892 pp. 211-2.

3   CL, 54th *Report*, 1900, pp. 314-4.
4   CL, 45th *Report*,,1891 pp. 193-4.
5   CA, CAN/5/1/3.
6   CL, 50th *Report, 1896*, pp. 291-2.
7   Journal of Mental Science, *Asylum Reports*, 1891-2, vol. 39, p. 276
8   CL, 51th *Report*, 1896, pp. 279.
9   CL, 54th *Report*, 1900, pp. 314-4
10 LMA, LCC/MIN/871.
11 CA, CAN/5/1/3.
12 LMA, LCC/MIN/870.
13 LMA, LCC/MIN/871.
14 LMA, LCC/MIN/869.
15 LMA, LCC/MIN/866.
16 CA, CAN/5/1/7.
17 LMA, LCC/MIN/873.
18 CA, CAN/5/1/7.
19 LMA, LCC/MIN/873.
20 LMA, LCC/MIN/866.
21 LMA, LCC/MIN/868.
22 LMA, LCC/MIN/869.
23 LMA, LCC/MIN/871.
24 CL, 54th *Report*, 1900, pp. 314-4
25 CL, 50th, 1896, p. 31; LMA, LCC/MIN/871; *The Times*, 21 September 1895; *The Times*, 28 September, 1895.
26 CL, 45th *Report*, 1891, pp. 193-4.
27 CA, CAN/1/6/1.
28 LMA, LCC/MIN/866.
29 LMA, LCC/MIN/868.
30 CL, 49th *Report*, 1895, p. 265.
31 CL, 50th *Report*, 1896, pp. 291-3.
32 CA, CAN/1/6/1.
33 LMA, LCC/MIN/871.
34 CA, CAN/1/6/1.
35 CL, 52nd *Report*, 1898, pp. 305-7.
36 LMA, LCC/MIN/872.
37 CA, CAN/1/6/1.
38 LMA, LCC/MIN/870.

The daily routine

1   CL, 53rd *Report*, 1899, pp. 314-5.
2   LMA, LCC/MIN/868.
3   LMA, LCC/MIN/869.
4   LMA, LCC/MIN/870.
5   LMA, LCC/MIN/868.
6   LMA, LCC/MIN/869.
7   LMA, LCC/MIN/870.
8   LMA, LCC/MIN/873.
9   CL, 54th *Report*, 1900, pp. 313-4.
10 CL, 54th *Report*, 1900, p. 30.
11 LMA, LCC/MIN/871.
12 LMA, LCC/MIN/872.
13 CL, 45th *Report*, 1891, pp. 193-4.
14 CL, 50th *Report*, 1896, p. 291.
15 CL, 55th *Report*, 1901, pp. 296-7.
16 LMA, LCC/MIN/868-72.
17 LMA, LCC/MIN/872.
18 CL, 50th *Report*, 1896, p. 291.
19 CL, 55th *Report*, 1901, pp. 313-7.
20 CA, CAN/5/1/3.
21 CL, 42nd *Report*, 1888, pp. 252-4.
22 CL, 45th *Report*, 1891, pp. 193-4.
23 CL, 49th *Report*, 1895, p. 265.
24 CL, 50th *Report*, 1896, p. 291.

[25] LMA, LCC/MIN/873.
[26] CL, 55th *Report*, 1901, pp. 296-7.
[27] CL, 48th *Report*, 1894, pp. 230-33.
[28] CL, 47th *Report*, 1893, p. 63.
[29] CL, 54th *Report*, 1900, pp. 313-7.
[30] LMA, LCC/MIN/872.
[31] LMA, LCC/MIN/871.
[32] LMA, LCC/MIN/866.
[33] LMA, LCC/MIN/873.
[34] CL, 54th *Report*, 1900 pp. 313-7.
[35] LMA, LCC/MIN/870.
[36] LMA, LCC/MIN/874.
[37] CL, 55th *Report*, 1901, pp. 296-7.

The new century 1900-1914
[1] CL, 66th *Report*, 1912, pp. 375-7.
[2] LMA, LCC/MIN/879.
[3] CL, 66th *Report*, 1912, pp. 375-7.
[4] LMA, LCC/MIN/882.
[5] CL, 54th *Report*, 1900, p. 30
[6] CL, 56th *Report*, 1902, pp. 34-5.
[7] *The Croydon Advertiser*, 4 July 1903.
[8] CL, 61st *Report*, 1907, pp. 329-31.
[9] CL, 60th *Report*, 1906, pp. 338-40.
[10] *Report of the London County Council for the year 1904-1905*, (London, 1906), p. 50.
[11] LMA, LCC/MIN/882.
[12] CL, 67th *Report*, 1913, p. 306.
[13] LMA, LCC/MIN/885.
[14] CA, CAN/1/12/1.
[15] LMA, LCC/MIN/882.
[16] LMA, LCC/MIN/885.
[17] LMA, LCC/MIN/886.
[18] LMA, LCC/MIN/882.
[19] LMA, LCC/MIN/874. Estamene was a woollen dress fabric, superior to serge, with a rough surface. Galatea, a strong plain weave of linen or cotton with a smooth finish, was similar to duck.
[20] CA, CAN/1/12/1.
[21] LMA, LCC/MIN/879
[22] LMA, LCC/MIN/885.
[23] LMA, LCC/MIN/886.
[24] LMA, LCC/MIN/877.
[25] LMA, LCC/MIN/885.
[26] LMA, LCC/MIN/876.
[27] CL. 65th *Report*, 1911, pp. 353-6.
[28] CL, 66th *Report*, 1912, pp. 375-7.
[29] LMA, LCC/MIN/874.
[30] LMA, LCC/MIN/876.
[31] LMA, LCC/MIN/879.
[32] LMA, LCC/MIN/882.
[33] LMA, LCC/MIN/885.
[34] LMA, LCC/MIN/878.
[35] LMA, LCC/MIN/885.
[36] LMA, LCC/MIN/880.

Law and disorder
[1] LMA, LCC/MIN/878.
[2] LMA, LCC/MIN/880.
[3] LMA, LCC/MIN/877.
[4] LMA, LCC/MIN/881.
[5] LMA, LCC/MIN/885.
[6] LMA, LCC/MIN/879.
[7] LMA, LCC/MIN/880.
[8] LMA, LCC/MIN/875.
[9] LMA, LCC/MIN/878.
[10] LMA, LCC/MIN/879.

[11] LMA, LCC/MIN/878.
[12] LMA, LCC/MIN/875.
[13] LMA, LCC/MIN/879.
[14] LMA, LCC/MIN/877.
[15] LMA, LCC/MIN/879.
[16] LMA, LCC/MIN/874.
[17] LMA, LCC/MIN/875.
[18] CA, CAN/1/12/1. *General Rules for the Management of the London County Lunatic Asylums.*

Progress and development
[1] LMA, LCC/MIN/874.
[2] *Report of the London County Council for the year 1904-1905*, (London, 1906), p. 50.
[3] LMA, LCC/MIN/881.
[4] LMA, LCC/MIN/882.
[5] LMA, LCC/MIN/885.
[6] LMA, LCC/MIN/875.
[7] LMA, LCC/MIN/876.
[8] LMA, LCC/MIN/877.
[9] LMA, LCC/MIN/878.
[10] LMA, LCC/MIN/880.
[11] LMA, LCC/MIN/879.
[12] LMA, LCC/MIN/882.
[13] LMA, LCC/MIN/881.
[14] LMA, LCC/MIN/882.
[15] LMA, LCC/MIN/882. Dr Cribb was a first assistant medical officer.
[16] LMA, LCC/MIN/875.
[17] LMA, LCC/MIN/876.
[18] LMA, LCC/MIN/877.
[19] LMA, LCC/MIN/878.
[20] LMA, LCC/MIN/881.
[21] LMA, LCC/MIN/885.
[22] LMA, LCC/MIN/874.
[23] LMA, LCC/MIN/878.
[24] LMA, LCC/MIN/882.
[25] LMA, LCC/MIN/879.
[26] LMA, LCC/MIN/880.
[27] LMA, LCC/MIN/882.
[28] LMA, LCC/MIN/875.
[29] LMA, LCC/MIN/876.
[30] LMA, LCC/MIN/874.
[31] LMA, LCC/MIN/875.
[32] LMA, LCC/MIN/878.
[33] LMA, LCC/MIN/881.
[34] LMA, LCC/MIN/877.
[35] LMA, LCC/MIN/875.
[36] LMA, LCC/MIN/877.
[37] LMA, LCC/MIN/878.
[38] LMA, LCC/MIN/876.
[39] LMA, LCC/MIN/877.
[40] LMA, LCC/MIN/878.
[41] LMA, LCC/MIN/876.
[42] LMA, LCC/MIN/879.
[43] LMA, LCC/MIN/881.
[44] LMA, LCC/MIN/874.
[45] LMA, LCC/MIN/879.
[46] LMA, LCC/MIN/881.
[47] LMA, LCC/MIN/882.
[48] LMA, LCC/MIN/884.
[49] LMA, LCC/MIN/886.
[50] LMA, LCC/MIN/882.

The patients' lot
[1] CL, 61st *Report*, 1907, pp. 7-15.
[2] The earliest surviving medical register for male patients begins in 1937.
[3] CL, 56th *Report* 1902, pp. 306-7.
[4] LMA, LCC/MIN/877.
[5] CL, 61st *Report*, 1907, pp. 329-31.
[6] LMA, LCC/MIN/880.
[7] CL, 62nd *Report*, 1908, pp. 346-8.
[8] LMA, LCC/MIN/877.

255

[9] LMA, LCC/MIN/882.
[10] LMA, LCC/MIN/878.
[11] LMA, LCC/MIN/876.
[12] LMA, LCC/MIN/882.
[13] LMA, LCC/MIN/877.
[14] LMA, LCC/MIN/878.
[15] LMA, LCC/MIN/882.
[16] LMA, LCC/MIN/881.
[17] LMA, LCC/MIN/875.
[18] LMA, LCC/MIN/877.
[19] LMA, LCC/MIN/878.
[20] CL, 67th *Report*, 1912, pp. 399-400.
[21] CL, 67th *Report*, 1913, p.306.
[22] LMA, LCC/MIN/882.
[23] CL, 67th *Report*, 1913, pp. 399-400.
[24] LMA, LCC/MIN/876.
[25] LMA, LCC/MIN/883.
[26] LMA, LCC/MIN/879.
[27] LMA, LCC/MIN/880.
[28] LMA, LCC/MIN/886.
[29] LMA, LCC/MIN/875.
[30] LMA, LCC/MIN/876.
[31] LMA, LCC/MIN/882.
[32] LMA, LCC/MIN/878.
[33] LMA, LCC/MIN/875.
[34] LMA, LCC/MIN/880.
[35] LMA, LCC/MIN/879.
[36] LMA, LCC/MIN/880.
[37] LMA, LCC/MIN/882.
[38] LMA, LCC/MIN/881.
[39] LMA, LCC/MIN/882.
[40] LMA, LCC/MIN/886.
[41] LMA, LCC/MIN/885.
[42] LMA, LCC/MIN/881.
[43] LMA, LCC/MIN/882.
[44] LMA, LCC/MIN/886.
[45] LMA, LCC/MIN/879.
[46] LMA, LCC/MIN/880.
[47] Kenneth S. Lynn, *Charlie Chaplin and his Times*, (London, 1997), pp. 55-7, p. 72.
[48] Lynn, *Charlie Chaplin*, p. 102.
[49] LMA, LCC/MIN/880.
[50] CL, 67th *Report*, 1913, p. 95.
[51] Vera Skultans, *English Madness. Ideas on Insanity, 1580-1890*, (London, 1979), pp. 17-8.
[52] 59th *Report*, 1905, pp. 338-9; 66th, 1912, pp. 399-400.
[53] CA, *Borough of Croydon*, 25, p. 966.
[54] CL, 67th *Report*, 1913, pp. 86-93.

World War One and its consequences
[1] LMA, LCC/MIN/887.
[2] LMA, LCC/MIN/888.
[3] LMA, LCC/MIN/887.
[4] LMA, LCC/MIN/888.
[5] LMA, LCC/MIN/887. In 1924, regulations had changed so that Miss K.L. Jones could be appointed as a locum dispensing chemist.
[6] CA, CAN/2/1/9.
[7] BC, 5th *Report*, 1918, pp. 5-6.
[8] LMA, LMA/MIN/888.
[9] LMA, LMA/MIN/890.
[10] LMA, LMA/MIN/892.
[11] LMA, LCC/MIN/891.
[12] BC, 3rd *Report*, 1916, pp. 8-10.
[13] LMA, LCC/MIN/888.
[14] LMA, LCC/MIN/889.
[15] LMA, LCC/MIN/888.
[16] LMA, LCC/MIN/889.
[17] LMA, LCC/MIN/890.
[18] LMA, LCC/MIN/887.
[19] LMA, LCC/MIN/888.

[20] LMA, LCC/MIN/889.
[21] LMA, LCC/MIN/890.
[22] LMA, LCC/MIN/889.
[23] LMA, LCC/MIN/890.
[24] LMA, LCC/MIN/887.
[25] LMA, LCC/MIN/889.
[26] LMA, LCC/MIN/891.
[27] LMA, LCC/MIN/889.
[28] LMA, LCC/MIN/890.
[29] LMA, LCC/MIN/887,
[30] LMA, LCC/MIN/890.
[31] *The London County Council Record of Service in the Great War 1914-18 by Members of the Council's Staff*, (London, 1922), pp. 189-90.
[32] LMA, LCC/MIN/887-8.
[33] LMA, LCC/MIN/890.
[34] LMA, LCC/MIN/891.
[35] LMA, LCC/MIN/890

War and asylum

[1] CA, CAN/2/1/8
[2] Information from Adrian Faulk and Peter Taylor.
[3] LMA, LCA/MIN/888.
[4] LMA, LCC/MIN/889.
[5] CA, CAN/4/3/4; CAN/2/1/1/3.
[6] CA, CAN/2/14.
[7] LMA, LCC/MIN/890.
[8] CA, CAN/2/14.
[9] LMA, LCC/MIN/890.
[10] Peter Barham, *Forgotten Lunatics of the Great War*, (New Haven & London, 2004, 2007 ed.), pp. 214-5.
[11] LMA, LCC/MIN/893.
[12] CA, CAN/2/14; CAN/2/6/1; CAN/2/1/1/3; CAN/4/34. Information from Adrian Faulks.
[13] *Croydon Guardian*, 16 November 2009.
[14] *Croydon Guardian*, 16 September 2009, 23 September 2009, 11 November 2009. Their bodies were among over 3,000 transferred to Croydon Cemetery in 1981 and cremated. Adrian Faulks has led a campaign to have their war service recognised.
[15] Barham, *Forgotten Lunatics*, p. 371; CA, CAN/2/14.
[16] Barham, *Forgotten Lunatics*, p. 272.
[17] Barham, *Forgotten Lunatics*, pp. 267-70.
[18] Barham, *Forgotten Lunatics*, p. 247.
[19] LMA, LCC/MIN/894.
[20] BC, 12th *Report*, 1925, pp. 243-5.
[21] CA, CAN/2/1/13.
[22] CA, CAN/2/4.
[23] LMA, LCC/MIN/900.
[24] LMA, LCC/MIN/888.
[25] LMA, LCC/MIN/889.
[26] BC, 5th *Report*, 1918, pp. 5-6.
[27] LMA, LCC/MIN/887.
[28] LMA, LCC/MIN/888.
[29] Barham, *Forgotten Lunatics*, pp. 185-6.
[30] Barham, *Forgotten Lunatics*, p. 400, note 10.
[31] LMA, LCC/MIN/890.
[32] BC, 5th *Report*, 1918, pp. 5-6.
[33] BC, 5th *Report*, 1918, pp. 24-8.
[34] Claude B. Ker, Claude Rendle (rev.), *Ker's Manual of Fevers*, (Oxford, 1911, 1927 ed.), pp. 177-235.
[35] BC, 4th *Report*, 1917, p. 44.
[36] LMA, LCC/MIN/888.
[37] BC, 5th *Report*, 1918, pp. 31-3

[38] BC, 6th *Report*, 1919, p. 30.
[39] CA, LS/00/521.
[40] LMA, LCC/MIN/893.
[41] LMA, LCC/MIN/894.

Portnalls
[1] LMA, LCC/MIN/875.
[2] LMA, LCC/MIN/876.
[3] LMA, LCC/MIN/881.
[4] LMA, LCC/MIN/882.
[5] LMA, LCC/MIN/886.
[6] LMA, LCC/MIN/887.
[7] LMA, LCC/MIN/888.
[8] LMA, LCC/MIN/889.
[9] LMA, LCC/MIN/891.
[10] LMA, LCC/MIN/892.
[11] BC, 8th *Report*, 1921, p. 5.
[12] BC, 8th *Report*, 1921, p. 29.
[13] LMA, LCC/MIN/893.
[14] BC, 8th *Report*, 1921, p. 110.
[15] LMA, LCC/MIN/893.
[16] LMA, LCC/MIN/894.

Attitudes in the 1920s
[1] CA, CAN/1/12/1.
[2] CA, CAN/1/12/1, CAN/1/12/15.
[3] BC, 6th *Report*, 1919, p. 15.
[4] A. Millicent Ashdown, *A Complete System of Nursing*, (London, 1917, 1924 ed.), pp. 336-51.
[5] Ashdown, *Nursing*, p. 342.
[6] LMA, LCC/MIN/893.
[7] BC, 11th *Report*, 1924, pp. 23-5.
[8] BC, 15th *Report*, 1929, p. 159-61.
[9] BC, 11th *Report*, 1924, pp. 250.
[10] LMA, LCC/MIN/892.
[11] BC, 11th *Report*, 1924, pp. 23-5. BC, 12th Report, 1925, pp. 243-5.
[12] LMA, LCC/MIN/891.
[13] LMA, LCC/MIN/896.
[14] Sir David Henderson & Ivor R.C. Batchelor, *Henderson and Gillespie's Textbook of Psychiatry*, (London, 1927, 1962 ed.), pp. 388-9.
[15] LMA, LCC/MIN/895.
[16] LMA, LCC/MIN/896.
[17] BC, 11th *Report*, 1924, pp. 246-7.
[18] BC, 12th *Report*, 1926, p. 17.
[19] BC, 15th *Report*, 1928, p. 31.
[20] BC, 12th *Report*, 1926, pp. 243-5.
[21] BC, 11th *Report*, 1924, p. 17.
[22] Ashdown, *Nursing*, p. 342
[23] Pamela Michael, *Care and Treatment of the Mentally Ill in North Wales 1800-2000*, (Cardiff, 2003), p. 89.
[24] LMA, LCC/MIN/894.
[25] LMA, LCC/MIN/895.
[26] CAN/2/2/1/1.
[27] BC, 12th *Report*, 1926, pp. 243-5.
[28] CA, CAN/2/2/1/1.
[29] CA, AN/2/2/1/7.

From asylum to hospital
[1] LMA, LCC/MIN/896.
[2] CA, CAN/1/11
[3] BC, 4th *Report*, 1917, p. 44. The private patients included two male and two female criminal patients
[4] BC, 5th *Report*, 1918, p. 16.
[5] LMA, LCC/MIN/891.
[6] LMA, LCC/MIN/892.
[7] BC, 8th *Report*, 1921, p. 110; BC, 10th *Report*, 1923, pp. 184-6.
[8] LMA, LCC/MIN/899.
[9] BC, 16th *Report*, 1929, pp. 205-7.
[10] LMA, LCC/MIN/895.

[11] LMA, LCC/MIN/896.
[12] LMA, LCC/MIN/892.
[13] LMA, LCC/MIN/896.
[14] BC, 8th *Report*, 1921, p. 5.
[15] BC, 15th *Report*, 1928, p. 1.
[16] BC, 16th *Report*, 1929, p. 9.
[17] CA, CAN/1/11.
[18] CA, CAN/1/12/15.
[19] CA, CAN/1/11.
[20] LMA, LCC/MIN/894.
[21] LMA, LCC/MIN/893, CA, GUA/1/2/28-9.
[22] LMA, LCC/MIN/895.
[23] LMA, LCC/MIN/900.
[24] CA, CAN/1/11
[25] LMA, LCC/MIN/897.
[26] BC, 13th *Report*, 1926, pp. 131-3.
[27] LMA, LCC/MIN/899.
[28] LMA, LCC/MIN/897.
[29] BC, 16th *Report*, 1929, pp. 205-7.
[30] BC, 22nd *Report*, 1935, pp. 297-9.
[31] CA, CAN/1/11.
[32] *T.C.A*, 6 March 1992.

The Board of Control
[1] BC, 10th *Report*, 1923, pp. 184-6.
[2] CA, CAN/1/11.
[3] BC, 11th *Report*, 1924, pp. 246-7.
[4] Pamela Michael, Care and Treatment of the Mentally Ill in North Wales 1800-2000, (Cardiff, 2003), p. 134.
[5] LMA, LCC/MIN/896.
[6] LMA, LCC/MIN/899.
[7] LMA, LCC/MIN/900.
[8] BC, 12th *Report*, 1925, pp. 243-5.
[9] LMA, LCC/MIN/897.
[10] BC, 13th *Report*, 1926, pp. 131-3.
[11] LMA, LCC/MIN/896.
[12] LMA, LCC/MIN/897.
[13] BC, 13th *Report*, 1926, pp. 131-3
[14] LMA, LCC/MIN/897.
[15] LMA, LCC/MIN/896.
[16] BC, 13th *Report*, 1926, pp. 131-3.
[17] BC, 13th *Report*, 1926, p. 5.
[18] BC, 11th *Report*, 1924, pp. 246-7.
[19] BC, 14th *Report*, 1927, pp. 148-9.
[20] BC, 15th *Report*, 1928, pp. 159-61.
[21] LMA, LCC/MIN/897.
[22] LMA, LCC/MIN/894.
[23] BC, 15th *Report*, 1928, p. 15.
[24] BC, 16th *Report*, 1929, p. 9.
[25] BC, 16th *Report*, 1929, p. 205-7.
[26] LMA, LCC/MIN/900.
[27] BC, 13th *Report*, 1926, pp. 131-3

The Estate
[1] LMA, LCC/MIN/896.
[2] LMA, LCC/MIN/897.
[3] LMA, LCC/MIN/900.
[4] LMA, LCC/MIN/891.
[5] LMA, LCC/MIN/892.
[6] LMA, LCC/MIN/894.
[7] LMA, LCC/MIN/892.
[8] LMA, LCC/MIN/895.
[9] LMA, LCC/MIN/897.
[10] LMA, LCC/MIN/895.
[11] LMA, LCC/MIN/897.
[12] LMA, LCC/MIN/895.

[13] LMA, LCC/MIN/896.
[14] LMA, LCC/MIN/895.
[15] LMA, LCC/MIN/897.
[16] LMA, LCC/MIN/900.
[17] LMA, LCC/MIN/892.
[18] LMA, LCC/MIN/891.
[19] LMA, LCC/MIN/901.
[20] LMA, LCC/MIN/897.
[21] LMA, LCC/MIN/896.
[22] LMA, LCC/MIN/901.

From gas to electric
[1] LMA, LCC/MIN/901.
[2] LMA, LCC/MIN/902.
[3] LMA, LCC/MIN/901.
[4] LMA, LCC/MIN/902.
[5] CA, CAN/1/11.
[6] LMA, LCC/MIN/902; BC, 22nd *Report*, 1935, pp. 297-9.
[7] LMA, LCC/MIN/902.
[8] LMA, LCC/MIN/901.
[9] LMA, LCC/MIN/902.
[10] LMA, LCC/MIN/903.
[11] LMA, LCC/MIN/902.
[12] LMA, LCC/MIN/903.
[13] BC, 24th *Report*, 1937, p. 5.
[14] LMA, LCC/MIN/903.
[15] LMA, LCC/MIN/904.

Freedom for some
[1] LMA, LCC/MIN/901.
[2] CA, CAN/1/11.
[3] BC, 16th *Report*, 1929, pp. 205-7.
[4] BC, 20th *Report*, 1933, pp. 7-8.
[5] BC, 18th *Report*, 1931, pp. 245-7.
[6] Information from John Wates.
[7] CA, CAN/1/11.
[8] BC, 18th *Report*, 1931, p. 21.
[9] BC, 17th *Report*, 1930, pp. 10-11.

[10] BC, 18th *Report*, 1931, p. 21.
[11] BC, 18th *Report*, 1931, pp. 245-7.
[12] BC, 22nd *Report*, 1935, p. 21, p. 297.
[13] BC, 23rd *Report*, 1936, pp. 295-7.
[14] LMA, LCC/MIN/900.
[15] LMA, LCC/MIN/902.
[16] LMA, LCC/MIN/903.
[17] BC, 18th *Report*, 1931, pp. 245-7.
[18] BC, 18th *Report*, 1931, p.11.
[19] LMA, LCC/MIN/903.
[20] LMA, LCC/MIN/901.
[21] LMA, LCC/MIN/902.
[22] LMA, LCC/MIN/900.
[23] LMA, LCC/MIN/901.
[24] LMA, LCC/MIN/902.
[25] BC, 18th *Report*, 1931, pp. 245-7.
[26] CA, CAN/1/11.
[27] BC, 18th *Report*, 1931, pp. 245-7.
[28] BC, 22nd *Report*, 1935, pp. 297-9.
[29] BC, 23rd *Report*, 1936, pp. 6-7
[30] CA, CAN/2/3/6.
[31] BC, 23rd *Report*, 1936, pp. 295-7.
[32] CA, CAN/1/11.
[33] BC, 23rd *Report*, 1936, pp. 295-7.
[34] LMA, LCC/MIN/902.

Occupational therapy
[1] BC, 16th *Report*, 1929, p. 207.
[2] BC, 18th *Report*, pp. 9-10.
[3] BC, 20th *Report*, 1933, p. 39.
[4] BC, 21st *Report*, 1934, p. 5.
[5] LMA, LCC/MIN/902; LMA, LCC/MIN/903.
[6] LMA, LCC/MIN/902.
[7] BC, 22nd *Report*, 1935, pp. 297-9.
[8] BC, 23rd *Report*, 1936, pp. 295-7.
[9] LMA, LCC/MIN/902.

World War Two and its aftermath
1. LMA, LCC/MIN/904.
2. CA, CAN/1/13.
3. LMA, LCC/MIN/904.
4. CA, CAN/1/13.
5. LMA, LCA/MIN/904.
6. CA, CAN/1/13.
7. LMA, LCA/MIN/904.
8. CA, CAN/2/3/1&7.
9. CA, CAN/1/13.
10. LMA, LCC/MIN/904.
11. CA, CAN/1/13.
12. LMA, LCC/MIN/904.
13. CA, CAN/1/13.
14. LMA, LCC/MIN/904.
15. CA, CAN/1/13.
16. CA, CAN/1/1/1.
17. CA, CAN/1/13.
18. LMA, LCC/MIN/904.
19. CA, CAN/1/13.
20. LMA, LCC/MIN/904.
21. CA, CAN/1/13.
22. LMA, LCC/MIN/904.
23. CA, CAN/1/13.
24. LMA, LCC/MIN/904.
25. CA, CAN/1/13.
26. LMA, LCC/MIN/904.
27. Miss Littlejohn died in 1956.

The National Health Service 1948-1960
1. CA, CAN/2/9.

Activity and rehabilitation
1. CA, CAN/13/10/1-14.
2. CA, CAN/1/13, CAN/1/1/1-9.

Planned reduction
CA, CAN/2/7/3.
1. CA, CAN/1/1/1/9
2. CA, CAN/1/1/1/10.
3. CA, CAN/1/1/1/11-12.
4. CA, CAN/1/1/1/13.
5. CA, CAN/1/1/1/14
6. CA, CAN/1/1/1/13.
7. CA, CAN/1/1/1/14
8. CA, CAN/1/1/1/15.

The Hospital Management Team
1. CA, CAN/1/1/1/16.
2. CA, CAN/1/1/1/17.
3. CA, CAN/1/1/1/18.
4. CA, CAN/1/1/1/19.
5. CA, CAN/1/1/1/20.
6. CA, CAN/1/1/1/21.
7. CA, CAN/1/1/1/22.

Planned closure
1. CA, CAN/1/7/2.
2. *Cane Hill News*, February 1986.
3. Sue Hutt & Pam Buttrey, *I've Got a Job to Do! A Study of the Clubhouse Model,* (Croydon, 1991).

Index

Adams, Night Attendant 53
Addington 39
Allen, Charles 76
Allport, Howard 215
Anderson, John 52
Arkle, F. 172
Arthur, Ellen 104
Ashfield, Edwin Toovey 32
Assistant matron 59, 107, 179
Asylum Cottages 89
Ayling, Stephen 93

B, Ethel 174-5
B., W. 33
Babot, Edward 122
Bailey, Florence Madeline 36
Baker, Alwyn 29
Baker, Henry George 101
Baker, Inspector 76
Balfour, Jabez 27
Bandon Hill Cemetery 120
Banerji, Dr Sudhindranath 173
Banstead Asylum/Hospital
.... 99, 119, 161, 179, 194, 196
Banstead 215
Barden, Elizabeth 9
Beadle, Martin 53
Bearman, Emma 26
Beckenham Hospital 202
Beckenham Mental Health
Association 226
Bedford, Mr 110
Bell, George, ... 73
Bermondsey 118
Berry, Joseph 31-2
Berry, Mrs 31-2
Berrywood Asylum 38-41

Bethlem Royal Hospital 224
Beverley 10
Bexley Asylum/Hospital
.... 71, 99-100, 115, 119, 140, 161
Birmingham 96
Bissidine, Mrs 97
Bond, Kathleen 195
Bond, Mr 87
Boniface, E.E. 116
Botley's Park Hospital 216
Bott, Dr W.G. 43
Box Hill 178
Bradshaw, Maria 97
Braintree 4
Bravery, Martha 34
Brighton 215
Brighton Road
.... 47, 78, 87, 130, 166
Brindley, Amelia 32
Bromley 222, 237-8
Bromley Area Health Authority
.... 225, 230, 232
Bromley Health Authority 238
Brook, Mr 19
Brooke, Mr Thomas
.... 19, 39, 44, 46, 52, 75
Brookwood Asylum/Hospital
.... 7-8, 10-11, 15, 164
Broomhall, Miss K. ....
Brown, Alfred James 52
Brown, Mary Ann 65, 98
Brown, William 57
Bunn, Alice 65
Burton, Thomas 77
Byron, Edmond 10

Cearn, C.H. 163
Callanan, Joe 237
Camberwell 8, 60, 118, 211
Campbell, Jane Ferrier 73

262

Canadian Army 191
Carey, John 118
Carpenter, Dr Alfred 7, 27
Carson, James 26
Casbolt, Frederick Charles 118
Cassidy, Dr 3
Caterham Asylum 8-9
Caterham Junction 19, 35, 38
Cemetery ... 14, 48, 164, 206, 229
Chamberlain, Mary Ann 99
Chaplin, Charlie 104
Chaplin, Hannah 104-5
Chapman, Florence 105
Chapman, Frederick Edward 26, 52
Chapman, Mr 203, 212
Chapman, Mrs 113-4
Chappell, J.T. 16
Charing Cross Station 99
Charlesworth, Mrs A.L. 124
Charlton, Dr 202
Chartham Hospital 161
Chelsea 60
Chertsey 8
Chipstead 163
Chipstead Residents Association .
....205-6
Chipstead Road 48, 61, 87, 91
Chipstead Valley Road
.... 148, 168, 231, 234
Clapham 8, 60
Clarke, Dr 122
Claybury Asylum/Hospital
.... 66, 99, 103, 140, 160
Clerk 75, 103, 109, 120, 165
Clothing 156-7, 180, 189-193, ...
.... 196, 209, 211
Cockman, Jemima 108
Colchester 31-2
Collis, Mr & Mrs 133
Colney Hatch Asylum/Hospital
.... 55, 90, 122, 140, 155

Coniston Road 174
Connington, Edward 121
Conolly, John 1
Coomber, W. 146
Cornwall 127
Cottage Hospital
.... 158, 202-3, 227, 229, 231
Cottages 48, 73
Cotton, Neil 97
Coulsdon House and Estate Agency
.... 87
Coulsdon Nursing Association 89
Coulsdon Railway Station 47
Coulsdon South Station 174
Course, James 52
Court Lodge Estate 163
Cozens, Mr A.W. 178
Crawford, Rev. John 25, 110
Cresswell, A.E. 163
Cribb, Dr 87
Croydon 6-9, 13, 15, 18, 29, 36, 39,
41-2, 46, 65-6, 68-9, 77, 91-3, 99,
109-10, 148, 225, 229
Croydon Airport 188
Croydon Area Health Authority 227
Croydon Mental Hospital 68, 106
Croydon Workhouse 36
Curtis, Selina 73
Cusack, George 74

D., Rose 54
Dalton, Kate 127
Darenth Asylum/Hospital 216
Davies, Catherine 179
Davies, Mr. G.K. 227
Davies, Rev. D.V. 217
Davies, William 26
Debenham, Suffolk 63
Dodds, John 63
Dollar, Mrs M.M. . 199, 201, 215
Donaldson, Dr W.I. 109, 124

263

Dore, Arthur Henry 118
Dorking 8, 13, 39
Dorrell,, Elizabeth Nichols 73
Dowling, Miss 173, 202, 224
Duke, James 117
Dulwich Hospital 218
Dunstans Cottages 164

E., Sarah 39
East Anglia 69
East Croydon Station 38
East Surrey Water Company 90, 93
Eastern Command 120
Eastern General Hospital, No 2 118
ECT 191, 193-4, 202
Edridge, Mr Thomas 26-7
Elgee, Dr Samuel Charles 109, 122, 139-41, 145, 147, 155-6, 159-60, 163-4, 168, 174, 179, 184
Ellis, Ellen 55
Ely, Miss 41
Emergency Hospital 189
Employment, patients 1, 60-2, 88, 122-4, 178-9, 190-1, 204, 223
Epileptic Colony 108
Epsom 13, 179
Epsom Hospital 179
Essex 15
Euston, Suffolk 50

Fahey, Dr 198, 216
Fair Dean Close 63
Fair Dean Down 63
Farm ...60, 101-3, 162-3, 169-70, 204, 222, 229
Farmer, Attendant 54
Farnborough Hospital ... 233, 238
Farnham 8
Farthing Down 14
Ferrier, Alfred and family 30-1
Ffitch, Frederick 63

Finch, Edward 55
Fire fighting 90-1
Fish, Mr 77, 111, 162-3
Fisherton House
.... 9, 15, 65-6, 68, 97, 132
Flude, Mary Ann 96
Food 56-9, 67, 101-4, 112-5, 124, 145, 149-50, 153-4, 190-5, 200-1, 222
Ford, William 110
Fountains Hospital 170
Fox, Edward 118
French, Mrs 110
Frost, Henry Thomas 178

G, Mildred 179
Gaffney, Julia ....
Garden House
.... 87, 101, 133, 157, 229, 231
Gardener's Cottage 44
Gas work's Cottage 44
Gates 45, 79-80, 152, 163, 174
Geary, W. 110
Geere, Mr 206, 220
Gentle, Horace........................ 60
Gibb, Dr 215
Gibraltar 189
Girling, Mrs 199
Girling, Sarah 62
Glencairn 164, 202
Glencross family 148
Gloucester Asylum 37-40
Goddard, Matilda 29
Godstone 8, 13, 39
Goom, Agnes 97
Goom, James Henry 97
Green, Mr 20
Greenwich 60
Greyhound Tap, Croydon 31
Grosvenor, Hon. R.C. 43
Grove Hall 41

Guildford 8
Guy, George 55

Hackney 60
Hailstone, Mrs 203
Haines, David 42
Hall, Eliza 34
Hampshire, Mr 173
Hanwell Asylum/Hospital
.... 20, 86, 99,122, 161
Hardingham, Charlotte 64
Hardy, Nelson 62
Harling, Miss 142
Harman, Mary 26
Harmsworth, Faith 141
Harris, A.A. 107
Harvey, George 11
Haywood, Clara 97
Henderson, Helen ....
Henson, William Henry 109
Henty, Attendant 116
Hertfordshire 118
Hibling, Louisa 148
Hickey, father 215
Hill, Dr 26
Hill, Kate 26
Hiscox, Mr 111
Holborn 60
Hollyme Oake Road
[Hollymeoake] 130, 166, 203
Hollymoor Asylum, Birmingham 97
Holmes, Frederick W. 11
Hooley 61
Horey, George Albert 52
Horne, Walter John 117
Horton Asylum/Hospital 100, 108-10, 139, 173, 181, 188-9
Hours of work
.... 51, 69-70, 86, 118, 143
Howell, Charles Henry
.... 10-12, 16, 37, 45

Hunt, Fanny 52
Hutchison, Dr 218
Hutchison, Ralph Henry 120

I., H. 40
Ill treatment of patients
.... 53-5, 72, 156, 178-9
Ingram, Joseph J., ... 41
Insulin treatment 197
Ireland 50

Jannes, Franz 98
Jauregg, Wagner 139
Johnson, Charles 42
Johnson, Esther 51
Jones, Florence 62
Joyce, Stephen 52

Kenley Aerodrome 126
Kenley Airfield 188
Kenley Police 205
Kennington 120
Kensington 60
Kilminster, Ann 29-30
Kilminster, Maud 30
King Edward's Hospital Fund
.... 203, 210, 212-4, 223
Kings Fund 231
Kirby, John G. 91

Laing, Mr 12
Lakeman, Miss 107
Lambeth 60, 118
Lambeth Infirmary 105
Lambeth Mental Health
Association 226
Lancaster 3, 45
Largactil 218
Larkin, Miss 203
Leicester City Mental Hospital 181
Leyfields Farm 169

265

Liddamore, Mary Ann 50
Liddamore, Sarah 50
Lilly, Dr George Austen 139, 160-1, 168-72, 180-1, 186, 189, 192, 194, 198, 201, 205-6, 209-11
Lingen, David 11-12
Lion Green 11, 48, 68
Lion Green Road 87, 101, 171, 222
Littlejohn, Dr Edward Salterne 109-110, 113-6, 119, 124, 127
Littlejohn, Miss 189, 198
Local Government Board 2, 3
London, City of 60
London Electric Supply Company 173
London Omnibus Company .. 167
Long Grove Asylum/Hospital 115, 124, 159-61

M., M. 33
Mackie, John 26
Madras 98
Malarial treatment 139-40
Mallet, Mr 215
Manor House 131
Marina, Princess..................... 220
Markwick, Mr 34
Marshall, Bertram Charles 73, 76
Marshall, Lord 163
Martineau, P.M. 43
Marylebone 97
Matron 55, 59, 72, 76, 109, 134, 169, 189, 198, 207, 215-6, 224
Mattresses 46, 86
Maudsley Hospital ... 139-40, 224
Maudsley, Henry 3-4
Maybank Cottages 89
McCoughlin, Miss 229
McCowan, Dr 139
McDougell, Mr 82
McKenzie, Alexander 120

McKeohan, J., Attendant 74
McLeish, Charles 99
Mead, James Arthur 163, 175
Medication 141-2, 197
Mental Aftercare Association 2, 96-7, 150, 183, 202, 222
Merstham Military Hospital . 116
Middlesex Hospital 159
Milne, Beatrice 109
Mitcham 39, 120
Mitcham Road Cemetery 230
Mitchell, Dr 202, 215
Monson, Lord 12-3, 27
Moody, Dr James 3, 16, 1, 14, 16, 19, 25, 29-33, 37-8, 41-2, 51-3, 55, 59, 63-78, 82, 86-90, 97-8, 100-2
Moody, Lady 108-9
Moore, Edward Charles 115-7
Moore, Edward J. 115
Morres, Dr Frederick 107, 173
Morrice, William 50
Morris, Charles 31
Morris, George James 120
Morris, Margaret Jane 127
Mott, Dr Frederick 106, 124, 139
Moule, Mr 113-4, 163
Moulsford 10
Mount Vernon Hospital ....
Muir, Mr and Mrs 79
Munro, Alexander 52
Mynott, Thomas 77

Napsbury War Hospital 118
National Asylum Workers Union 135, 146, 149
Netherne Mental Hospital 181, 223
New, William 131
Newman, William A. 76
Norfolk 15, ... 103
Northamptonshire 15
Norwood 74

266

Nurses Home 166, 169-71
O'Brien, Nurse 54
Oaks Wood 87, 113, 116
Oakwood Hospital 237
Old Manor House 129
Old Town, Croydon 131
Old Tram Road 13
Onslow, Lord 98
Orchard, Percy 118
Ovaltine 142
Owen, Mabel 110

Pacey, Nurse 54
Packham, Jim 152
Paddington 60
Paine, Frederick 26
Parker, patient 54
Parks, Emily Grace 55
Parole, patients 157, 175-6, 201, 205
Pasmore, Dr 106
Pathe Freres 101
Patrick, Nurse 54
Paver, A.G. 165
Pearn, Dr Napier ....
139, 150, 160, 163, 173, 192, 198
Pearson, patient 55
Peckham House 29-30, 105
Peer, Mrs A. 174
Penge 29, 41
Philand, Mr 114
Physiotherapy 202
Plumstead Infirmary 98
Pollack, Anna 215
Poplar 60, 72
Porter, Dr Winifred 173, 195
Portnalls 11-12, 111, 128-33, 158, 164, 172, 190, 230
Portnalls Road 79, 113, 131, 163, 203-6, 228, 234
Portsmouth 15, 177, 203
Postern House/Villa .. 78, 87, 101, 163-4, 174, 202, 205
Posterns Wood 216
Potterton, Horace 73
Powell, Eliza 25
Preece, Alice 41
Preece, Marion 41
Pre-frontal leucotomies . 197, 202
Price, John 120
Pritchard, Alfred 131
Psychotherapy 202
Pumping House Cottages 35
Purley 34

Railway 12, 19, 38,
.... 45-9, 91, 103, 206
Raistrick, Miss Kathleen 168, 186
Ralph, Mr James 11, 25, 75
Ramsdale, Clara 42
Ramsgate 124
Ransom, Attendant 74
Reardon, Edward 118
Red Lion Hotel 19, 47, 52, 91, 233
Redhill Hospital 218
Reigate 8, 13, 215
Reynolds, Thomas 26
Rice, Harry Charles 117
Rice, Joseph E. 179
Richard, Ernest G................... 146
Richardson, Hannah 74
Richmond 8
Riddell, Jane 38
Roberts, Moorson 63
Robins, Fanny 52
Robinson, Nathaniel 43
Roehampton Military Hospital ...
.... 116-7, 122
Ross, John 50, 52
Ross, Nellie 50
Ross, Nurse 53
Rotterdam 98
Royal Bath Hospital, Harrogate 148

Russell, Mrs 165
Russell, Peter 116
Ryall, Lilian 179

S., G. 61
S., J. M. 64
Salisbury 9, 15
Samoo, Ramasammy 98
Samuel, Henry 195
Sargeant, Emily 26
Saunders, Emma 33
Schoolenart, Samuel 118
Scotland 50
Sears, Mr 64
Selsdon Park Farm 163
Semprini, Mr 220
Sennett, William 109
Sewell, Jessie 29
Sewerage 92-3
Seymour, Lt. Col. Leopold 27
Shanks, Miss 41
Sharpe, Miss Alice . 198, 201, 214
Sheriff, Alexander 195
Sherwell, Mr 169
Shoreditch 60
Shorter, Nurse 72
Sibley, Major Gen. Thomas ....
.... 27, 38, 43
Sinclair, Sir J.G. Tollemache .. 100
Skeets, Attendant 54
Slattery, Mr 54
Slaughter Mr 31-2
Smith, Mr 75
Smith, patient 54
Somerset, William 53
Southerns Farm 163, 169
Southwark Infirmary 97
Spanish influenza 127
Sports and Social Club
.... 191, 207, 210, 223
Springfield Hospital 216

St Dunstans Cottages . 88-90, 164
St Saviours Union 8, 60
St. Bernard's Hospital 191, 193
St. Giles Hospital, Camberwell 202
St. Giles, Camberwell 67
St. Joseph's Orphanage, Orpington
.... 148
St. Olave's Union 13, 38, 60
St. Olave's Hospital, Rotherhithe
.... 202, 218
St. Pancras 66
Stacey, Henry 41
Stanley, Anne 26
Starcross (Western Counties Idiot Asylum) 38
Stelazine 218
Stepney Workhouse 66
Stepping Stones 222
Steward, House 57, 61, 67, 75, 87, 89, 101, 109, 146-148
Stewart, Rev. 13-4
Stirling, Dr Pauline 173
Stoats Nest Station 12, 19, 38
Stoney Cottages .. 130-1, 164, 227
Stores, Sarah 66
Storthes Hall Hospital 164
Stott, John Davis 50
Stratford Station 103
Streatham Park Cemetery 120, 206
Strong, Richard 43
Styles, Daniel 32
Sussex 69
Sutton Water Company 91
Swansea 177
Sykes, Dr 111

Tanfield Dairy 19
Tanner, Mr 159
Taverner, Mr 77
Taylor, Frederick 120-1
Taylor, Henry R. 29

268

Taylor, Mrs 110
The Edinburgh Castle 97
The Manor 108
The Manor Asylum 99
Thefts 76-80
Thienpoint, Dr 110
Thomas, Henry 29
Thomas, Richard 29
Thomas, Robert 118-9
Thompson, Dr David 25
Thomson, Mr George Gilbert 16, 25
Thornton, John A., ... 73
Thrower, Dr 225
Todd, Ellen 29
Tofranil 218
Tollers Farm 113-4, 163, 169
Tooting Bec Asylum/Hospital
.... 170, 203, 222
Treatment 64, 137-42, 160, 218-9
Trenowden, Mr 216
Tripp, Maxwell 52
Trish, Thomas ....
Troy, Esther 96
Tubbs, Mr 189
Tucker family ....
.... 10-12, 48, 61, 89, 129-32
Tuke, Dr 20
Tuke, William 1
Tuohey, Joseph Herbert 26
Tupper, Emily Clara 26, 52
Tupper, Esther Ann 52
Turner, James 131
Turney, Alexander 64
Tushey, Attendant 54
Typhoid 124-8, 55, 160, 190, 194, 197, 202

Ultra-violet radiation 140
Uniforms 70-1, 149, 176-7
Utrecht 98

Valuer 48, ... 164
Vincent Road 234
Vines, Barry 227-9, 233

Wages 51
Wales 29, 50, 69, 145, 197
Walk, Dr Alexander
.... 173, 198, 202-9, 212, 215-9
Wallington 91
Wands As 44
Wandsworth 8, 13, 60
Wandsworth Asylum 6-10
Ward, Robert 83
Warlingham Park Hospital
.... 212, 216, 223
Warne, Mary 26
Warren, Alfred 116
Warren, Mrs 228
Warwickshire 15
Waterloo Station 97
Watkin, Sir Edward 12
Watney, Mr 48
Watson, Henry 68
Watson, John 53
Webber, Miss 198, 202, 207
Webster, Peter 227
Welch, Attendant 54
Well Cottage 101
Well House 164
West Norwood 120
West Park Hospital 122
Western Counties Idiots Asylum ..
.... 15, 36
Westminster Workhouse 98
Wheeler, Mr 103
Wheeler, Thomas 146
Whipsnade Zoo 215
Whitechapel 66
Whyclift 34
Wickens, Mr 179
Wilkinson, J. 107, 117

269

Williams, George 74
Williamson, Mr 215
Wilson, Isabel 191
Wilson, Sarah 29
Windebank. Mr........................ 79
Winson Green Asylum 96
Wood, Bessie Matilda 34
Woodhall, Esther Ann 26
Woodmansterne 48, 89
Woodmansterne Road 79, 92
Woodward, Miss..........................
Woolworths 178
Worcester Hospital 164
Wynter, Andrew 2, 33

X-ray 190

Yandle, Richard 77, 107, 173
York Retreat 1